# 1,000,000 Books

are available to read at

# Forgotten Books

www.ForgottenBooks.com

Read online
Download PDF
Purchase in print

ISBN 978-1-331-64696-9
PIBN 10217472

This book is a reproduction of an important historical work. Forgotten Books uses state-of-the-art technology to digitally reconstruct the work, preserving the original format whilst repairing imperfections present in the aged copy. In rare cases, an imperfection in the original, such as a blemish or missing page, may be replicated in our edition. We do, however, repair the vast majority of imperfections successfully; any imperfections that remain are intentionally left to preserve the state of such historical works.

Forgotten Books is a registered trademark of FB &c Ltd.
Copyright © 2018 FB &c Ltd.
FB &c Ltd, Dalton House, 60 Windsor Avenue, London, SW19 2RR.
Company number 08720141. Registered in England and Wales.

For support please visit www.forgottenbooks.com

# 1 MONTH OF FREE READING

at

www.ForgottenBooks.com

By purchasing this book you are eligible for one month membership to ForgottenBooks.com, giving you unlimited access to our entire collection of over 1,000,000 titles via our web site and mobile apps.

To claim your free month visit:

www.forgottenbooks.com/free217472

\* Offer is valid for 45 days from date of purchase. Terms and conditions apply.

English
Français
Deutsche
Italiano
Español
Português

# www.forgottenbooks.com

**Mythology** Photography **Fiction** Fishing Christianity **Art** Cooking Essays Buddhism Freemasonry Medicine **Biology** Music **Ancient Egypt** Evolution Carpentry Physics Dance Geology **Mathematics** Fitness Shakespeare **Folklore** Yoga Marketing **Confidence** Immortality Biographies Poetry **Psychology** Witchcraft Electronics Chemistry History **Law** Accounting **Philosophy** Anthropology Alchemy Drama Quantum Mechanics Atheism Sexual Health **Ancient History Entrepreneurship** Languages Sport Paleontology Needlework Islam **Metaphysics** Investment Archaeology Parenting Statistics Criminology **Motivational**

# AN AMBASSADOR OF
THE VANQUISHED

# AN AMBASSADOR OF THE VANQUISHED

VISCOUNT ÉLIE DE GONTAUT-BIRON'S
MISSION TO BERLIN, 1871—1877

*FROM HIS DIARIES AND MEMORANDA*

BY

THE DUKE DE BROGLIE

*TRANSLATED, WITH NOTES, BY*
ALBERT D. VANDAM
AUTHOR OF "AN ENGLISHMAN IN PARIS"

LONDON
WILLIAM HEINEMANN
1896

*[All rights reserved]*

UNIV. OF
CALIFORNIA

Replacing 211809

| | PAGE |
|---|---|
| THE LIBERATION OF THE TERRITORY ... ... ... | 1 |

## PART II
THE MINISTRY OF MAY 24, 1873 ... ... ... ... 79

## PART III
THE EPISCOPAL CHARGES AND THE CRISIS OF 1875 ... 141

## PART IV
THE EASTERN QUESTION AND THE BERLIN MEMORANDUM—THE ELECTIONS OF 1877—THE RESIGNATION 241

 588

# THE LIBERATION OF THE
TERRITORY

## THE LIBERATION OF THE TERRITORY

I

VISCOUNT ÉLIE (Elias) de Gontaut-Biron represented France at Berlin in the capacity of ambassador from December 4, 1871, till the last days of 1877. At the time that mission was confided to him, part of the Treaty of Peace concluded with Germany in consequence of our disasters was already being carried out. Two out of the five milliards of the war indemnity stipulated for by Clause 2 of that Treaty were on the eve of being paid, by means of a loan subscribed with marvellous rapidity by the resources of the country in the way of savings and national energy. But three more remained to be paid, and six French departments were to be held in pledge by the troops of the victor until the whole should have been settled. Moreover, the new limits of our territory, so sadly mutilated, were not exactly defined. In other words, nothing was finally concluded, and the possibility of new conflicts, or rather of fresh misfortunes, had by no means vanished from the horizon. The slightest disagreement with regard to the manner and time of payment, or in connection with the mapping out of the contested districts, a scuffle between the victorious soldiers and the vanquished populations on this or that occupied spot, any or all of those contingencies might place us once more, just as during the negotiations for peace itself, in the alternative of having to make painful concessions, or of resuming a hopeless resistance; we were, in fact, under the heel of the victor, who was still the master, to interpret according to his own will the conditions he himself had dictated.

It was that victor whom the representative of France had to go and confront at Berlin, *i.e.* at the seat of his power, in order to discuss with him questions still pregnant with so much stress and storm. No one was more surprised than M. de Gontaut himself at being called upon, or rather condemned to assume that perilous honour. He himself takes care to remind us in *Recollections*, which his kindly confidence has enabled us to read,[1] that nothing, absolutely nothing, had prepared him for that task. Until he was well advanced in life, he had stood aloof from all public office.[2] Sprung from one of the oldest and most illustrious families of France, his fealty to hereditary traditions and convictions had kept him from all participation in politics during the whole

[1] The memoirs in question have, it appears, not been published as yet.
[2] M. de Gontaut-Biron was born in 1817.—TRANSLATOR.

of the Second Empire. It was only after our defeats that the suffrages of the electors of the Lower Pyrenees had gone in search of him in that retreat to send him to the National Assembly. The sympathy he had never felt towards the dynasty that came to an end on September 4 was equally conspicuous by its absence with regard to the Republic which was improvised that day, and under ordinary circumstances he would have had no desire to take service under it.

But the word "ordinary" had lost its significance at that critical hour. The possibility of rendering the slightest service to the land of one's birth, fallen into such a depth of misfortune, imposed on men of all parties the duty of forgetting, at any rate for the time being, their dearest attachments. Hence, it had been agreed from the very first days of the opening of the Assembly, that, in order to facilitate the patriotic concord, the Republican form, adopted in the hour of intense excitement by the population of Paris, should be considered merely as a temporary label, and that all questions bearing on the definite constitution of the Government should be postponed to the day when France should be free from the foreign yoke under which she was smarting. In the parlance of those days, which is gradually being forgotten as they recede, this was called "the Bordeaux pact." It was M. Thiers himself who had solemnly proclaimed the conditions of that truce of parties. It was on the occasion of his investiture with the supreme power by the unanimous suffrages of the National Assembly, and the words he used left apparently no room for ambiguous interpretation. He promised *on his honour*, and on the penalty of being considered as *guilty of treason*, to attempt nothing himself against that truce, nor to allow others to attempt anything against it. Did he deceive himself with regard to the sense of his words and the extent of his engagements? It is a delicate point, on which I should be reluctant to insist, and only then if the exposition of facts made it absolutely necessary.

In this instance it is sufficient to remind the reader that, whether it was justified or not, M. de Gontaut's confidence was as complete as that of others placed in a similar position, and to whom M. Thiers made analogous offers, or rather on whom he imposed the same duties. Not one of these would have lent himself to them if for a single moment they could have supposed that the smallest renunciation of their monarchical convictions was required of them in consequence. Those who, like M. de Gontaut, had been entrusted with a seat in the new Parliament would have been particularly scrupulous not to desert it if they had thought that their absence was calculated to compromise the cause which in their opinion constituted the hope of the country.

It was in that frame of mind, and not without a good deal of hesitation and repugnance, that M. de Gontaut, an ambassador greatly surprised at being one, took the road to Berlin. The very mixed feelings that animated him on the day he was to take his first official step in handing the new Emperor his credentials, cannot be better described than he himself has described them in terms rendered eloquent by their sincerity. "Behold me then," he says, "compelled to don a uniform for the first time in my life. I may own that I felt more or less uncomfortable at my own appearance in a coat with gold lace on every seam, a sword getting between my legs, and a cocked hat with white feathers on my head. Mingling with the serious and sad reflections of the moment there come some less grave and more humorous impressions at the sight of my costume, or at the sound of 'Your Excellency' from the grand seigneurs, as well as from the subalterns. I rubbed my eyes in order to ascertain whether I had been taken with a sudden access of giddiness, or whether my eyesight was perfectly clear. I asked myself whether it was I, a descendant of those who warred in the Crusades, who, in the name of the President of the French Republic, was about to present myself as the ambassador of my sadly disturbed country to the new Emperor of Germany in all the glitter of his success, surrounded by triumphant generals like himself;

whether it was I who was going afterwards to pay court to the Empress amidst her ladies of honour attired in all their splendour as on gala days? I asked myself all this as I stood alone amidst a crowd of unknown faces, and listening to a language I did not understand. Was it a dream? Was it a nightmare? It was both the one and the other; it was a multitude of diverse sensations such as one might experience during a troubled sleep, in which brilliant scenes become complicated by impossible, unlikely, and ridiculous situations, from which one is relieved only by becoming awake."

The procession and escort that came to take the ambassador made their way along the Unter den Linden, lined by a sight-loving population, whose demeanour was, however, becoming throughout, and the military of all grades in particular stood at the salute, and deferentially put their hands to their helmets. "I thought in a melancholy way," said M. de Gontaut nevertheless, "that I resembled those kings of antiquity vanquished and despoiled by the Romans, and who came to swell the triumphs of the victors."

I am pleased to be able to say in common fairness that there was nothing calculated to increase the bitterness of those thoughts in the subsequent interviews with the Emperor and the various members of the Imperial family. On the contrary, every one of them visibly tried to spare the dignity of the vanquished one and to make his position bearable. "When the doors of the reception-room were thrown open I entered alone, and beheld in the centre of the apartment a tall, martial, and kindly-looking man, standing upright, bareheaded, and wearing the ribbon of the Legion of Honour. I advanced towards him bowing deeply. He on his side advanced to meet me." This was the opportunity to deliver a little speech drawn up under the supervision of M. Thiers, and of which the following was the principal sentence: "Invested by the eminent man who actually presides over the destinies of France with a mission than which none could be more honourable, that of renewing regular and pacific relations between two great nations, I make bold to trust to your Majesty's goodwill to help me to discharge my task with all the loyalty I am anxious to bring to bear upon it. Peace with honour is an essential thing to nations."

At the sound of the words "loyalty" and "honour," particularly emphasized by the speaker, the Emperor slightly inclined his head in token of assent. "I share every one of those sentiments," he said afterwards. "I will endeavour to make your stay in Berlin as agreeable as possible."

From the Emperor M. de Gontaut had to pass to the Empress. All those who knew that Princess are aware of the particular liking she displayed from her youth for French literature and society, and the graceful ease with which she spoke our language. It is not surprising, then, that it should have pleased her to prolong with marked goodwill the official interview, and to become so forgetful of the etiquette of a first audience as to make the ambassador sit down. She recalled little details from M. de Gontaut's family history which she had heard from her Paris friends and acquaintances, and dwelt especially on particulars connected with his respected mother whom he had recently lost. "You have no doubt made a great sacrifice in accepting the embassy to Berlin, but you have done the right thing, and you may depend on me to prevent your repenting of the step."

One did not expect similar assurances of goodwill from the heir to the throne, afterwards Emperor Frederick, one of the combatants in the struggle that had just come to an end, and for that very reason those assurances assumed a greater significance. Nevertheless, the words he uttered, full of generous and lofty thoughts, will astonish no one who has since then watched with deep concern the last phase of that noble prince's life. He also spoke of France and of the recollections he had left behind him there, without avoiding speaking of the very latest.

"I know lots of people in France; I have even seen some during the late events." "Yes," replied M. de Gontaut, "you have seen the Bishop of Orleans, who has a very vivid recollection of the sentiments expressed by your Imperial Highness." "Yes, that's just it, Monseigneur Dupanloup," remarked the Prince with great animation; "unfortunately he was just going away to Bordeaux, and I was only able to talk to him for ten minutes. Our two countries have had a terrible bleeding," he went on; "like yourselves, we have had some considerable and very bad losses. Now we must stick to peace." "That is the feeling with which I have come to Berlin," said M. de Gontaut. "There is some merit on our side in wishing for peace, for we are paying a heavy price for it, but peace is useful to Germany as it is to France." "Yes, you are right, peace is good for everybody."

And the Princess, whom at present we call Empress Victoria (Empress Frederick), repeated the words "with a kind of gentle energy."

The consideration one shows to the weak, and which sadly marks their position, may touch but do not console them. To be the object of such consideration amidst the discreet surroundings of private interviews was sufficiently painful to M. de Gontaut; still more painful was it to find himself their object amidst the brilliant receptions and entertainments which succeeded one another during that year at the Court of Prussia, the splendour of those entertainments being enhanced by the feeling of triumph of the entertainers. The first of those entertainments was a magnificent concert.

"When the Emperor and Empress made their appearance," says M. de Gontaut, "there was a deep silence, and the first strains of the music rose on the air. Up till then I was mainly swayed by curiosity, but at that moment my heart sank, and I began to analyze my own sensations. I began to account to myself for the scene at which I was looking; they were our conquerors I had before me, they who had beaten, humiliated, and pitilessly treated us. I was seated at the foot of their throne; I represented vanquished, diminished, lowered France. I may own that my heart's anguish was such as to find almost vent in tears, and that for the first time in my life the sounds of a magnificent orchestra, as they fell upon my ears, were odious to me. To revive my courage, I ceased looking at the scene before me, and turned my thoughts to those higher regions where serenity and peace hold undivided sway—towards that heavenly court, very different in its brilliancy from the brilliancy of earthly courts; towards that heavenly court which knows neither the insolent triumphs of mere strength, nor sorrows that cannot be healed; towards that heavenly court, where the vanquished, the disinherited, and all those who have fought the good fight of life are at rest.

That moment of introspection comforted me. About a quarter past eleven the concert was over, the princes retired, the company slowly left the White Room, and at midnight I was at home, chewing the cud of my own thoughts with regard to that brilliant entertainment, amidst a silence unbroken by any sound without, and in a room flooded with moonlight. My mind dwelt unconsciously on all those harmonious chords, on all those princes, on the interchange of compliments; in one word, on everything that had caused so much noise and commotion but one short hour ago, and which, at the time I write, is gone for ever, like everything that is merely of this world—gone, vanished, lost into eternity."

In diplomacy, the period for the interchange of mere compliments, while it should not be treated with indifference, passes quickly by to make room for that of transacting business, consequently for entering into discussions. The first discussion M. de Gontaut had to sustain with Herr von Bismarck, or rather the first meeting he had to face (discussion was out of the question), was on a subject that could not be broached without emotion on the ambassador's part. All the French prisoners had by no means been given up at the conclusion of peace. Prussia still kept within her fortresses not only some of the regulars accused of having committed, during their captivity, acts of insubordination or other offences, but also those who, forming no part of the regular army, had been taken "arms in hand"; for, by a more than doubtful interpretation of international law, the Prussian generals never consented to look upon the freely-organized contingents (*les corps francs*) as entitled to the consideration which, according to the usages of all civilized nations, is due to belligerents. They, the Prussian generals, would not concede those rights even to the corps organized under official approval. As a consequence, they had often punished with death acts of legitimate defence, and flattered themselves that they were showing great clemency when inflicting an indefinite term of captivity on those whom they considered guilty of such defence. Among those prisoners were some of the flower of our country.

M. de Gontaut, acting on instructions from M. Thiers, resolutely set to work to plead their cause. The greatest difficulty, however, lay in doing this with Herr von Bismarck himself, who, after having welcomed the ambassador at a first interview with a brusqueness to which he wished to impart the semblance of cordiality, made himself generally invisible, referring the more delicate questions at issue to his Minister for Foreign Affairs, Herr von Thile, who in his turn had never sufficient latitude given to him to settle them; hence M. de Gontaut never did more than draw a few individual concessions from him, which, moreover, were limited to the lot of the purely military captures. M. de St. Vallier, who was at Nancy at that time, charged by M. Thiers with the communications between himself and General von Manteuffel, commanding the army of occupation, and who pursued assiduously a similar course, was not more lucky than M. de Gontaut in that respect.[1] Months went by, and there seemed to be no end to the hardships borne by the ill-fated captives. At last, one day at a dinner-party, M. de Gontaut happened to be seated by the side of the terrible Chancellor. It is a well-known fact that his somewhat forbidding aspect and his colossal height (M. de Gontaut says, "He gives one the impression of a Goth or a Visigoth,"), whence he, as it were, dominates his interlocutor, make it rather difficult to open a conversation with him. Nevertheless, this was an opportunity it would have been unwise not to embrace, and M. de Gontaut made up his mind to seize it, and to get the load from off his heart. It was a by no means easy task, for his powerful neighbour, who saw no doubt what he was aiming at, deliberately interrupted him by a long monologue on the best way to obtain good vintages, and treated the conveniently-handy subject with

---

[1] M. de St. Vallier was Minister Plenipotentiary at Stuttgart at the outbreak of the war, and succeeded M. de Gontaut-Biron as Ambassador to Berlin. It was during his mission that the French Embassy on the Pariser Platz was rebuilt, at a cost of £24,000.—TRANS.

an inexhaustible flow of language, testifying to a deep study of the question. It was only just before the party broke up that M. de Gontaut was enabled to slip in a word, which was immediately taken up most animatedly. Herr von Bismarck insisted energetically on the necessity of *curbing French ardour*, and to guard by examples of just severity his troops which were still in France from the dangers to which they were exposed every day in their contact with the inhabitants of the "occupied" provinces. Had he not just heard that some peasants tried for having killed two German soldiers in a quarrel had been acquitted by juries of two departments (Aisne and Seine et Oise)? It was therefore useless to depend on French justice; he was compelled to provide his own police.

"After all," remarked Herr von Bismarck, "what you are complaining is the consequence of war." "All the more reason," replied M. de Gontaut, "not to prolong the thing beyond the war itself."

The conversation ended, though, with a word of hope, which M. de Gontaut construed into a kind of promise. He was wrong, for, the fulfilment of the supposed promise being delayed, he thought he might venture to refresh the Chancellor's memory by a letter addressed to him directly. "I was but a novice in diplomacy," he said ingenuously. And, in fact, though he had carefully avoided every expression that might read like a reproach, Herr von Bismarck pretended to be offended at being accused of breaking his word, and made the pretext the opportunity for deferring the hoped-for amnesty until the conclusion of a more important negotiation, which was not terminated until several months later.

That negotiation aimed at nothing less than at the alleviation, in advance of the date fixed beforehand, of the enormous burden that weighed upon us, and to accelerate the moment of our complete deliverance. The painful treaty signed at Frankfort the year before had fixed May 12, 1874, as the latest date for the payment of the three milliards still due, and for the cessation at the same time of the occupation of the territory which was held as a guarantee for that payment. Truly, a special clause gave France the option to discharge her debt before that day by a series of advance payments on account, but no provision had been made as to the consideration that should accrue to us in return for those advanced payments, if made, whether in the extent of the territory occupied or the number of troops, whose maintenance devolved on the French Treasury. M. Thiers intended to claim a proportional and gradual decrease of those two burdens.

There was nothing excessive in that claim, for in every kind of transaction natural equity prescribes that the value of the pledge shall be kept proportionate to the amount of the debt. But it would have been neither prudent nor feasible to ask for more. Truly, in an analogous situation the Duc de Richelieu, speaking in the name of Louis XVIII. at the Congress of Aix-la-Chapelle, had, by sheer weight of character and by the benevolent support of Russia, obtained an immediate and unconditional termination of a similar period of trial which was not to expire for a long while, but the condition of things and the states of mind were far different. Herr von Bismarck had none of the generous feelings of Alexander I.; we had no aid to expect from any of the European Powers. The new Emperor of Germany could not be asked to show the consideration for the uncertain and provisional state of Republican France, which the allied Powers of 1815 had shown to the monarchical principle represented by the envoy of royalty restored. This time we could look for no other attenuation of our lot than that of our own forestalling of the sacrifices exacted from us.

But in that particular direction one might advance boldly and make the largest offers without the least fear of being embarrassed in their performance. The ease with which the first loan had been subscribed attested a strength of the national thrift that promised as easy a response to a second, no matter how short the interval between the two, and even if the second should considerably exceed the first. M. Thiers felt perfectly safe in announcing that the first of the three still outstanding milliards would be at the disposal of Germany in the first half of 1872, and the last two in the course of the following year. The next thing to do was to obtain a proportional reduction in the extent of the occupation after each payment. Those were the terms in which the negotiations were to be opened by M. de Gontaut at Berlin, and in Paris by M. Thiers with the ambassador of Prussia, Count von Arnim.

But at the first word uttered, it became patent that this unexpected proof of the financial resources of France—which astonished Europe, and inspired us with a justified revival of hope—was received by our victors with very different feelings. The surprise showed them the mistake they had made, and they were scarcely able to hide their annoyance. In fixing the amount of the indemnity at a figure hitherto unprecedented, one which appalled the imagination, the idea had been to deal at the wealth and credit of the nation, already so cruelly tried, a blow from which she would not recover for a long while, if ever. This turned out to be a mistake, seeing that the burden was so lightly borne, but the error they secretly regretted was that of not having asked for more. Then when they saw the wounded one, whom they believed to be utterly prostrate, get up and recover his strength in a marvellously short time, there was the annoyance of having to give him his liberty to make use of that strength. Moreover, was not this very hurry to pay at once and at any price somewhat suspicious? Did not the hurry to be rid of the German troops hide the design to embark in military preparations away from their surveillance, with the view of having recourse as soon as possible, and in the hope of a prompt revenge, to the chances of another war? That fear, on the face of it, seemed confirmed by the activity with which, at the same moment, the National Assembly assiduously devoted itself to the task of reconstructing our shattered army, with an ardour such that M. Thiers himself appeared unable to restrain it, inasmuch as he dissented on several points with the parliamentary commissions, notably on the points of compulsory service, and the inordinate increase of the effective number of troops which would be its result. The conclusion was that, in the interests of peace, Germany should be in no hurry to relinquish the means to check the intention to provoke her, the signs of which she fancied she could detect.

Sincere though this feeling of uneasiness was with some, it was, if not altogether assumed, at any rate considerably exaggerated by others, who were not unwilling to take advantage of it; for this near renewal of hostilities on France's part which they professed to dread was almost openly and eagerly desired by a powerful party, especially among the military *entourage* of the Emperor. Convinced, as they said they were, that the feeling of irritation prevailing in France would inevitably lead to a renewed struggle, whether sooner or later, was it not wiser to face it at once, when their heel was still on the throat of the enemy, and all the roads to the capital practically open? Moreover, seeing that the operation which was meant to weaken her for ever had failed in its aim, this would be the moment to make it complete. Truly, some of them remarked, that even with the prospect of a more or less imminent renewal of the war, it would be to Germany's interest to begin proceedings by getting hold of the three milliards, which would serve to cover the cost of that war, instead of leaving the money to the French Treasury. But the majority were in favour of keeping the territory due to their victory, and in military circles it was over and over again repeated, that if France had paid 4,999,999,999 francs of her debt, not a single German ought to leave the ground occupied until the last franc was in Germany's pockets. The reports of this provoking language were so widespread, that one day an English paper, as a rule well-informed, gave the news that if France refused to give her promise to suspend her armaments, the German ambassador would be recalled, and the army of occupation would take the field once more.

The extreme coolness with which M. de Gontaut's first references to the subject which he was instructed to make, in the form of discreet hints, were received is explained by the somewhat complex views which have just been alluded to, and it became the ambassador's business to disentangle them and to make them understood. This, as it were, constituted the moral part of the negotiation, which only he was in a position to pursue, amidst the surroundings in which he was placed. With regard to the material difficulties of all kinds hampering a hitherto unparalleled and gigantic financial operation, M. Thiers brought to bear upon this solution all the inexhaustible resources of a mind and a promptness and at the same time suppleness of decision which astounded even the experienced financiers whom he made his instruments. Unfortunately, the only one to confront him was the German ambassador in Paris, Count von Arnim, a peevish and unbusiness-like interlocutor, who, as was suspected then already and proved afterwards, only reflected very impartially the mental disposition and intentions of his masters. In Berlin only was it possible to read their real feelings clearly and to probe their inmost hearts. Truly, to do this it required the subtlety of observation with which M. de Gontaut found himself all at once endowed, and which at the first trial must have left him thoroughly convinced, in spite of what he said himself, that his diplomatic apprenticeship would not be a long one. In a profession in which a knowledge of men is of infinitely greater value than mere book-learning, there has been no more convincing proof than his, that the thing one is likely to know is that which one would have never known if an apprenticeship to it had been necessary. In judging M. de Gontaut to be fully fitted for the delicate task that had been confided to him, without the need of adding anything to his natural gifts, developed by the practice of polite society, M. Thiers had judged correctly, and been served by his luck.

The capacity to listen and to understand, however, was one thing, to get hold of an interlocutor was another, and the more difficult of the two. "Prussian interiors are very much walled-in," wrote M. de Gontaut on January 29, 1872, "and this holds good of the higher as of the less elevated sections of society. The great distrust of foreigners has been a tradition here since the time of Frederick the Great. The princes never talk politics, and one never sets eyes on them except at official receptions. Herr von Bismarck is practically invisible. The representatives of the German courts quiver in their shoes before the Chancellor, and those of other courts are scarcely more free of speech. Those are the elements by the aid of which one is compelled to look and to judge, and you will admit that there is a great risk of venturing too far, especially to one who is so little seasoned as I am as yet."

If, as M. de Gontaut subsequently says, the ice was broken very soon, his rapid advance into a midst which lent itself so little to it, was due to a union of good qualities which are sure to be appreciated quickly, not only in social intercourse, but on the scene of the most important transactions; namely, a prepossessing manner, which did not detract from the dignity, the charm, and the firmness of his intercourse; secondly, a great delicacy of feeling, and even the advantage of being a delightful talker. Besides, M. de Gontaut was not the only one that was thus endowed, and who utilized those gifts. He was seconded by his numerous and lovable family, the members of which, owing to grand alliances contracted previously to the war, met at once with an affectionate and almost familiar welcome in the higher spheres of Prussian society, and who in that way were enabled to approach several royal personages on a footing of respectful intimacy. Thanks to those facilities, and to the art of keeping an open door to all sorts of communications, M. de Gontaut managed to gather in a short time, and from the best sources, many bits of information exceedingly useful to his purpose, of giving those in Paris an exact idea of what was being said and thought and occurred in Berlin.

First of all came the great banker, the financial

auxiliary of Herr Von Bismarck. "I am bound to tell you" (says Herr Bleichroeder in a confidential interview) "that Herr von Bismarck is very pleased to see you here, but he is not pleased with M. Thiers." "But why?" I asked. "Because M. Thiers is increasing the French army to an inordinate extent. Prince Bismarck is anxiously watching the reorganization of your army. He finds that the war budget is eighty millions of francs in excess of the preceding budgets. He assures us that the new 'effective' exceeds that of the Empire, which would be contrary to the promises given to him personally at Versailles by M. Thiers. That is the dark point at the horizon; the only one, perhaps, that worries Prince Bismarck with regard to the maintenance of peace."

A few days afterwards came the turn of one of M. de Gontaut's colleagues, the Minister of a great foreign court. He went still further in his revelations. "The military party," said that envoy, "will always reproach Bismarck with having given up Belfort to France, and they have not altogether abandoned the idea of prolonging the military occupation, perhaps to make it permanent. They are well aware that this would be altogether at variance with the treaties, but they are counting on some imprudent act on your part, on some delay in the fulfilment of your engagements; also probably on troubles among yourselves, which they would convert into a pretext for their designs. At all events that party is strongly inclined to occupy your departments as long as possible, and, after what I have just told you, you will not fail to understand the reason of it."

"A little while after that," adds M. de Gontaut, "a member of the *Bundesrath* (the Federal Council of the Empire) said to me, 'There is a strong wish here to keep Belfort. The war, according to calculations, has cost Germany about four milliards; they would be very willing to cry quits with you for the fifth milliard if you would let them keep Belfort.'"

To cap the whole, there was an interview of the same kind with a personage more important than all the rest, with him who, perhaps, to a greater degree than Lazare Carnot, had deserved the title of the organizer of victory, in effect, with Marshal von Moltke. The interview was of M. de Gontaut's own seeking. Aware of the exaggerated terms in which the efforts of the National Assembly to replace the scattered army were being discussed by the Prussian Staffs, the ambassador broached the subject point-blank to Moltke, by asking him if he had any knowledge of the report on the new military law presented by M. de Chasseloup-Laubat.

"I have read it," replied the Marshal; "he reports in favour of compulsory service. Do you think he will get it?" As will be seen directly, that question bore directly on the chief preoccupation of the Prussian Government. "I am unable to say," I remarked to the Marshal; "I am unable to say; opinions are very much divided. M. Thiers is scarcely inclined to compulsory service; but you have got it here, and the majority of the European states are adopting it one after the other. Hence there is a general tendency in France to apply it." "I cannot deny it," said the Marshal; "still as yet I fail to see in what direction the Assembly will decide. . . . Meanwhile," he went on, rather more vivaciously than was his wont, and with a slightly bitter smile, "meanwhile, M. Thiers seems pretty busy in reconstructing that army. Next spring it will be in a position to commence war."

Then, as if afraid that he had gone too far, he warmly disclaimed all desire for a renewal of hostilities, and even emphatically mentioned his own wish that the occupation should come to an end as soon as possible, in the interest of the German troops themselves. He in that way confirmed, as it were, seriously what he had said a few days previously in a jocular manner, namely, that material existence in France was so easy and sweet that it had the effect of spoiling his soldiers for their profession.

Contrary to the habits of most diplomatic agents, M. de Gontaut says very little of himself in his dispatches. From an innate feeling of modesty (sufficiently rare among our countrymen), he seems to be convinced that, with reference to the advice he was called upon to give, that which was said to him was of greater interest than his own replies or remarks. In spite of that reserve, one cannot help being struck by the justness of perception and promptness of reply which enabled him to show more than once (and that notwithstanding his slight practical knowledge of military matters) that the measures at which Germany professed to take umbrage were, after all, only the indispensable minimum of endeavour on the part of France to reconstruct her shattered "*cadres*," and precaution to repair her broken lines of defence. Gontaut's loyalty, which was admitted on all sides after a little while, and the character of good faith that stamped all his words, gave great weight to his statements. They were, moreover, confirmed by M. Thiers in a very sustained correspondence, in which, warned of the nature of the difficulties that were obstructing his hopes, he brought to bear upon the removal of those prejudices and obstacles that mixture of clearness and dash that invested truth from his lips with an almost irresistible strength.

But whatever the effect of those protestations, the choicest passages of which M. de Gontaut carefully communicated with a view to their reaching the Emperor himself, every eye remained, nevertheless, fixed on our Assembly, and every ear strained to catch the sound of the debates on the law of recruitment, which were at that moment just beginning to occupy the attention of the Chamber. It was patent that the decision for which we were being kept waiting would depend on the turn of those debates; and I have already indicated the capital point which aroused the most anxious curiosity to the whole of military society, but to the Emperor himself more than to any one, namely, the introduction so ardently desired by a section of the Assembly of compulsory and personal military service. Not that the generals, who had practical proof of what in reality constituted the strength of the French soldier, were seriously alarmed at the enormous cipher which in consequence of that general call might somewhat indefinitely multiply their quantity. In reality the number caused them no anxiety, for they felt certain that Germany would always be able to place more men in line than we; and besides, more than one of those generals had his doubts with regard to the system of compulsory service in itself. But the ardour displayed by the French in their rush to meet a sacrifice, the burden of which would be especially felt by the better provided classes, the enthusiastic shouts that had greeted the fiery words of the Duc d'Audiffret-Pasquier, enjoining on every citizen the duty to learn the practice of arms; all these, according to them, were the signs revealing, still according to them, not an impulse of lofty patriotism, but an impatient thirsting for reparation and revenge. It was like the bugle sounding a general uprising. They were awaiting the final resolution of the Assembly as the touchstone which would enable them to judge of the degree of confidence they were to place in our pacific intentions.

At the same time, this was the very subject on which M. Thiers felt the most easy, not only with regard to offering the most formal assurances, but, as it were, to lavish them, for there was no subject on which he had a more decided opinion and a more deep-seated conviction. It is well known that he clung to both these in his retirement, and till the last day of his life, and that on the eve of his death he gathered his friends around him to beseech them not to lend themselves to a mode of recruitment the unavoidable consequence of which was the shortening of the term of service, which shortening would, according to him, spoil the mechanism of no matter what army by swamping it in a confused and indisciplined mass. Therefore it would be absolutely beside the truth to say that he authorized M. de Gontaut to promise in his (Thiers') name that he would not allow the system of compulsory service to be legally adopted. If there were such a pledge at all, he had taken it beforehand, not with regard to Germany, but with regard to

France and to himself, in the patriotic interest of a national defence. But he made no secret of his resolve, and assured the Prussian Government that he felt sufficiently strong to overcome all resistance. Hence on April 26, 1872, the report spread that he was about to give way to the repeated instances of the Parliamentary Commission. "I am told," he writes, "that M. de Bismarck is displeased at two things." (The first being only an insignificant detail as to the mode of payment of the various sums to be paid, I think it unnecessary to reproduce it.) "But the second," he goes on to say, "is an agreement between me and the Commission, entitled the Army Commission on the principle of compulsory service. Those two things are absolutely untrue (*sont fausses*). I am in favour of an army which knows its business, and am against a revolutionary army, as unfit to wage war within as without. I shall, perhaps, be obliged to make concessions in the way of words, but I will make no concessions whatsoever with regard to things. Whosoever has had business dealings with men knows that one is, as a rule, compelled to the former, even under circumstances of the sincerest and staunchest convictions."

Truth to tell, his able and clever minister for Foreign Affairs, M. de Rémusat, did not altogether share his confidence. "I doubt," he wrote on May 12, "if the King of Prussia would have felt particularly assured if he could have heard the speech of M. le Duc d'Audiffret-Pasquier,[1] who, as far as talent went, unquestionably deserved his immense success, but who at the same time, I fear, is not quite as prudent as he is eloquent. He drew thunders of applause in favour of compulsory service, and I have no need to tell you with what suspicion Germany views the system which, nevertheless, would probably give us an army more anarchical than warlike. You may boldly give it forth that M. Thiers has come to an understanding with the Assembly, and is under the impression that he will really obtain what he desires by means of a concession of words and an amendment which will be accorded to him. He is very sincere in that assurance, but I may tell you in all confidence, that this question of the reorganization of the army has always impressed me as being the most critical of all, and if there be a rock on which we are likely to split, I am sadly afraid it will be that one."

M. de Rémusat's mistrust was not devoid of foundation. Every one, in fact, has heard of the strength of will and energy it wanted on M. Thiers' part to restrain the generous impetuosity

[1] M. d'Audiffret-Pasquier made two speeches during that memorable month of May 1872. The first, that of May 4, 1872, which is evidently that alluded to by M. de Rémusat, caused intense excitement, and raised him in public opinion to the front rank of parliamentary orators. It drew a violent reply from M. Rouher, whom he answered in a second speech (May 22), which was considered even more powerful than the first.—TRANS.

of the Assembly. The compromise arrived at between him and the Parliamentary Commission consisted in the acceptance, fundamentally, of compulsory service combined with the maintenance of active service for five years, which combination obliged the authorities to take only half the contingent each year, lest the effective number of troops should exceed the proportions which the budget could possibly bear. But from the moment that mutual understanding was established, M. Thiers refused to overstep his concession by so much as a hair's-breadth. He even opposed with all his strength a modest amendment to reduce the active service from five years to four, and went as far as to declare in the Tribune itself, that if the law were modified in that direction he would decline the responsibility of applying it. It was in the fear of a crisis which no one cared to provoke that the amendment, already withdrawn by its author and re-introduced by a rather obscure member, only secured an insignificant number of votes.

A comparison between two dates is in itself sufficient to show the effect of that sitting, the recollection of which is still vivid in the minds of all who were members of the Assembly. The final vote was given in the evening of June 10, and a fortnight afterwards—namely, on the 29th —a negotiation, the delays and indecision of which had been prolonged for months, could be promptly terminated at Versailles by the signing of a Convention, the clauses of which partly responded to M. Thiers' hopes and wishes.[1]

I say "partly," for there were still several points wanting to complete the satisfaction of M. Thiers. The Convention stipulated clearly enough that two departments should be evacuated immediately after the payment of the first half-milliard (of the remaining three), and two other departments after the integral discharge of the second, which was fixed for March 1, 1874. But although there was a clause which implied clearly enough the successive reduction of the number of troops in consequence, nothing precise had been stipulated in that respect, and the relief of this or that department might entail a heavier burden on another. The evacuated departments, moreover, were to remain (according to the Treaty) neutral ground in the military sense until the final execution of the operation, that is, there could be

---

[1] There is evidently a slight mistake on the author's part, which I do not feel justified in altering in the text. He distinctly says a fortnight (*quinze jours*), but, according to his dates, nineteen days went by between the passing of the law and the signing of the Convention by M. de Rémusat and Count von Arnim. He is distinctly correct in his dates ; the law passed on the 10th, and was promulgated on June 27. The Convention was also signed on the date he assigns. Inasmuch as he lays great stress on the shortness of the interval, the error may be a slip of the pen, or a printer's error, or he has merely used the words *quinze jours* in a more or less accurate sense. I am translating from the first, and what appear to me *not* finally corrected proofs, for the sake of dispatch.—TRANS.

no agglomeration of troops nor erection of new fortresses. Finally, a delay for the discharge of the third milliard had been granted until May 1, 1875, although such delay had not been asked for. Truly, there was also the option on France's part to substitute before that period financial guarantees of recognized weight for the territorial guarantees. Those various conditions attested a persistent and by no means gracious mistrust, and betrayed the secret hope, maybe, to take advantage of possible complications. Hence, when the text of the Convention became known, there was a rather visible disappointment on the part of the nation which had hoped for better things.

Charged by the Commission of the Assembly, to which the Treaty had to be submitted, with the report thereon, I did my utmost to hide that feeling, but the assent, which could not be withheld, was given in a sad and silent manner, although unanimously. Truly, a popular ratification of a different character, and of much greater importance, followed close; namely, the issue of a loan of three milliards, covered in a few days by subscriptions which attained nearly forty times the amount asked for. The ill-humour of the creditor mattered little after that to the debtor, who, holding his ransom in the palm of his hand, might safely believe himself to be nigh his hour of deliverance.

For the nonce, in fact, the proof admitted of no

reply. Verily, France was resuscitated, and she would have to be reckoned with once more, a nation which, scarcely recovered from so terrible a fall, showed herself capable and disposed to use the sinews of war in such a large-handed manner. The success was beyond all expectation. The very lively impression it produced in Europe came in the nick of time, perhaps, to modify the character of a solemn meeting which was to be held at Berlin, and in which M. de Gontaut would be called upon to take a greater part than had apparently been reserved to him.

In the course of the previous year the Emperor of Austria had received at Gastein a visit from the new Emperor of Germany—a doleful act of politeness, only tending to establish beyond a doubt the triumph of an erstwhile rival who had become all-powerful, but which, nevertheless, was all the more significant, and at the same time equally necessary to return.

The arrival, then, in Berlin, of the Sovereign and Prime Minister of Austria, timed to take place about the very beginning of the autumn, seemed perfectly natural; but what caused greater surprise was the news that Czar Alexander II., either as a self-invited or bidden guest, intended to make a third at the interview. Was it to be a real congress, that meeting? And if so, what would be its meaning and aim. The English and German papers immediately swarmed with comments of all kinds on the subject. Given the place of meeting, it could not be admitted for a moment that the host called upon to preside at that meeting would permit in his very presence a discussion of the extraordinarily important facts that had been accomplished but a short time since to his glory and profit. There remained, then, only one supposition, namely, that he intended, on the contrary, to ask for, nay to demand, perhaps, their consecration by means of the sanction of his fellow-monarchs, in order to make those facts the starting-point and basis of a new European code of the law of nations.

The conjecture was all the more natural, inasmuch as that mode of conferring legitimacy of a certain sort, by a general assent after the fact, on possessions more or less regularly acquired, tallied sufficiently well with past traditions, and in particular with those of the grand Congress of Vienna, which were still vividly imprinted on everybody's memory as the heroic days of diplomacy. In fact, was it not in a similar manner that the powers which foregathered on that memorable occasion, after dividing among themselves the spoil of the vanquished one of Waterloo, and allotting crowns and territories at their own sweet will, had affixed their collective guarantee to their work, and by so doing reciprocally pledged themselves to allow no attempt against it except by their unanimous agreement and consent. In reality, that was the rule which had prevailed for nearly forty years; the treaties of 1815 figuring meanwhile as the charter of an international pact, which had not been deviated from save on very rare occasions, and after protracted negotiations and a series of conferences and protocols. Was that the *rôle* reserved now for the Treaty of Frankfort? Was it to be converted into the principal clause of a new policy of mutual insurance between the three great Powers of the North? Those proposed articles of European partnership might appear somewhat belated on the part of Herr von Bismarck, for no one more than he had openly made it a point not to be trammelled by any consideration for conventions, or of interests other than those of his master. No one had been more assiduous in dissuading Wilhelm to admit of intervention or even of comment that might hamper him in the most rigorous and extended application of his rights as a victor. In that way he had twice re-arranged the map of Central Europe without permitting witnesses, even those most interested in that new distribution, to as much as lift their voices. It did indeed seem strange that, after having kept his neighbours at arm's-length during the action, he now wished to induce them to guarantee the identical points with regard to which he had conspicuously abstained from consulting them. Was this a reason, though, why the new German Empire, after having allotted to itself everything it deemed fit to take, should not seek to secure for itself, in order to keep what it had taken, the eventual co-operation of those whose counsels were neither asked nor probably would have been listened to if offered? Not at all. In thus changing his tone and carriage in accordance with altered circumstances, the Prussian Minister was only imitating once more the grand model whose example it has always been his boast to reproduce. In order to understand Bismarck thoroughly, one must before everything else study Frederick the Great. The invader of Silesia, after having laid violent hands on his prey without taking advice or listening to remonstrance, was nevertheless most anxious afterwards to obtain the recognition and guarantee of his possession by all the united Powers, which assembled a few years later at the Congress of Aix-la-Chapelle.

What we really had to fear, then, was a confirmation and even an aggravation of the painful position in which we were placed, for it was not a matter of indifference to us to see the chain of our conquered provinces riveted still more tightly by two additional links, and a restriction of the chances which the unexpected whims of Fortune keep in reserve for the just causes she has allowed to be defeated. M. de Gontaut, who had come to spend a few days in France after the signing of the Convention, received orders to return immediately to his post with instructions to watch everything in order to ascertain whether the conversation between the royal (? imperial) personages would result in something more than an interchange of friendly assurances, and, above all, whether it would lead to anything like a verbal convention or a written instrument.

It did not take M. de Gontaut long to become practically sure that, if an idea of that kind had been entertained at Berlin, the reception of the first overtures in that direction had not been of a nature to encourage it. The first dazzling effects caused by the brilliant Prussian victories were beginning to wear off, and the spectators, struck for a moment with stupor, were gradually coming to their senses, and felt more or less ill-at-ease. All those who sooner or later would be bound to have dealings with the favourite of fortune looked with apprehension at the preponderant power looming in front of them, and with which no one would be sufficiently strong to cope. On every frontier of the German Empire there became evident the kind of uneasiness caused by the lateral pressure of a volume of water, even when undisturbed, which is too vast for its banks, and ever ready to overflow them. Seeing that France, which people imagined to be utterly crushed, seemed to be reviving, the idea presented itself to many that one day she might be called upon to assume a part that would serve as a basis of resistance against the colossus whose growth has been so complacently watched; and that presentiment was not without its influence on the friendly welcome M. de Gontaut received from the two imperial visitors to Berlin and their ministers, a welcome the very reverse of that of Herr von Bismarck, who was disagreeably surprised at M. de Gontaut's hurried return.

On the part of the Austrians, however, the expression of that feeling was, though sufficiently patent, more or less reserved and not unmixed. This was but natural; Austria was strongly suspected, and not without reason, of having expressed sincere wishes for our success during the whole duration of the war. Recent revelations have even shown that she had promised us her aid on certain conditions, the fulfilment of which the ministers of Napoleon III. had the incredible imprudence not to await. Any mark of sympathy would have given umbrage, which in her actual isolated and unsupported position it was highly important to avoid; hence M. de Gontaut's conversations with the Emperor always took place in the presence of a numerous gathering, and although they were sufficiently prolonged to arouse the attention and displeasure of certain witnesses of them, nothing was ever said beyond vague general statements and remarks. Different was the attitude of Russia, simply because her situation was equally different. She had rendered good service to the victor during the war, inasmuch as the constant dread of her ever-threatening intervention had deprived us of all support from the outside; she had reaped the fruit of her good offices by freeing herself, in virtue of the Convention recently signed in London, from all the consequences of her Crimean defeats, and by recovering for her navy the free run and the empire of the Black Sea. At the end of the game the parties to it were quits, and at liberty to regulate their future relations with one another as best they liked. The perfect frankness of the Czar's language during the interview he granted M. de Gontaut attested that independence.

After having, according to diplomatic custom, inquired about the health of the Chief of the State, the Czar went on, saying—" I hold M. Thiers in the most profound esteem. Be kind enough to convey to him my assurance that he has nothing to fear from what is going on here. France might have been certain beforehand that I would bear no share in anything that might be attempted against her."

In his turn, Chancellor Gortschakoff considered it his duty to add his comments to those professions already so reassuring. "His Majesty's language conveys very accurately the sentiments of the Russian Government," he said. "We are interested in and sympathetic to France. France must be both strong and wise: she must be wise in order to play the part assigned to her in the world; she must be wise just because she must be able to play her part with authority, and in order to make her action yield beneficent results. Take heart for yourself, and also reassure M. Thiers. If you fulfil the engagements undertaken by you nothing else will be required of you. People are talking of your army and its reorganization, it is but natural that these matters should not be looked at with indifference here; but on that point Germany has not the faintest right to address the slightest objection to you. You do what you please, and you are right. . . ." Then he went on—" With regard to what has passed between us here, there may have been an interchange of views and ideas, but there has been no protocol. We are parting without the smallest scrap of writing between us. Do not fail to inform your Government to that effect."

It was the same idea that was expressed a few days later, and in a somewhat more epigrammatic manner, by a Russian agent who occupied a most important position. All those who have had occasion to meet with him will recognize him by the somewhat thoughtless animation of his utterances.[1] " Russia and Austria," he

[1] I have an idea that the Russian agent referred to was M. Hamburger, who was sometime, and may be still, as far as I know,

said, "have no wish to intervene in the question of the annexations that have been accomplished. Prussia began the war without consulting the other European Powers; she has had the luck of being victorious; she has made use of her victory according to her own will, without inviting the assent of Russia and Austria. She has acted on her own absolute responsibility. (*Elle a agi à ses risques et périls.*) What has been won by war may be lost in war. She has conquered; if she should be conquered when her turn comes is none of our business."

At the still troubled period, when those assurances of a sympathetic support on the part of Russia were given to us, there might have been a doubt as to their sincerity and durableness. Subsequent facts have proved that France was right in trusting to them. We know how brilliantly and firmly the successor of Alexander II. persisted in his line of conduct, which was as loyal as it was sensible. An attempt to show what were its origin and starting-point may not be without interest, if for no other purpose than to divide equally between the father and the son the honour and gratitude due to them.

And now let us glance for a moment at the

---

the Russian minister in Switzerland. But it is nothing more than an idea, for the author's description, except in one point, is too vague to go by. M. Hamburger was somewhat famed for his clever but nearly always ill-considered speeches. He was, nevertheless, greatly liked by the *entourage* of Alexander II.—TRANS.

*finesse*, utterly devoid of presumption, with which M. de Gontaut, at the termination of the imperial visits, summed up his judgment on the dispositions he had been able to fathom.

"I am disinclined to believe that Germany has obtained what she desired. Without aiming exactly at anything hostile against France, she tried to extract from a very cordial and confidential meeting of the three most powerful sovereigns of continental Europe, a manifestation which would have somewhat turned to the confusion of France. Whatever she may still say to the contrary, it would have flattered her pride in a certain sense if those sovereigns, by an explicit act, had recognized the territorial modifications that have taken place in consequence of the last war. Has she been successful on those two points? I do not think so. Russia and Austria consider France to be necessary to Europe. It is their opinion that France has suffered enough, and they are evidently bent on encouraging her in her happy efforts to reinstate herself in her old position. In proof whereof are the praises bestowed by Alexander and Francis-Joseph, and by the Chancellor of the Russian Empire, on the reorganization of our army. Hence we may take it that Russia and Austria desire to see a France that shall be strong, and that Germany would like to keep France feeble. This constitutes a capital difference between the policies of the three

Powers, a difference of which Germany, do whatever she will, will be compelled to take notice."

"Since her victories," he adds, "the Press of this country treats with disdain the idea of a European equilibrium. It will have no more of it, because it aims at its own preponderance. Nobody, therefore, dared to pronounce the word since the misfortunes of France, and, behold, the word has reappeared in the language of politics. There is, as yet, no occasion to say that it means a victory for our country; but, at any rate, a proof that justice is beginning to be dealt out to her."—*Souvenirs*, pp. 85, 86.

Assuredly nothing was better calculated to make us look impatiently forward to our complete deliverance than this clear patch on the European horizon; hence M. de Gontaut, acting upon orders from M. Thiers, was just preparing to open negotiations for the elimination from the last Convention of the clause dealing with the delay in the occupation, which was no longer justified by our financial condition, and consequently with the clauses of guarantee that had been added to it. Everything led him to believe that he would have no difficulty in making himself listened to, when a grave accident in our home politics brought unexpected trouble around him, and even prevented for some time the mere mention of the matter in conversation.

## II.

The 13th November, the day on which the National Assembly resumed its work, after a short recess, M. Thiers, taking possession of the rostrum himself, read a presidential message, in which, after having summarized with his wonted precision and clearness the whole of the financial and political transactions over which he had so ably presided, he proposed without the least circumlocution to proceed at once to the final establishment of the Republican Government. "The Republic," he said, "exists. The attempt to establish something else would mean another revolution, and the one most to be feared. . . . The Republic," he went on to say, "is bound to be the government of the nation, which, having for a long while and in good faith left the divided direction of her destinies to a hereditary power, but which, not having succeeded, through mistakes which it would be impossible to judge today, decides at last to govern herself, and by herself, through the men she has elected." Truly, he immediately added that the Republic, such as he conceived it, must be and remain essentially Conservative, and he claimed the proper institutions which, according to him, would enable it to keep up that character, *i. e.* the extension of the prerogatives of the executive power, the constitution of a Second Chamber, an electoral law regulating the exercise of universal suffrage; but, disguise it as he would, the blow had been aimed. It was the rupture of the truce of parties known, as I have said, by the name of the Bordeaux pact; it was the open declaration of war to the Monarchical party of the Assembly. The prompt reply of M. Audrec de Kerdrel to the challenge is already a matter of history. Striding to the rostrum there and then, he moved and carried instanter the appointment of a commission to draw up an answer to the message of the President. Those who were present on that memorable day are not likely to forget the state of indescribable excitement that prevailed after that unexpected passage of arms, and until the adjournment of the Assembly.

It would be an exaggeration, perhaps, to say that the news of this stirring incident was received with a like emotion. Our affairs did not command as much attention as that, but, to say the least, people were equally surprised. No one expected this unforeseen outbreak of a parliamentary civil war. M. Thiers' provocation caused as much surprise as the reply that had followed it, if not more. People were aware that differences, which sometimes assumed a grave character, had before now broken out between the Assembly and the illustrious man invested by it with the supreme power. The threats of resignation on M. Thiers' part, when the intentions of the Assembly seemed to be at variance with his, had preoccupied the public mind more than once; but people reflected that, after all, those threats had never been carried out, the differences having always been adjusted by an arrangement, in which the Assembly generally got the worst. That was what had occurred particularly in connection with the military laws. Compulsory personal service having been, as I remarked before, the only one of the more or less marked preferences of the Assembly that might have hampered M. Thiers in the course of his patriotic negotiations, the Assembly made up its mind, regretfully it is true, to sacrifice it to him. On all the other points that might contribute to the grand task of the national deliverance, the agreement had been as cordial as it was complete, in spite of the statements to the contrary propagated subsequently by the unskilful panegyrists of M. Thiers. Whatever he had asked, or merely expressed a wish for, in connection with that sacred cause, had been accepted without either debate or discussion by all parties. In one word, France, whatever may have been the already too perceptible effect of her interior divisions, had always shown herself resolved to remain united while the alien had possession of her soil, in order to look him boldly in the face. Surely, he who spoke in her name had the greatest interest in seeing France prolong that attitude full of dignity as long as possible, for in that way he could truly claim to be the representative of the whole nation, and could make himself the surety for the fulfilment of all the engagements he might enter into for her, no matter what those engagements would be, and without reference to the chief France might place at her head later on, or the institutions that should govern her. Why then this haste to trouble a condition of unanimity of which, even if it were but an apparent one, he more than anybody reaped the credit and the honour? Why that unjustified haste, which exposed him to the risk by placing his power at the mercy of a stormy debate, impairing not only the authority of his charge, but even the value of his signature? Why had he not waited a few months longer, to put the seal on the final act of what was to constitute his future title to glory?

That was the question which everybody asked himself, and for the reply to which people looked above all to M. de Gontaut. "The message of M. Thiers is altogether republican then?" said Herr von Schlemitz, the President of the Council of Ministers, with evident trouble. "But it implies the violation of the Bordeaux pact. What does it mean, and whither will it lead?" Taken by surprise, like every one else, the ambassador was least of all able to answer, for during his recent short stay in Paris, M. Thiers, aware of his sentiments, had (probably in order not to hurt those sentiments) not given him the least hint with regard to his personal intentions. Far from it. Though he talked to him in an apparently confidential manner about the message he was preparing, his language had remained sufficiently vague to convey the impression, that though he might ask for some legislative measures they would be solely in the direction of guaranteeing the conservative spirit from the invasion of revolutionary ideas and passions. M. de Gontaut's illusion on the subject had been such as to convince to the same effect Chancellor Gortschakoff, with whom he had had another interview previous to the latter's departure from Berlin. Unfortunately, the telegram recounting the sitting of the Assembly happened to reach Berlin on the evening of and but a few hours after the interview; and the Chancellor meeting the ambassador next morning, "could not help showing me his surprise, which I could not help noticing, and which, in reality, I shared to the full, *plus* a feeling of sorrow." These are M. de Gontaut's own words. Then he goes on—"He had just left Emperor Wilhelm, and I have reason to believe that their feelings on the subject are the same. I had only had a summary of the presidential message; I endeavoured to justify its tone by replying to Prince Gortschakoff that I was enabled to gather two things from it: the virtual acknowledgment of the existence of the Republic *de facto*, which it was impossible to deny; and the absolute necessity to hedge it round with conservative guarantees. The last declaration constituting the capital point of the message, every one both in France and Europe ought to be pleased at it."

For a man who practically did not know what to think, much less what to say, M. de Gontaut got out of the difficulty pretty well. Meanwhile, it was necessary to convey to Paris an account of the uneasy feeling prevalent at Berlin, and M. de Gontaut would have been wanting both in dignity and frankness if he failed to show clearly his own awkward position at being suspected of wishing to deceive or of having been deceived himself, and of having been compelled to account for his error by explanations which would satisfy no one, seeing that they failed to satisfy himself. I may admit that to this day, reason as I will on those facts with the calmness and impartiality of history, to which indeed they belong, I understand no more than I did at the first hour (perhaps less than I did at the first hour) what induced M. Thiers to select that critical moment to anticipate, as it were, an explanation with the monarchical party—an explanation which sooner or later would have been unavoidable, but which was most inopportune just then. Did he really imagine that a number of colleagues, several of whom were his friends, and with nearly all of whom he had lived for two years on a footing of intimacy, did he really imagine that all these would allow him to disregard in the most cavalier fashion all the promises he had made them without the least protest on their part? To think this would be to suppose him as utterly bereft of that knowledge of men which constitutes an essential part of the art to govern them. Truly, he may have been encouraged in that illusion by the resignation with which that royalist majority had allowed him, from the very morrow of the engagements taken by him at Bordeaux, to interpret those engagements in a sense absolutely contrary to the ordinary sense of his words, and such as we understand them. It was, in fact, patent, and we were all aware of it, that far from maintaining with regard to constitutional questions the scrupulous neutrality which (if he did not misunderstand him) he had sworn to maintain *on his honour*, he had considered himself as entitled to lean overtly to a republican solution, and never neglected a means to ensure its success.

It was in order to secure to the Republic the legal title as distinct from the *de facto* one which she already possessed, that he had used all the influence due either to the fame of his happy genius or to popular favour; in furtherance of that view, he had put in operation all the mechanism of that administrative power which is always so great in France, and all the fascination of his brilliant conversation. If it be true, that his relations with each of us had remained most kindly, his confidence, his heart, his innermost feelings belonged, nevertheless, to the Republican Left. Not one of us fostered any longer the faintest illusion in that respect. Assuredly, it was painful to watch day by day the progress and accomplishment of a hostile and, according to us, destructive work. But the urgency of the national crisis, and the importance of not complicating it by an inward crisis, had compelled us to let things take their course, and to shut our eyes even to proofs. But the great and decisive question was not to be solved without us, that much had, at any rate, been promised, and unambiguously promised, to us. We were not so far wrong, then, in exercising patience pending the day of reckoning. And behold, before that day had come we were being told, not only that the question would not be put, but that we were haughtily refused the right to discuss it. There was something particularly offensive in that unceremonious treatment, the effect of which, it is difficult to believe, M. Thiers had not felt beforehand. He could all the less easily be mistaken in that respect, seeing that he was perfectly aware of the nature of the feelings that animated us all, and the sincerity of which not only deserved his consideration but his esteem. Among the most devoted partisans of royalty, some, in order to remain faithful to the principles dear to them, had foregone from their youth the advantages of a high position, and spent the best years of their lives in retirement, whence they had only emerged at the appeal of their country in distress, and with that modest devotion of which M. de Gontaut had set the example; others were the pupils of M. Thiers himself, inasmuch as they had been taught to consider the perils to which a great nation is exposed by the system of removing, at will of the chief power, the very school of parliamentary chiefs of which M. Thiers was the most illustrious survivor.

And it was on the whole of those convictions and affections of diverse origin and character, it is true, but all equally entitled to respect, it was on those glorious recollections of the past, it was on all those lessons experience had taught us, on all the apprehensions of the future, that we were asked to proceed "to the order of the day[1]" with

---

[1] "The order of the day" of an Assembly is the order it has established for the regulation and transaction of its business. When the Assembly fixes a day for the discussion of a question (or bill), it is called "inscribing the question on the order of the day." "To pass to (to proceed with) the order of the day" means to resume the course of business inscribed on that order, which has been interrupted by an interpellation or an unforeseen incident. In a wider sense a motion voted by the Assembly is also called "the order of the day." "The order of the day pure and simple" is

a disdainful oblivion of antecedent events, and by a kind of motion to resume the "previous questions."[1]

Our irritation was but natural. We were, perhaps, wrong to yield to it too much by interpreting the conduct at which we were offended, and justly offended, in a more offensive manner than we interpreted the fact itself. On several occasions we had seen M. Thiers bend the Assembly to his will by the mere threat of a resignation which would have interrupted and compromised the course of the vital negotiation with which he was entrusted. We were under the impression that he intended to have recourse once more to that means of influence, or rather of intimidation, to carry by sheer compulsion our

---

the decision arrived at by the Assembly to "close the incident," and to proceed purely and simply "with the course of its business." "The motived order of the day" indicates, on the contrary, the motives for which the Assembly proceeds with "the order of the day"; that kind of "order of the day" frequently marks the conclusion of an interpellation, and may mean the wish of the Assembly, its approval or its censure of the Government.

[1] "The previous question" (*question préalable*) takes also and always precedence over the principal motion. "To move the previous question" is, as a rule, a means to shelve from the very outset and before everything a proposition considered dangerous, offensive (injurious), unconstitutional, or unworthy of being examined. A member may always move "the previous question" save in the matter of a rule affecting "the order of the day." When "the previous question" has been voted with regard to a proposition, that proposition is considered as non-existent; it is only inserted in the report of the proceedings if it has been read; it is neither printed nor distributed among the members.
—Alphonse Bertrand, *L'Organisation Française*. (TRANS.)

adhesion to the Republic, and we were led to suppose that in order to deprive us of the liberty of refusal he did not want to await the departure of the last German soldier; when, his task having been accomplished, his continuance in power might have seemed less necessary to us, and we should therefore resign ourselves more easily to his withdrawal from it. That would in reality have been an indirect way to make us Republicans in spite of ourselves, and from sheer dread of a new complication with the alien. To attempt to resolve a question which to us was a matter of conscience in such a manner, was after all but the exercise of a moral pressure distinctly calculated to inspire people who professed to have a heart with a feeling of revolt. A calmer judgment makes me reluctant to-day to attribute to M. Thiers a design that would not have been worthy of him. In any case, if a like calculation entered his mind for a moment, he never cherished a more completely erroneous one; for by provoking a debate, the gravity of which he must have foreseen, he did not acclerate the advent of the Republic; but by an absolutely contrary effect he delayed and even compromised for a moment the solution that was to liberate us, and the accomplishment of which was as near to his heart as it was to ours.

What could not fail to happen was this. The struggle that had begun between the Assembly and the President threw all those who from across the frontiers, and especially from Berlin, endeavoured to comprehend the nature and to follow the course of it into a state of mental confusion, of which M. de Gontaut in his *Souvenirs* gives an exact and living picture. Betwixt the two parties at strife people no longer knew on which side was right, reason, the chances of success, in whom to take an interest, in whom to place confidence. In principle, nearly all the hopes gathered round a Monarchy. The establishment of a great Republic in the centre of Europe found no favour in political circles. With the exception of Herr von Bismarck, who wished to keep France republican owing to reasons which he did not attempt to disguise, but which were neither flattering to the Republic nor to France, there was no one who did not think that the restoration of royalty was the reasonable and desirable issue to our long revolutionary crises. But people fancied they knew (and unfortunately it was not a mere fancy on their part), that between the Royalists of the Assembly and the only possible representatives of the hereditary principle the understanding was by no means perfect; the fusion of the two branches of the royal house of France, which had been attempted several times, had not been accomplished; the hopes of the Monarchists were considered doubtful, and held in suspense in that way owing to a reason which it was difficult to understand, but which from that fact gave rise to much anxiety and still greater astonishment. Moreover, the men who spoke in the name of the Monarchical party were little known; their protracted opposition to the imperial *régime* had prevented them from acquiring either the notoriety or the experience gained by the exercise of power. M. Thiers had the advantage over them of a reputation acquired long ago, and which had increased in a favourable sense from the line of conduct, both loyal and sensible, he had of late adopted in the most thorny of negotiations. There were but two reproaches against him, for one of which, in fact, he was in no wise responsible, namely, his advanced age, which precluded a long lease with him; the other was that to which his inopportune message lent consistency, viz. his predilection— the motive of which it was so difficult to understand—for the Republican idea, and the encouragement given by him to the party which from its doctrines and its past was looked upon as hostile to conservative interests. There existed in particular one name, the legend of which has, as yet, not been destroyed by the opportunism of its bearer, and which was regarded as a bugbear by every friend of peace—it was that of M. Gambetta. It was with a certain dread that his presence was noted among the allies of M. Thiers in the latter's struggle against the Monarchists.

In that condition of uncertainty which scarcely requires explaining, those who still held us at their mercy adopted a mode of dealing with us which was, after all, not surprising; it was that of not discussing anything with us, to allow no step towards our deliverance while the quarrel between the two Powers lasted. The reason, which is not difficult to guess, was that before treating with France it was necessary to know who was entitled to sign in her name, and who would be there to execute the articles of a new Convention on the morrow of their having been granted. " Try to come to an understanding between yourselves if you wish us to listen to you;" such was the advice, unquestionably prudent and wise, that was given to us, and there is reason to believe that the advice was mainly due to the practical sense and kindly feeling of the old Emperor. Herr von Bismarck would have, perhaps, preferred to have the discord prolonged, and may have proposed to himself to embitter it in order to take advantage of it. Be that as it may, it was M. de Gontaut who returned to the charge, by informing the chiefs from whom he still derived his authority, as well as the friends whom he had left in the Assembly, that a superior interest commanded them to put an end to their differences, or at any rate to moderate their tone in discussing them.

It was M. Thiers who, receiving the first hint, was also the first to perceive his error, and with the natural pliancy of his mind soon found a means to repair that error. The opportunity that presented itself, and which he did not fail to seize, was provided to him by a motion of M. Gambetta aiming at the immediate dissolution of the Assembly. That hazardous expedient, which smacked of suicide, being to the taste of no one, whether of the President or the Assembly itself, became a neutral and, as it were, unpremeditated ground for the better understanding of the two parties. The Keeper of the Seals, M. Dufaure, who by his personal predilections and well-known disinclination for the relations M. Thiers had created for himself among the members of the Advanced Left, inspired us with more confidence than the chief, was entrusted with the opposing of the motion, and M. Thiers, perhaps in order to give him a freer hand, even abstained from putting in an appearance at the sitting. M. Dufaure's eloquence, springing from the depths of his inmost convictions, assumed on that day a character of unwonted emotion, which aroused a genuine enthusiasm. This was one of those sittings of reconciliation, "over-flowing with tenderness," of which the first National Assembly of France had furnished more than once the example, and the character of which is unfortunately more touching than lasting. The Assembly unanimously voted the appointment of an extraordinary commission, which, without attempting to solve or even to broach the question of a definite form of government, would offer M. Thiers for the whole duration of the provisional *régime* personified by him, the means of governing which he desired. The conditions of this veritable "Lamourette's kiss"[1] were clearly put by M. le Duc d'Audiffret-Pasquier in the following terms—" Inasmuch as we do not wish to divide the country against herself under the present circumstances, we loyally accept the discussion of certain organic laws tending to perfect and to consolidate the actual condition of affairs. But do not ask us either to recant our past or to subscribe to any confession of faith that would close the future to us. We are simply adjourning the realization of our hopes."

The man most satisfied with a result that enabled him to breathe freely was assuredly M. de Gontaut, but he was not the only one in Berlin who experienced that feeling of relief. Every one, in fact, congratulated him on the subject. "We feel reassured," said the Under-Secretary of State for Foreign Affairs to him; "as late as yesterday we were practically uncertain towards which side M. Thiers was leaning; he has the Right with him now; his wisest course is to march with

---

[1] An allusion to the all-round embraces which terminated the sitting of the Legislative Assembly on July 7, 1792, at the conclusion of a speech by the Abbé Lamourette, Constitutional Bishop of Lyons, who preached unity and fraternity at the threatened approach of the Prussians and Austrians.—TRANS.

them." Even Herr von Bismarck would not be left out of the chorus of congratulations.

"In fact," he said, in that semi-placid, semi-jeering tone which he adopted in his brighter moods, "in fact, seeing that they have as yet not arrived at an understanding among themselves, the only thing they can do is to support the actual condition of affairs. You will stick to Adolphe I." "We are willing enough to do that," I replied, "provided he leave no heir."

In short, the general tension became so conspicuously less, that during the first days of January 1873 (the vote of reconciliation had taken place on the preceding 15th December) M. de Gontaut was enabled to obtain a hearing for his overtures, tending to remove the last obstacles to the earlier withdrawal of the troops of occupation than was stipulated in consideration of an advanced payment.

Nevertheless, the task of the famous Commission of Thirty (to give it the title by which it was as famous then as it has ceased to be to-day) was not so easy as it seemed on that day of oratorical excitement. Its line of conduct had been traced for it by M. d'Audiffret-Pasquier with all possible clearness, for all that it was narrow and slippery. Practically, the terms in which the question had been presented were, if not contradictory to, at least difficult to reconcile with, each other. The object was the organization of a provisional situation. Now, it so happens that the provisional, from its very nature, and born under the stress of circumstances that constitute the reason of its being and determines its conditions, does not admit of organization. Organic institutions assume, on their part, and naturally enough, a definite look; hence the result, that each of the two parties, the reconciliation of which it was the Commission's task to promote, and which had in its midst representatives ever on the alert, endeavoured to interpret in its own sense the somewhat hybrid character the measures proposed. M. Thiers' evident aim (which he did not disguise) was to make the Commission draft the principal outlines of a Republican constitution; but the majority, which was very distinctly Monarchical, steadfastly refused to say anything, or to let anything pass which eventually might be construed as prejudicial to the solution which, perhaps, it would not have been in a position to propose immediately, but which it wished to be left free to propose at the end of the stipulated interregnum that was clearly drawing nigh. In this conflict of opposing designs there was therefore, I will not say not an article, but not even a word or a syllable of all the measures under discussion that did not give rise to a debate on the substance as well as on the form; and after several weeks of deliberation they were as little advanced as ever, and more than ever confronted by the probability of not coming to an understanding at all.

There is no such a thing as secrecy with regard to the debates in committee of a Commission, especially if that Commission be a numerous one and divided against itself. I remember as it were to-day the door of the committee room in the palace of Versailles where our meetings were held, I remember that door besieged by the reporters of the newspapers of various shades, who with their pencils in hand came to take notes of every incident of our sittings. All those notes were so much copy communicated at the same time to the foreign and especially to the German press, and all our alternatives to proposed decisions, whether accepted or rejected, produced their counter-effect on the parallel discussion, going on two hundred leagues away from them, between the ambassador of France and the Prussian ministers. The negotiation progressed or receded according to M. Thiers' agreement with the Assembly becoming more probable or remaining problematical. But for the fear of employing a somewhat hazardous metaphor, I should say that the greater or lesser rapidity of the march of the German troops towards the frontier they were to cross eventually depended on the slower or quicker steps of the two home Powers towards one another.

The embarrassment, and to a certain extent nervous agitation, of the unhappy negotiator at the slightest mishap to this badly-horsed chariot may be easily conceived. Worried beyond endurance, he made up his mind after a few weeks to lay the awkwardness of his situation before a friend, a member of the Commission of Thirty, in a letter, the terms of which would have remained graven on my memory even if the text of the epistle had been lost. "You are gradually losing the ground you have gained during the last months," he wrote, with a view of having his words communicated to us. "The German Government, in common with most of the foreign Governments, having little or no sympathy with the proclaiming of the Republic, even a Conservative Republic, all those Governments applauded your resolution to secure a dominant Conservative influence in the direction of affairs, and the firmness you displayed in keeping the Government to that ground. Much apprehension was felt with regard to the intrigues of the Left, and the sway it might exercise on the President's mind by the adroit flattery of its members; hence, M. Thiers' union with the Right was regarded with conspicuous favour. But M. Thiers' foreign policy, his efforts to restore order at home, to re-establish the finances and the army, have inspired people with a real sympathy for him, and even a sincere admiration, and, in sum, a great confidence in him personally. There is, therefore, no disposition on people's part to approve of anything that seems intended to lessen that personality, to restrict the power of which, according to every one, he has made such good use up to the present. Still less are people disposed to approve of anything that might lead to withdrawal of his Presidency. In consequence of all of which, people fail or refuse to understand those long and subtle discussions of the Commission of Thirty, and express their surprise at the importance you would attach to normal and deeply-pondered institutions in connection with an abnormal and evidently transitory situation and circumstances. They accuse the majority of the Commission, *i.e.* the Right, of a design to hamper the much-desired agreement between the Conservatives and M. Thiers. One of the most important aims of my mission," he added in conclusion, "is to reassure Germany, not only with regard to the payment of our debt, but also with regard to the appeasement of the public mind and its legitimate consequence, the revival of business, on the restoration of a feeling of tranquillity in France; or if not altogether able to reassure Germany completely, to draw her attention to our reasons for hoping that those benefits will not be withheld from us for long. Do not make my task more difficult than it is, and is likely to be, under no matter what circumstances. Take it for granted that the prolonging and emphasizing of the disagreement during the latest sittings of the Commission are producing a most damaging effect here, the counter-effect of which we are certain to feel in our negotiations for the liberation of the territory."

When this letter was communicated to me by our common friend to whom it was addressed, the Commission had just appointed me its reporter. I do not know exactly to what I owed that honour, for though my monarchical convictions left no doubt in any one's mind, I by no means figured among the most ardent to share either the most confident hopes in nor the lively resentment against M. Thiers. My fellow members were, perhaps, under the impression that, being more or less used to writing by profession, I should be more apt than any one else to mark the delicate shades of the situation in which we found ourselves. I was greatly struck by the justness of M. de Gontaut's arguments so nobly expressed, and by the picture of his patriotic grief, and I made up my mind there and then to spare no possible concession to make the labours of the Commission lead to the pacific solution on which depended the restoration of our country to her complete independence. I communicated that intention to some of my most intimate friends, who associated themselves with it.

We apprised M. Thiers through several intermediaries of our conciliatory intentions. I myself opened direct intercourse with several ministers I knew, MM. de Rémusat, de Goulard, and Dufaure, and was finally allowed to discuss with

M. Thiers himself the various formulas that might be employed to respond to his requirements, though I managed to husband all our reserves by shifting the ground of the contest once more to that mapped out by the Bordeaux pact, on which ground he, at any rate, apparently consented to meet me. I even seem to remember that on one occasion he introduced me without warning into the Ministerial Council assembled in order to afford his own friends a better understanding and appreciation of my explanations. In spite of an ever-perceptible look of constraint, he made it a point to listen very patiently to my remarks, to place himself in my position, amidst the difficulties I could not help submitting to him, to lend himself to the expedients I proposed to overcome them; and I was all the more surprised at this, inasmuch as I received far from the same amount of attention even when, as his ambassador in London, I had to give an account of the difficulties I might and did meet with in the course of the business with which I was entrusted. I vaguely suspected the motive of disposition, and did not attribute the credit of it to my good intentions, and least of all to my eloquence. The secret of it has, however, been more completely revealed to me ever since the dispatches of M. de Gontaut showed me how conscientiously that worthy agent of France lavished his warnings on him as well as on us without being discouraged by the surly receptions accorded to them now and again. M. de Gontaut played in reality the part, so frequently to be met with in the comedies of Molière, of the faithful servant who, in order to effect a reconciliation between the lovers that have quarrelled, goes in turns from one side of the stage to the other to dispense good advice. In this instance, however, he had to contend with this difficulty: the lovers, being in no way in love with one another, only shook hands reluctantly in the end. I am inclined to think that the occasion of that particular display of confidence to which I alluded just now must have coincided with the reception of a letter like the following—

"*Berlin, February* 1, 1872.

"I ought to give you an account of a conversation I have just had with a friend of the King. . . . This friend has already been to see me twice or thrice under circumstances analogous to the present one, and has unburthened himself to me with a sincerity and trust which in return demand on our side great circumspection. . . . He broached at once the question of France's situation with regard to her home affairs. . . . He then recurred to the immense perils to the whole of Europe with which the triumph of Gambetta and the Left would be fraught, and warmly expressed the hope that an understanding would be arrived at between M. Thiers and the

Right. He went so far as to say, 'It is the King's ardent wish, and you may be sure that if such an understanding were established, there would be no difficulty on his part with regard to the withdrawal of the troops.' I told him that his hopes on that point were well founded. ' In politics,' I added, ' one should avoid using the word "certainty"; but the tendencies towards reconciliation have been too marked during the last few weeks, they are getting too emphasized every day, they are too necessary and too consistent with reason for me to deny the logic of things, and refuse to say, " The understanding will be brought about."' 'So much the better,' remarked Count ——; 'but I have not the slightest hesitation in telling you that everything depends on M. Thiers; the understanding between Prussia and France is in his hands.'"

To which letter M. Thiers, who had perhaps been talking to me in the meanwhile, sent the following reply:—" Make your mind easy, the Thirty are given to worrying, teasing, and cavilling, but they will prove themselves sensible at the right moment, and in a few days all will be over."

And when, on the 23rd, the Report of the Commission was submitted to the Assembly in the terms stipulated beforehand, he wrote at once, " The agreement arrived at with the Thirty is producing a genuine gladness."

We had, in fact, succeeded in coming to an agreement with regard to a formula that commended itself to the majority of the Commission, and subsequently to the majority of the Assembly itself. Unfortunately that majority was not constituted as I could have wished. A considerable part of the Right refused to belong to it, and had to be replaced by a nearly equal number of M. Thiers' personal friends. That division grieved me deeply; and to this day, when re-reading the text it fell to my lot to defend and comment upon, I fail to understand how, under the given circumstances, one could have gone to work otherwise in order to arrive at the immediate understanding necessitated by so supreme an interest, and at the same time leave the doors ajar for the Monarchy even within the immediate future. The constituent power of the Assembly was fully recognized and placed at the head of the project itself, while the institutions the Assembly promised to establish before the termination of its labours, the respective attributes of the executive and the legislative powers, the establishment of a second Chamber, were one and all perfectly compatible with the Monarchy, and presented nothing that implied the relinquishment or the neglect of the hereditary principle.

Hence, I fail to account to myself for the scruples which not only prevented part of the Royalists to adhere to the project, but lent to their discussion of it a character of lively remonstrance and bitterness which was sufficiently painful, and grieved me the more inasmuch as I perceived well enough that my momentary friendly intercourse with M. Thiers gave rise to unjust and rather puerile suspicions, and that I was debarred from pointing out, even by casting looks in the direction of our frontiers, still occupied by alien troops, the principal motive that had prompted me.

In vain had I tried to make that motive plain by the words of the passage that wound up the Report—"France centres all her hopes in the union of the public Powers." I had said, "It is that union cemented by sacrifices and efforts made in common which will soon efface the last signs of the foreign invasion." Dignity forbade me to speak more clearly from a French rostrum.[1]

[1] Being essentially anxious not to refer to questions of home policy except in their connection with France's diplomatic position which was so critical at that period, I am bound, as it were, to keep silent on a whole part of the project elaborated by the Commission of the Thirty, which, nevertheless, gave rise to very lively debates. I am alluding to the rules established for the limitation of the direct communication of the President of the Republic with the Assembly to fixed cases, and under special conditions. Those regulations (rules) applying to an essentially transitory and exceptional condition of affairs, aimed solely at preventing incidents similar to those that had occurred already at various times; viz. an unforeseen altercation between the Chief of the State and the parliamentary majority, and his resignation in consequence of a hasty (*irréfléchi*) vote, bringing in its wake at a moment's notice two extremely grave political crises. Of course, at present nothing of the kind is necessary, inasmuch as under the actual Constitution, the President of the Republic does not belong to any parliamentary assembly, and has therefore no claim to make his appearance in

Before long I was amply rewarded for those few hours of worry and annoyance, for as soon as the project[1] was voted, M. Thiers brought a new and final Convention, which left nothing to desire, to the Assembly. In fact, the votes on the preamble and on the first clauses of the Bill, attesting, as it were, the establishment of the parliamentary agreement, had been sufficient to dispel at once, so to speak, the difficulties at Berlin which until then had been the subject of a sustained correspondence between M. de Gontaut and M. Thiers; and everything had been prepared for the signing of the whole, which (the signing) took place exactly forty-eight hours after the passing of the whole of the project of the Commission of the Thirty. Never was there a more rapid and at the same time more complete result. The final payments having been fixed for September 5, every spot was to be free on the previous July 5, save Verdun and a zone of four kilomètres, which was to be held in pledge until the later date, the short space between the two being considered necessary to provide the last measures to efface the traces of the occupation. The question of keeping Belfort for the

---

it. Without that wise precaution, presidential crises, which would put the whole of the State in suspense and interrupt its progress, would become as frequent and as sudden as ministerial ones. It was that danger threatening the Assembly at every moment which the Commission of the Thirty was entrusted to remove.

[1] A *projet de loi* is a Government Bill, a *proposition de loi* is a private Bill.—TRANS.

same period, and in virtue of the same title of guarantee, had been broached for a moment, the military party at Berlin being evidently reluctant to part with that stronghold. Some, more obstinate than the rest, wished to pretend that that precaution was absolutely necessary in order to prevent the revolutionary movements that might burst forth at the ferment caused by the joy of deliverance. But both M. Thiers and M. de Gontaut having indignantly repulsed that offensive supposition, Herr von Bismarck made up his mind to strike out a condition the suspicious appearance of which would have compromised the whole effect of that grand moral success. Moreover, the Chancellor, having expressed the wish to sign the Convention personally (perhaps in order not to leave the honour of it to his ambassador, Herr von Arnim, his dissentiments with whom were becoming public), it was to M. de Gontaut that fell the well-deserved luck to affix his name to the text that was to liberate us, and to bequeath in that way the most touching and most glorious memorial to a family which could already boast so many illustrious ones.

While sharing the general joy, I could not help indulging in some personal gladness for having contributed, in a modest and small measure, to the removal of some of the obstacles that might have encumbered the road to that most desired goal. M. Dufaure was kind enough to congratulate me to that effect in a letter which I have preserved. I was not quite so fortunate with M. Thiers. In common with one of the members of the Commission of the Thirty who had lent me the most constant support, I considered it my duty to join the many who on that evening went to congratulate him. I verily believe that at the first moment he would have been glad to ignore our presence, and he acknowledged our congratulations in a manner scarcely calculated to encourage a renewal of them. As we descended the staircase of the Presidency, my companion and I could not help looking and smiling at one another. It was evident we were no longer wanted; I myself was more or less cognisant of the fact, but for decency's sake they might have waited a few days before letting us feel it. If, as had been maliciously supposed, I had expected a reward of some kind in return for my assistance, such as, for instance, the offer of a fresh ambassadorial mission, or even that of a portfolio, I had assuredly reckoned without my host.

The impression I felt at this change of tactics (which, I need scarcely say, left me absolutely callous on my own account), that impression I meet with once more in the reminiscences of M. de Gontaut, who had altogether different reasons for feeling the same. Treated with all the distinction so amply due to him, seeing that he was invested with the highest insignia of the national order of knighthood, in deviation of all the rules of that order, and in virtue of an exception, applauded by every one, M. de Gontaut came to spend a few days in Paris, where he met with an equally distinguished welcome from M. Thiers, and from the latter's friends in the Assembly.

"I soon became aware," he says, "that though we had reached a halting-point in our preoccupations with regard to our foreign policy, there was no similar point in our home divisions. In fact, the peace that had made his task possible, and to the restoration of which he had so actively contributed, was only a truce to be broken very shortly. This was particularly brought to him during a reception at the Presidency attended by many members of the Assembly, and belonging to the different parties. He was struck by their reserved and hostile attitude. It was, I believe, at a dinner to which I was invited. I forget the reason that prevented my going, but my nephew, M. d'Haussonville, who had been my fellow-member of the Commission of the Thirty, went. After the dinner the conversation turned on an incident that had just occurred, and was making a good deal of noise; it was the expulsion of Prince Napoleon, carried out by the order of M. Thiers, although there was no legal provision in virtue of which the members of the late

Imperial Family could be banished from France. Hence there could be no question as to the arbitrary character of the measure. But M. Thiers defended it very emphatically, affirming that, law or no law, a Government always had the right to remove those whose presence constituted a threat to its existence, "and that," he added, "is the rule I am determined to apply to all pretenders, so you know what you have to expect, M. d'Haussonville."

If M. de Gontaut happened to hear those words, there could be no cause for surprise at his returning to his post his heart full of dark foreboding. "I had several interviews with M. Thiers before my departure," he wrote. "On the very day I took leave of him we had a somewhat emphatic conversation on the subject of his attitude, and though I failed to find the note relating to that conversation, I remember very well having said to him as I stood on the threshold of the door, 'You do not intend, then, to throw in your lot with the Conservatives?' To which M. Thiers replied curtly, 'No.' 'Well, you had better consider. This may prove your ruin,' I retorted, but I did not think that I should turn out to be so good a prophet."

## II

## THE MINISTRY OF MAY 24, 1873

# THE MINISTRY OF MAY 24, 1873

THE National Assembly, of which M. de Gontaut was a member, and in which I was his colleague, has often been reproached with having waited until the liberation of the territory was completed to engage upon the conflict with M. Thiers, the result of which was his withdrawal from the Presidency of the Republic. Those censors say that, with the blackest ingratitude, we watched for the moment of his having concluded the task he alone was capable of accomplishing for us to divest him of the chief power. Only a little while ago that accusation has been repeated in the bitterest terms by one of the most eloquent of M. Thiers' friends.

I know of no accusation less justified than that one. Those who prefer that charge simply forget that, as I have already said more than once, M. Thiers himself, when placed at the head of the State by the suffrages of the Assembly, had expressly requested it to raise no question calculated to lead to serious dissensions in the home policy, and least of all that touching the definite form of government, as long as shackled France had not thrown off the alien's shackles. It was he who, in most eloquent and impassioned terms, had pledged all parties to that truce. If he imagined subsequently that that engagement, to which he had subscribed more explicitly than no matter whom of us, need not prevent him from favouring a republican solution openly, and even to propose the adoption of one before the stipulated time, that assuredly was no reason why those who did not interpret their promise in the same sense should have considered themselves justified in following his example. Besides, we have already seen that that precipitate course had by no means been crowned with success. The home crisis which his republican message of November 12, 1872, prematurely provoked, had delayed and well nigh compromised a matter of paramount national interest. By abstaining from a similar error in the opposite direction, the Royalists could claim to have acted loyally and at the same time patriotically. But as soon as the condition had been completely fulfilled, and the stipulated delay had expired, they recovered, in virtue of that fact, the plenary right pertaining to the members of a constituent Assembly, and no scruple whatever could any longer prevent them from using that right. As for the reproach of having, from sheer ingratitude, ignored the incontestable services M. Thiers had rendered, I can only express my surprise that such a word should have been uttered seriously in connection with constitutional or even legislative matters. Neither institutions nor laws are made in obedience to gratitude. To those who have served her well a nation owes proofs of her gratitude. She cannot heap the measure of honours and advantages too high; the only mark of deference she has the right to withhold is that which would allow them to decide at their will the institutions that should govern her. To establish a constitutional pact whence would depend the future of several generations, out of deference to the merits or services of one man, would be an act not less imprudent than culpable. Neither a people nor an individual is bound to sacrifice her or his reason, her or his conscience, to no matter whom. England has never been considered an ungrateful nation to those who served her well. But what Englishman ever dreamt of securing power to any man, were he the victor of Waterloo himself, for a day longer than the free movement of parties had naturally conferred that power on him?

Therefore a conflict between the Monarchical party of the Assembly and M. Thiers must have sprung up sooner or later, unless the one consented to forego its old convictions, or the other abandoned its recent conversion, a concession which, considering the positions taken up or maintained, was not to be expected, either from one side or the other. The shock was unavoidable, yet, as is well known, it was not the question of a definite form of government, it was not the choice between the Republic and the Monarchy that caused the explosion; what gave rise to it was the alarm caused, not gratuitously, and not only among the Royalists, but among a very considerable part of the French nation, by the kind of alliances M. Thiers was compelled to accept, and even to seek, in the furtherance of his republican aims. Truly, his position, as defined by himself one day in the Assembly, was a singular one. Unable to establish the Republic by himself, he was perforce obliged to look for republican auxiliaries. As it happened, among those he was enabled to enlist there was not one from whom he was not divided by a radical divergence of views except on one sole point, that of the suppression of the hereditary Monarchy. While on all other matters, such as administration, finances, public worship, and public education, the Republicans of old and by profession claimed reforms conceived from an often very advanced democratic point of view, he alone among them remained imbued with a conservative spirit, which he carried now and again to the length of routine, and which was opposed to any and every kind of innovation. "Do you know why the Left applauds me?" he asked the Assembly on November 23, during the discussion that followed upon his republican message. "It is not because I share the opinions of the honourable members occupying those benches; it is not because I share the opinions, not of *the most advanced among them, but of the most moderate.* They know that on most of the political, social, or economic questions I do not share their opinions. No, *neither on the questions of taxation, the army, social organization, nor the organization of the Republic,* do I think like them."

The consequence of that avowal was that he entered upon the campaign for the establishment of the Republic at the head of an army which he would have to disband as soon as his success was secured, without calling them to share any of the fruits of the victory. No General ever held similar language to his soldiers. How would he have contrived that operation which, at the first blush, seemed to partake of the nature of a miracle? How would he have solved the problem of administering either the Republic without Republicans, or the Conservative *régime* without Conservatives? The question was difficult to answer then, it is not less difficult to-day. The far from encouraging results obtained by those of his friends who attempted the same undertaking without him, the deplorable concessions they were compelled to make, with so little profit, do not tend to dissipate that want of faith on my part. Truly he may have considered himself more apt than others to get out of a difficulty. Without being so simple-minded as to believe in the absolute disinterestedness of his casual friends, he may nevertheless have flattered himself that he had sufficient influence, at any rate over some, to obtain great sacrifices from them, and the suppleness of his talent may have made him confident of being able to turn round against those who proved refractory. But whether that confidence in himself was justified or not, it was excusable not to share it, and that was the case with a considerable fraction of the Assembly, which would have resigned itself, although without enthusiasm, and even without inclination, to accept the Republic at his hands, but who, before subscribing to this, made it a condition of their assent that he should not deviate from the narrow line of conduct he had mapped out for himself. Those Conservatives had neither a dislike to him personally, nor the design to attack his power, but they dreaded the influence on him of alliances, the hazardous and precarious character of which he himself had admitted; and it was against that pressure, the signs of which they believed they recognized, they were anxious to take precautions and demand guarantees.

The incident that invested those alarms with a character of urgency, and those demands with a form of pressing insistence, is well known. It was an unforeseen consequence of that very negotiation, the slow elaboration of which I have retraced here, and in particular of the part played in its last phase by the agreement between the Chief of the State and the Commission of the Thirty. The satisfaction caused by the act that put an end to the occupation was so general and emphatic, that M. Thiers conceived the very natural idea to have the act consecrated as it were by a kind of plébiscite. A vacancy having occurred in the parliamentary representation of Paris, which, as our readers may remember, formed at that time only one constituency, M. Thiers made up his mind to put up his Minister of Foreign Affairs as a candidate for the suffrages of the capital. It was but just that M. de Rémusat, who had lent his chief a useful aid, should share the honour of the result. A fraction of the Republican party, and that the most numerous, was of a different opinion. With their eyes fixed more intently on the Parliament than on our foreign relations, those Frenchmen of narrow views had become uneasy at the even momentary *rapprochement* between M. Thiers and part of the Assembly's Right. The same fact occurred once more, a few days later, in connection with the passing of a law[1] which assimilated the municipal *régime* of Lyons to that of Paris. That was unquestionably a tendency that might degenerate

---

[1] That law, if I am not mistaken, was abrogated, as far as the city of Lyons goes, at least thirteen years ago. I am astonished that the author does not mention the fact.—TRANS.

into habit, and which, it seemed to them, had better be stopped at once. M. Thiers needed a warning to make him desist from seeking henceforth to support himself by suffrages other than those he might find in their ranks. Consequently, an obscure candidate, whose sole merit consisted in the extreme character of his democratic opinions,[1] was opposed to M. de Rémusat, and defeated him by a crushing majority. If ever there was an act of ingratitude, it was surely committed on that day.

I will not undertake to explain the interpretation put by M. Thiers on a check which must have filled him with sorrow. Was it to allay the umbrage of the Republican party that he considered it expedient on that occasion to remove from his Cabinet the minister who seemed to come closer to the right-hand section of the Assembly than any of the others by affinities of origin and community of sentiments? Perhaps,

---

[1] M. Barodet (Désiré). His biography, if written, would prove nearly as amusing as that of the late M. Tirard, sometime Minister of Finances to the Third Republic. Far better educated than the erstwhile dealer in mock jewellery, Barodet, like Tirard, had been a Jack of all Trades and seemingly a master of none, for he was everything in turns and nothing very long. The author is not quite correct in saying that he was utterly obscure; what he ought to have said was that Barodet would have been practically unknown in Paris but for the chance the Conservatives themselves gave him to hoist himself into notoriety by their passing of the law providing for the municipal organization of Lyons. That deprived Barodet of his mayoralty, and, clever as he was, he utilized his pseudo-martyrdom to enter Parliament, and to inflict at the same time a lesson on Thiers.—TRANS.

but though that ministerial reconstruction may have reassured the Republican party, it had by no means the same effect on the Conservatives, nor could it have. In trying to soothe the former, he only succeeded in making the latter more uneasy. This was the unavoidable consequence of the unstable equilibrium by which he endeavoured to maintain himself. The concession made to those very exacting allies was only looked upon as so much proof of the ascendency they were gaining over him, and the condition of dependence to which they might flatter themselves they had reduced him.

Great was the consternation (the word is not an exaggerated one) especially among the group of which I spoke, and which, though ready to follow M. Thiers, dreaded to see his headlong course down a revolutionary slope; and it was that very ardent and somewhat widespread public feeling that gave its character to the event of May 24. The parliamentary motion which M. Thiers chose to construe into a vote of want of confidence was strictly confined to a request for a *determinedly Conservative* policy. And it was in those terms, foreign to all allusions to dynastic or constitutional questions, that the discussion was maintained to the end, in accordance with the position I had been instructed to take up when entrusted with the opening of the debate. I was sufficiently familiar at that moment with the feeling that prevailed in the Assembly, and with the uncertainty that swayed our own ranks until the last hour, to affirm that, if M. Thiers had announced his intention to take count of the visible emotion of the country and the Assembly, if he had uttered one word calculated to reassure his affrighted partisans, he could have easily detached from the feeble majority that appeared hostile to him a sufficient number of votes to secure a majority in the opposite sense. He deemed it inconsistent in him to make the slightest concession even in speech. On that very evening he tendered his resignation, and M. le Maréchal de MacMahon, who did not in the least expect to be made the recipient of that honour, or—to speak by the card—to have that sacrifice imposed on him, was called to replace M. Thiers as the President of the Republic.

I was bound to recall briefly those facts—a more complete recital of which would involve a great many details and comments that would be out of place here—because the conditions under which the new power was constituted could not fail to influence (as we shall see) the character of the relations M. de Gontaut had to keep up with the Prussian Government, and above all with Herr von Bismarck. M. de MacMahon having, moreover, entrusted me at that moment with the portfolio of Foreign Affairs, all the representatives of France had to enter into communication with me. I shall therefore have occasion to appeal, during that short space of time, to my personal recollections in order to confirm, and on certain points to complete, those of M. de Gontaut.

It was highly important to bring home to all our agents before everything the fact that the Marshal assumed power under the exact conditions M. Thiers had exercised it. For the moment there was to be no change either in the character or in the attributes of the elevated functions with which the one and the other had been invested; and the point on which it was essentially desirable to insist was, that no modification whatsoever had taken place in the direction of the foreign policy, which had in no way been mixed up with the crisis at its origin, and which was still more to be kept distinct from the result.

The following is the text of the circular I had drawn up on the morrow after my admission into the Ministry.

"The dissension between the majority of the Assembly and M. Thiers had no bearing on any point in connection with the foreign policy. You will please remember, that during the two years that have just passed the line of conduct adopted by M. Thiers, in view of the re-establishment of our relations with the foreign Powers after the disasters of 1870, has never been the subject of any debate in the Assembly. On the contrary, a large number of votes have approved the efforts—invariably successful—of that illustrious man to obliterate the traces of our misfortunes, and to secure once more to France her thorough independence as a nation. Hence the instructions you received from the preceding Government remain practically unchanged, and we trust you will adhere faithfully to the line of conduct it has traced for you."

I need not point out that, while holding this language to the envoys of France to all the Courts, I was thinking above all of Berlin and M. de Gontaut. Speaking to a friend, my relations with whom had never ceased, in spite of his absence, I had nothing new to tell him with regard to my intentions, nor the least effort to make to convince him of their sincerity. The support I had fortunately been enabled to lend him by removing the parliamentary obstacles to the conclusion of the last treaty had been too highly appreciated by him, he had too affectionately thanked me when we met again in Paris, to need a fresh assurance of the good faith I should bring to bear on the execution of that treaty; and as for himself, his signature having been appended in the name of France and not in behalf of M. Thiers personally, he was not disturbed by the dread of having its validity questioned.

It is but right to say, however, that this constituted only the apparent and to some degree the superficial aspect of the situation. In all the relations of life, whether international, political, or private, we should often attach less importance to the outward regularity of acts and conduct than to that inmost foundation of certain feelings that only remain hidden and silent, to find vent and show themselves in a single instant, and in consequence of the slightest incident. It would have been exceedingly imprudent to forget this, especially in the constant and always thorny relations which we had to go on maintaining with Germany. The smooth execution of the treaty itself still depended on the good understanding, one might even say on the graciousness of the agents commissioned to take it in hand. There was also this; between the respective populations, still filled to bursting with the recollection of a recent struggle, the very fact of being neighbours tended to keep up a spirit of reciprocal animosity the expression of which, ever ready to burst forth, might easily be envenomed. In short, it was difficult to enumerate the many points on which the as yet unrelinquished interests of France were likely to be confronted with the ambitious activity of the new empire. It was, then, essentially important to know the impression produced at Berlin by the parliamentary revolution that had been accomplished in Paris, and whether the Marshal might at least reckon on the comparative goodwill which for many reasons M. Thiers had managed to secure for himself during the latter part of his Presidency. That was the point on which, without loss of time, I made it a point to interrogate M. de Gontaut in a private letter, dated May 27, and though I could not have known then what I gathered subsequently, from the perusal of M. de Gontaut's dispatches, with regard to the complexity of sentiments of Wilhelm I.'s political and military *entourage* concerning ourselves, from the manner in which I put the question I seem to have foreseen the answer. "How is the event of the 24th May *really and truly (au fond et en réalité)* looked at in Berlin?" I asked. "I am not talking of the more or less lively regrets which M. Thiers' references may have caused from a purely personal point of view. I feel convinced that yourself share those regrets, because those whose dealings with him were solely confined to his foreign policy, and who experienced the charm of his conversation, cannot cherish any other impression. Nor do I refer to certain apprehensions that may be aroused by the presence of a Marshal of France at the head of affairs. You will do me the honour to take it for granted that I could not have been for a whole week at the Ministry for Foreign Affairs without letting every one at Berlin and in Europe know that all our engagements will be strictly kept; in one word, that the policy dictated to us by the most elementary common-sense will be pursued and even publicly announced without delay. But what I am anxious to know is the impression produced by a Conservative reaction in France? Which of the two sentiments predominates—that of the identity of interests of all the Governments in view of their being equally threatened by the self-same revolutionary spirit, or the fear that this happy event which, preserving France from the possible chance of anarchy, provides her with a much greater one to recover her old position? Was not the goodwill shown to M. Thiers mixed with a more or less profound calculation? Do not people think without saying it, nay, without admitting the thought to themselves, that the presence at the head of affairs of an old man dominated by bad counsellors could only afford France a material rest of a short time, necessary to the discharge of our debt, but which rest would be the lull before the outbreak of new crises, of which they reserved themselves the right to take advantage? You will most probably tell me that the sentiment varies, and is complex or simple according to the persons. Unfortunately, though, there is only one man at Berlin, and perhaps even in Europe, whose sentiment counts, and it is above all with regard to him that I am anxious. Have you any means of getting at his real thought, and of telling me what it has in store for us in the way of goodwill or the reverse? Tell me your own opinion in that respect. I know it is difficult to analyze impressions which even in the person who experiences them may be very confused."

"The two sentiments to which you allude," wrote M. de Gontaut in reply two days afterwards, "exist simultaneously at Berlin; that of the identity of interests of all the Governments in view of their being equally threatened by the self-same revolutionary spirit, and the fear of seeing France recover her splendour of old. Which is the more powerful of the two? It is a difficult question to answer; the sentiment varies according to the individual. You must not run away with the idea that the influence of the King is not considerable; he is greatly loved, liked, and considered, and he is frequently at issue with the Chancellor, for he is naturally and on principle much more conservative than he. I feel confident that the event of May 24 has been favourably viewed by the King; he feels particularly sympathetic towards M. de MacMahon, and every one in Berlin who lays claim to the title of Conservative is of a mind with the King. There is no doubt that he views the re-awakening of France with a certain feeling of apprehension, but his reluctance with regard to the Conventions of June 29 and March 15 sprang far more from his dread of the revolutionary spirit casting its shackles than from the fear of the projects of revenge. In fine, the two sentiments are there in his case, but the first dominates the other. The reverse is the case with Herr von Bismarck; and you are perfectly correct in saying, that no influence is equal to that of the Chancellor of the German Empire in the balance of European destinies. In conclusion and in reply, the check inflicted on Radicalism by the advent of the new Government has been hailed with joy here; nevertheless, they would like the convalescence to be a long one, and they are not at all anxious for the complete recovery of the patient. That is Herr von Bismarck's sentiment, and the boldness of his mind as much as the ingenuity of it will neglect no opportunity to prevent that recovery."

That prospect was not encouraging. I was not even allowed the time to prepare myself for it. When I received M. de Gontaut's letter I was already in a position to verify the correctness of his remarks.

I had apprised the foreign Governments of the advent of the new President by means of a simple notification to their representatives in Paris, and transmitted at the same time by our own diplomatic agents to the various Courts. In addition to that formality, which I considered sufficient, I had, according to custom, left my card with all the ambassadors. The English and Turkish ambassadors immediately acknowledged my act of politeness by calling personally. But I neither saw nor heard anything for several days from those of Germany, Austria, and Russia. I was all the more surprised at this coolness, seeing that Count Arnim and I had been on cordial terms when we met at M. de Rémusat's receptions; that Prince Orloff and I were frequently thrown together at the houses of common friends; that Count Apponyi and I had been on a truly intimate footing when we were colleagues in London. It was he, in fact, who sent me the explanation of his attitude of reserve through a friendly intermediary.

He had been obliged to submit to a rather unexpected demand by Herr von Bismarck, who, it appears, was not satisfied with a simple notification. The Chancellor contended, that in order to resume diplomatic relations with the new Government of France, new credentials from Marshal MacMahon to all the diplomatic agents were required, those they held from M. Thiers having, as it seemed to him, become void. That claim upset all notions of international law I had been taught during my diplomatic apprenticeship. The practice of renewing credentials at the commencement of each new reign applies to Monarchies alone, because the sovereign power itself changes with the person of the monarch who is its representative; but in the case of Republics the sovereign is practically the nation, which does not undergo a corresponding change, and of which the Chief of the State is only the temporary delegate. It is the nation that accredits the agents, and they are accredited to it. Herr von Bismarck, who did not dispute the principle, gave M. de Gontaut two reasons for not wishing to abide by it. Our Republic was only provisional, and to treat it like Switzerland or the United States would have been tantamount to an acknowledgment of its definite character. Besides, he added somewhat emphatically, he did not care to bind himself to recognize indiscriminately all the "elects" it might please us to put at our head; and by an allusion to the recollections of the last war, he conveyed clearly that there was a certain personage whose position might lead to his assumption of power, or, to speak correctly, to his resumption of power, with whom he would object to enter into diplomatic relations.

Of those two motives alleged in justification of a diplomatic novelty without precedent there was one with which I had no reason to be displeased. I had no objection whatsoever to anything that could bring home to people's minds the provisional character of the republican form of Government, but I had serious objections to recognize—even on a hypothesis which was farthest from my wishes —the right of a foreign State to exercise no matter what control and veto over the choice of the chief whom it might please France to give herself. Divided as I was between these two considerations, I caused M. de Gontaut to formulate express reservations with regard to the question of right, but after having taken those precautions, not to run the risk, for the sake of a simple formality, the interpretation of which was ambiguous, of prolonging a suspension—vexatious under all circumstances—of the diplomatic relations which urgently required resumption. I reckoned on his customary skill to save with dignity a delicate situation; Herr von Bismarck did not facilitate his task. At M. de Gontaut's first syllable at a second interview on the subject, Herr von Bismarck, instead of discussing the matter, cut him short with a haughty "Very well, so be it then; but remember, I have warned you. *Salvavi animam meam.* But Count von Arnim has asked me for leave of absence on account of his health; and inasmuch as he will have no credentials to present, he can come back. I'll authorize him to do so."

After which he gave M. de Gontaut to understand, that with the withdrawal of his reservations those of Austria and Prussia would also come to an end, but probably under the same conditions, and added that, after all, these Powers had only adopted his course with a repugnance which he professed to treat very cavalierly.

He was not averse to showing the close and at the same time dependent relations of those two states with their formidable neighbour. It was evident that he eagerly seized the opportunity to place the new Government in a kind of interdict with regard to the great Powers of Europe. The game was clear, but the trap was visible; it would have been stupid indeed to fall into it.

Hence, in order to satisfy a whim, the foundation of which consisted mainly in a display of ill-will, we had an exchange of credentials. Herr von Arnim was to hand his to the Marshal, and the envoy gave an account of the first interview in a dispatch published a few years later among the documents of the trial he had to undergo.[1] The terms of that account are curious, and as others may not have had the same reasons I had for noticing them, I cannot resist the temptation to reproduce them.

"*Paris, June* 2, 1873.

"ILLUSTRISSIME (very illustrious, or most illustrious?), most puissant Emperor and King, gracious Emperor, King, and Sovereign,

"Yesterday I had the honour to hand to Marshal MacMahon my new credentials, also the reply of His Majesty to the letter of notification. The Marshal, who still inhabits his private apartment, Rue de Grenelle, at Versailles, has requested me to repeat to Your Majesty, that he considered it his duty (*sa tâche*) to maintain the

---

[1] Herr von Arnim was, as is well known, recalled the year after the events above described, and subsequently indicted for having illegally kept and published confidential State documents.

good relations subsisting at this moment with Germany, and that he had a grateful recollection of the kindly reception he had met with at Berlin at his mission thither, as Envoy Extraordinary, on the occasion of Your Majesty's coronation. He also remembers the considerate manner in which he was treated in Germany during his captivity. The Marshal told me at the same time, that after Sedan he was left free to go whither he liked. He went at first to Givet, I believe. When the condition of his wound allowed him to be removed, two French battalions presented themselves to take him away. The temptation to follow them was indeed great; he had, after all, given no promise to constitute himself a prisoner, but in virtue of the consideration that had been shown him, he felt himself bound to observe great scruples, and he sent the battalions back. He adds that this incident was known to no one. The reception, which went off very simply, was nevertheless essentially different from the entirely free-and-easy manner adopted by M. Thiers. The Marshal, who was in uniform, received me standing, in the presence of his minister, and dismissed me (*me congedié*)[1] with the dignified bearing of a sovereign. I have seen few Frenchmen looking less like the typical

---

[1] The author says "dismissed," and the expression in French is absolutely correct. To English ears it may sound somewhat harsh, but I did not care to use the alternative, "intimated that the interview was at an end," in the text.—TRANS.

Frenchman than the Duc de Magenta. It may be, though, that the dry, simple, and the somewhat non-loquacious manner of the Marshal is more apt to govern the French properly than all the brilliancy of his predecessor."[1]

In my capacity as a witness I can guarantee the accuracy of this little picture, for I experienced a similar impression, and, to tell the truth, a similar surprise to those of Herr von Arnim. My knowledge of the Marshal at that period was very slight, and I knew that until then he had avoided entering into the slightest relations, even those of mere politeness, with the representative of Germany. I was therefore not altogether at ease as to the manner in which the conversation would be opened. Everything went off with a noble simplicity that impressed me very much. The slight timidity of speech which now and then hampered the Marshal in ordinary conversation seemed to have disappeared; and I fancied more than once that it was, on the contrary, his interlocutor who was suffering from it. The Ambassador Extraordinary of 1867,[2] and the captive of Sedan,

[1] "*Pro Nihilo*," *Antécédents du procès d'Arnim*, p. 94. I have an idea that *Pro Nihilo* and *Vorgeschichte des Arnimschen Processes*, to which the author seems to refer as one, are two different publications. I remember reading them both.—TRANS.

[2] This is evidently a slip of the pen on the part of the author, or a printer's error. The coronation took place in 1861, I believe, when Wilhelm declared himself "King by the will of God alone."—TRANS.

recalled his good as well as evil days with a truly rare mixture of dignity and kindly grace; his words betrayed neither the discouragement of misfortune nor the regret of a brilliant position, which had not dazzled him. The remark I made then; I have had occasion to review it more than once since. Everything in the shape of homage, and especially of compliment, referring exclusively to him and to noteworthy military performances, was received by the Marshal with ill-disguised annoyance, and a modesty which frequently bordered on the awkward. On the other hand, he was perfectly at his ease when it became a question to receive in the name of France the eminent foreign personages, or even princes, who came to pay their respects to him as Chief of the State. It was because on these occasions he forgot all about himself, and only thought about his duty. The loftiness of his sentiments became naturally at one with the loftiness of the rank which he had neither sought nor solicited.

Herr von Bismarck's rough treatment, and for which he had assigned so little reason, made M. de Gontaut and me expect similar treatment before long. And if it was not Herr von Bismarck himself, it was his Press, known to be in his pay and at his call, which undertook to leave us no breathing time, for before the new Government could possibly commit any act lending itself to comment or criticism, the word went round, in defiance of all etiquette, to increase in invective and violence against France, and all those who represented her, whether at home or abroad, and the order was obeyed by all the papers of which the Chancellor could dispose. M. de Gontaut, who subsequently was to suffer more than any one else, was, however, comparatively spared at that moment.

It was against me, against my very inoffensive personality (for until then Germany had had no cause to complain of or concern herself with me more than of or with any other Frenchman), that a very avalanche of insults was directed. There was no slander running riot in the lowest section of our revolutionary press that was not taken up and granted a conspicuous place in the foremost papers of Berlin, Frankfort, or Cologne. Neither the story of my life nor, above all (though I have never known why), my private means were spared in those attacks. I was both bankrupt in morals and in money, and had only accepted the Ministry to redeem, by means of speculation, my estates, which were mortgaged up to the last acre, and to prevent the threatened seizure of my stipend as a deputy. On that subject there was such perfect harmony between the French writers of the lowest category and the German ones of the highest that it became a question which should have the palm for invention. I have always professed great indifference for personal attacks, no matter whence they come and what they may be, and I am of opinion that he who has the misfortune to be sensitive in that respect should hold aloof from public life. But I may add that in this instance, and in virtue of the "certificate of origin"[1] of those renewed attacks, I went further still than being merely callous, I was tempted to look upon those attacks in the light of a flattering distinction.

On one particular occasion I was enabled to determine beyond the shadow of a doubt the quarter whence the arrow intended for me came. Monseigneur le Duc d'Aumale, in pursuance of the preliminary investigations to that deplorable *Bazaine trial* at which he presided with such extreme conscientiousness and eminent superiority, was desirous to examine personally the spot on which were enacted the scenes of the drama, the actors of which were to appear soon before him. He requested me to apprise the German authorities of his intention to visit the battlefields around Metz. I felt practically certain that the notice would not be well received, hence I sent it directly to Herr von Bismarck, either through M. de Gontaut or Herr von Arnim, I do not remember which, asking that the thing might be kept secret. But before the refusal, which was a foregone conclusion, could reach me, all the

---

[1] A certificate of origin (*un certificat d'origine*) is a document accompanying imported merchandise, attesting the place of their manufacture, and declaring that they do not come within the category of prohibited goods.—TRANS.

officious papers resounded with comments on the arrogance of a French prince wishing to make a triumphal progress through the annexed provinces, and the unseemly conduct of the minister who had lent himself to the design. This indelicate publicity had only one advantage, that of providing me with a reply, which I imagine must have struck home ("topical," says the author), when, a few days later, Herr von Arnim came to complain of certain articles in the French papers, the responsibility for which he wished to fasten on me, and which had spoken with more or less disregard of the Chancellor.

More singular was the fact of that unexpected ebullition of hostility and acrimoniousness in no way subsiding, when the acts as well as the attitude of the new Government had convinced the most incredulous that the sensitive and pacific policy of M. Thiers would in no wise be departed from. In vain were all the provisions of the Treaty of March 15 scrupulously observed; in vain did the evacuation of the territory proceed amid the profoundest calm of the populations; in vain did M. de Gontaut, in accordance with his instructions, carry the spirit of conciliation to its farthermost limits, amidst the sufficiently serious difficulties engendered by the execution of that Treaty. In short, the most praiseworthy perseverance from their point of view, the least praiseworthy from ours, looked in vain for a reproach to confront us with; the gall, nevertheless, persistently bubbled over. It was enough to induce the belief that the fall of the late President had inflicted a pain and almost personal wound on Herr von Bismarck to which he could not resign himself. But when the restoration of the Monarchy in France began to dawn on the political horizon, as the natural consequence of the vote of May 24, then the ill-humour increased to a degree as to become positive exasperation.

That was a result to be expected. In truth, as I have already pointed out, the new presidential combination had ostensibly taken its stand on the ground of neutrality and the pact of Bordeaux, and Marshal MacMahon, more careful and anxious to maintain his position there, had intentionally chosen his ministers from among all the shades of the Conservative majority, not excepting that section which for a moment, in the track of M. Thiers, had inclined towards the Republic. Royalist opinion prevailed, nevertheless, in a conspicuous degree, both in the Cabinet and among the party that had carried the Cabinet to and was maintaining it in power. There was no doubt, then, that the Royalists, having met with the favourable opportunity they had been waiting for till they were tired of waiting, would eagerly turn it to account to realize at last the wish so dear to them. Their constitutional right to restore the Monarchy admitted of no discussion, and the visit of M. le Comte de Paris to Frohsdorf on August 5 following, sealing as it did, and in so signal a manner, the reconciliation between the two branches of the House of France, seemed to justify the ardent hopes.

There is no need to resort to conjecture to form an idea of the impatience—to put it mildly —of the nervous irritation of Herr von Bismarck at the prospect of a monarchical restoration in France. It was the Chancellor of Germany himself who thought fit to inform us, by means of a document, the publication of which was due to his good offices, of his constant desire that we should keep to the Republic, that form of government being in his opinion best calculated to perpetuate our isolation and weakness. That object having constituted the principal motive for the Chancellor's goodwill to M. Thiers' government—as the Chancellor himself undisguisedly admits—it was but natural that M. Thiers' fall should have particularly affected him in a contrary sense. That charitable wish was printed in identical terms in the document of which I am speaking, and which caused a certain noise at the time of its publication. M. Thiers himself lived long enough to take cognizance of it, but I am unable to state what impression it produced.

A few traits, which may prove not without interest, will suffice to let in a retrospective light on the delicate situation in which M. de Gontaut and I found ourselves while our friends were proceeding with a task as dear to our patriotism as to theirs, but which left both the one and the other exposed to the relentless ill-will of the greatest and most formidable enemy to France. For there was not a moment's doubt in people's minds (and they were practically right) that the representative of France at Berlin, and the vice-president of the Council of Ministers in Paris, were associated from the bottom of their hearts with the generous design that was being worked out around them, albeit that their official position prevented them from taking an active part in the execution of that design.

For the strange revelation of Herr von Bismarck's feelings with regard to us we must look once more to the documents pertaining to the lawsuit instituted a few years later by the Chancellor against Herr von Arnim, his diplomatic agent with M. Thiers. The official dispatch containing that revelation was inserted with a kind of cynicism among those documents. It would appear that Herr von Arnim, a witness and perhaps a confidant of M. Thiers' republican designs, had refused to associate himself with them, nay, had gone the length of expressing some fears—from the monarchical and conservative point of view—with regard to the possibly contagious effect of the triumph of the Republic in France on the rest of Europe. This drew upon

Count Arnim the severest reproof a diplomatist ever received from his chief. "It is assuredly no part of our duty to make France powerful by strengthening her situation at home, and by the establishing there of a regular Monarchy, by enabling that country to conclude alliances with the Powers with which up till now we are keeping up friendly relations. The enmity of France forces upon us the wish for her continued weakness, and I consider that we are already giving proofs of great disinterestedness in not opposing resolutely and by force the establishment of solid monarchical institutions as long as the Treaty of Peace of Frankfort has not been completely carried out. I feel convinced that no Frenchman would ever dream of helping us to recover the blessings of a Monarchy if God saw fit to inflict on us the miseries of Republican anarchy. To show such kindly concern with regard to the fate of a hostile neighbour is an eminently Germanic virtue. But his Majesty's Government is the less justified to follow that unpractical inclination, seeing that every attentive observer must have noticed how numerous the political conversions have been and still are in Germany since the experiments *in corpore vili* of the Commune in the sight of the whole of Europe. France is a salutary hobgoblin to us. So long as the monarchies march shoulder to shoulder, the Republic cannot harm them. Such is my conviction, and it prevents my advising his Majesty to support monarchical rights in France."[1] This is the haughty language of the instructions sent to Count Arnim on December 20, 1872.

That manner of seeing things, which I suspected well enough, has since then been perfectly summed up by a Russian diplomatist, to whose humoristic way of putting matters I have already alluded. "You may take it for granted," said that caustic observer, "that Herr von Bismarck wishes you nothing so much as a *dissolving* Republic." I could scarcely imagine, however, that the day would come when I should see the barefaced avowal of Herr von Bismarck's real sentiments towards us.

I still doubt whether he would have imbued —supposing he tried, which I equally doubt—with a similar sentiment either his sovereign or the political master-minds of Europe, who continued to nourish against the republican form a prejudice amply justified by its past adventures. In spite of his arrogant ascendency, he would have experienced great difficulty to induce them to follow his lead. Hence, the design to restore the Monarchy of which we were suspected was never alleged among the number of grievances against us. The subject was never alluded to in the still very rare interviews between M. de Gontaut and the Chancellor or the Prussian ministers; it was

---

[1] The French version of the Arnim trial, pp. 79 *et seqq.*

not mentioned by Herr von Arnim in the daily complaints he brought to my door either with reference to the polemics of the papers, with which he fancied he had cause for dissatisfaction, or with regard to the coolness and the awkwardness of his intercourse with Parisian society. Only once, I believe, and in connection with some incident I do not remember, Herr von Arnim asked me, casually as it were, why we were in such a hurry to restore the throne, and began dwelling with praise on the advantages of maintaining the Republic in the position France had been placed by events. He pleaded that cause very badly, he spoke without conviction, like one who fulfils a disagreeable task, and I was not surprised to learn subsequently what I did not know then—that he was talking not only without, but against his personal conviction, that on that point he disagreed *in toto* with his chief. I simply replied to him laughing, and without appearing to attach any more importance to the matter than he did. "But if the Republic seems such a good thing," I said, "why not introduce it among yourselves?" He smiled, and did not refer to the subject again.

Herr von Bismarck, then, felt well enough that he could not prevail on monarchical Europe to look favourably on the Republic even in virtue of the harm the *régime* might do to France. But M. de Gontaut had warned me that, for all that, his ill-will would be as wary as it was active, and he could not have found a more fertile ground for the seed of distrust and hostility he was sowing among us. He hinted, if he did not say it, that we were not only Royalists, a crime all the crowned heads would have easily forgiven us, but we were also Ultramontanes and Clericals. And the Monarchy which we wished to establish would be Ultramontane and Clerical to the same degree, and consequently a threat to any and every neighbour not animated by the same spirit, and as a second consequence a threat to the maintenance of general peace. It is but just that every inventor should reap the credit of his own invention. There was nothing original in the cry of alarm, "Clericalism, that is the real enemy," which M. Gambetta was to thunder forth from the rostrum of the French Chamber a few months later. It was the self-same cry of Herr von Bismarck from the other side of the Rhine, and the echoes of which he meant to be heard beyond the Alps.

The diversion was all the more clever on Herr von Bismarck's part, in that it seemed the natural explanation of the struggle upon which he had just entered with the Catholic Church in Germany. Germany was at the commencement and in the first ardour of what since then has been termed the *Kulturkampf*, that relentless war against Catholicism, the motive of which has never been clearly known, and the issue of which has so ridiculously disappointed the man who yielded to the brutal whim to undertake it, but which for a period of ten years troubled German society most deeply. A series of laws intending to despoil as well as to persecute both the secular and regular clergy were proposed to the Diet, and the moment they were adopted their rigour was aggravated by confiscation and arbitrary proscription. The spectacle was scarcely calculated to arouse much admiration in France; but the Conservative and Monarchical Press in particular, while drawing pictures of those violent proceedings, could not refrain from expressing its indignation against the executors and its sympathy with the victims. Those very openly manifested dispositions easily provided Herr von Bismarck with a motive for pretending that, if restored royalty in France were animated by the same sentiment as its partisans, the simple fact of the advent of that royalty would afford the Catholic minority he was trampling upon as he pleased a moral support and a cause of hope of which he felt bound to take note. Was that danger real? was the fear he so noisily proclaimed sincere? My doubts are as strong as ever. Neither during nor after the war did the German Catholics show the least sympathy with France, and a patriotic scruple, which I should be the last to blame, has always prevented them from appearing to expect, still less from asking, assistance of the alien. The apprehension, nevertheless, might argue its justification from, to say the least, specious motives, and of a character to impress the aged Emperor, for though less ardent than his minister in the pursuit of the anti-Catholic campaign, Wilhelm I. had practically allowed of its being begun, and when once the struggle was engaged in he supported it from a feeling that his prestige was involved, being determined that the event should not turn to the disadvantage of the National Church, of which he was the chief and the representative.[1]

It was in consideration of quite a different nature, and of a much more urgent character, that weighed on the mind of another sovereign, whose terror of the Clericals so adroitly invoked by Herr von Bismarck was calculated to trouble that sovereign's. I am alluding to the King of Italy. Established in spite of himself at the Quirinal, almost facing the pontifical sovereign captive at the Vatican, Victor Emmanuel, as is well known, always felt himself ill at ease there, and the dread of being compelled to evacuate the place in consequence of some sudden reverse of fortune never ceased to haunt his mind and that of his retainers.[2]

[1] The author is perfectly right; here is a proof of it. "No measure is taken without my previous approval," Wilhelm I. wrote angrily to Pius IX. on September 3, 1875. The Holy Father had insinuated that the persecutions against the Catholics had probably been decided without the Emperor's knowledge.—TRANS.

[2] What is not so well known is, that this horrible fear on the part of *il ré galantuomo* sprang from a quasi-prophecy, dating, I believe, from the eve of Novara, to the effect that the Quirinal

Their anxious looks were strained in the direction of France.

France, in fact, had more or less cause to complain of the somewhat incorrect proceeding (to put it mildly) of her erstwhile allies of Solferino, who, instead of coming to her aid in her misfortunes, had profited by them to force an entry into Rome contrary to all engagements, and the moment the French troops had taken their departure. Would not France, at some future time, endeavour to exact a reckoning for that treatment the reverse of friendly, and recur to a fact the accomplishment of which her misfortunes for the time being had alone compelled her to accept? And what if that day of reckoning were made to coincide with that of the restoration of the Monarchy through the efforts of a party which numbered in its ranks the most zealous and most faithful champions of the temporal power of the Papacy?

A like supposition was practically void of all foundation, for the best and at the same time saddest of reasons; namely, that France, whether under a monarchical or republican *régime,* was too exhausted, too mutilated to attempt for a very long time to come any hostile movement against

would be fatal to him. The prediction had almost been forgotten, but recurred to Victor Emmanuel when he took up his residence at the palace. For a very long while after that Victor Emmanuel left Rome at night by the Porta Pia for the villa of Rosina Vercellana, Comtessa de Mirafiori.—TRANS.

no matter whom. She had quite enough to do to defend her own security; no sane person could harbour the thought of her attacking any one. The proof whereof is, that when some zealous Catholics petitioned the National Assembly to send to the captive Pius IX. an expression of their sympathy, there had not been a single voice requesting M. Thiers to add either a promise or hold out the faintest hope of effectual aid. But it did not matter a jot; an uneasy conscience makes cowards of us all, even with regard to mere phantoms. The dread that the restoration of the French Monarchy might prove the signal for an aggressive movement against the unification of Italy took hold quickly throughout the peninsula of the alarmed imaginations. Is it not said that even to this day they are not completely reassured? One thing is certain; not so very long ago I had a letter from a big Italian Review, a letter expressing in all seriousness the suspicion that Leo XIII.'s manifest goodwill to the Republican form of government (so little inclined to Clericalism indeed) with which we are blessed, evidently pointed to a secret understanding with MM. Ferry, Spuller, and even in case of need with MM. Brisson and Goblet, for the eventual restoration of the temporal power.

Be this as it may, from the moment Italy became seriously alarmed, and fancied that the restoration of a Monarchy in France meant danger to itself, Bismarck's purpose was virtually attained.

Monarchy in prospective appeared from that time forth like a black spot on the horizon; it was the spectre which was going to prevent Europe from enjoying in peace the rest to which she was just settling down; comment was rife; public opinion almost taxed us with preparing a vast reaction in favour of Catholic authority and the dogma of Legitimacy in order to re-establish Don Carlos at Madrid, the proscribed heir of the House of Bourbon at Naples, and all the dispossessed in Germany as well as Italy. It was to denounce and at the same time to avert the danger that Victor Emmanuel, in the beginning of September, repaired in something like state to Berlin and then to Vienna, to show the peoples of Europe that the great Powers stood united and hand in hand, ready to defend them against the Clerical agitation. But the union of the sovereigns was as nothing compared to that established immediately between the three Presses, German, Italian, and French: It was a concert with a triple band and loud ringing of bells, in which our Republican journalists took the dominant note and gave the key. Truly, a certain feeling of shame prevented them as yet to play too manifestly in open unison with the well-known organs of the Prussian Foreign Office. But there were no such scruples with regard to those of the Quirinal; there was a regular understanding between those two, a daily exchange of false or true communications, a tactical system combined with method— in one word, a cordiality which went to the length of effusiveness and sentimental affection. It was an understood thing that a friendship, nay, the closest intimacy, between Italy and France was simply a matter of course, and could only be frustrated and transformed into corresponding feelings of distrust by the threatening "papalin" Monarchists in power. But for the designs of which we were suspected, the two Latin sister-nations, intended by nature to understand and love one another, would have flung themselves into each other's arms, and Italy was only waiting for our disappearance from the political arena to show her grateful recollection of the services rendered to her unification by French arms. There is no need to show how subsequent events have belied the assumption which at that time, and even from sheer *naïveté* or calculation, commanded belief in every Republican mind.

But how could people, nay, the best disposed, help being seriously alarmed at the rumour of that Clerical peril, re-echoed as it was on every side; how could they help being alarmed when they even beheld one of the principal authors of the Education Bill of 1850, and the erstwhile accredited champion of the temporal power of the

Papacy, namely, M. Thiers, profess to share the general emotion to such an extent, as to promise in an open letter to resume his seat in the Assembly, in order to defend *threatened religious freedom;* how could they help being alarmed, when most intelligent women belonging to the immediate circle of M. Thiers' friends repaired to the public places in the South of France, in order to persuade the peasantry that the first act of a restored Monarchy would be the reviving of tithes, accompanied by a law of enforced monthly confession? Finally, in common candour as well as fairness, we are bound to admit that our own monarchical, but above all our religious Press caused us every now and again a good deal of embarrassment. The manner in which it took up the provocations coming from Italy was calculated to invest them with a show of justice; the prominence it gave to most laudable religious manifestations was calculated to invest them with the appearance of a political character. It was not sufficiently cautious in its appeals for divine protection to escape the garbling of those appeals, and their transformation at the hands of those of bad faith into petitions for other than spiritual weapons for the defence of religion.

Without allowing himself to be affected beyond measure by a situation, the painful nature of which was mainly manifest around him, M. de Gontaut kept me informed of all its evolutions with his usual frankness and clear-sightedness. "There is a point," he wrote to me on August 12, "which has always caused me anxiety, and I fancy I talked it over with you in Paris; I am alluding to the religious question in Germany. Herr von Bismarck, carried away by his passion, has made it one of the bases of his policy. The resistance he has met with, and which is becoming more accentuated every day, irritates him, and far from proving a discouragement, it seems to act like a stimulant on his will. His mind is fertile in resources, he has few or no scruples, he is bold to a degree, and I feel convinced that his principal occupation at this moment is the devising of new means of victory. He is, moreover, afraid of France; he dreads the awakening of the religious spirit there, and would look upon it as a possible encouragement to the resistance the Catholics oppose to him. In short, he views with apprehension the clearing of the horizon in favour of a probable return of the Monarchy in France; and, thanks to the gossip of the Press, to the inopportune and indiscreet comments—to put it mildly—of the journals and of certain members of the extreme Right, as well as to the cries of alarm on the part of the Republican papers, even of the most moderate, he is under the impression that the Comte de Chambord, if he did ascend the throne, would before all adopt a Pope-ridden and religious policy of reaction, etc., etc. The triumph of the Carlists in Spain would frighten him no less from that particular point of view. Impelled by those surmises, he cannot help being bent on giving us serious trouble. How will he contrive it? that is the question. It will probably not be by declaring war against us, at any rate not for the present. . . . I repeat; there lies the dark and dreaded point. How is it to be cleared up? That again is very difficult."

A month later, the chances of restoring the Monarchy having become more probable, and above all more imminent, he warned me of possible dangers of a more serious nature, and calculated to give me greater concern. He had had the opportunity of a conversation with the Empress Augusta, who throughout never ceased to honour him with her goodwill. That noble woman was far from sharing all the views, and least of all all the passions, of Herr von Bismarck, whether with regard to France, whose ruin she had never wished for, or with regard to the Catholic religion, towards which she was accused, even in Germany, of entertaining a secret leaning. On that particular day M. de Gontaut was surprised to find her sad, more reserved than usual, and visibly shaken by the noise around her.

"Without departing from the reserve arising from the conventions of our reciprocal situation, I endeavoured to reassure her with regard to the tendencies that cause such a gratuitous anxiety in

Germany. In spite of her friendly disposition, in spite of the natural elevation of her character, she is not personally free from the prejudices against us that are being so cleverly exploited at present. I was not in the least surprised at this, for that distrust is as it were in the air we breathe here, and with which apparently the most distinguished cannot help being impregnated. I may add, that this anxiety, arising from the dread of a new 'lifting of bucklers' in France, and particularly by the excessive development of religious manifestations, is not confined to Germany alone, but may be noticed in nearly every foreigner, if I am to judge by the conversations I had during my stay at the watering-places in Germany. This is a symptom to the existence of which we should not close our eyes, and which is calculated to make us think. The Empress, moreover, said something to me, from which I may safely conclude that henceforth my position will be fraught with greater difficulties, and be more delicate than hitherto it has been, *that is, while there were outstanding accounts between Germany and France.* While pointing this out to me, in, I am bound to admit, a very kindly tone and manner, did she mean to allude to some plan Germany is hatching, to this or that trouble she may endeavour to fasten upon us a little later on? I doubt it, because she remains altogether outside the sphere of politics. Hence I am inclined to believe, that in talking to me as she did she was simply impressed by the sad and general view we had both arrived at a little while before when discussing the whole of the situation, and the social dangers hanging over us in the future. Nevertheless, I fancy that certain words of hers might be construed into an allusion to the uneasy dispositions of Europe, face to face with the religious manifestations of our country, and particularly to the dispositions of Prince Bismarck."

I need scarcely say that those grave warnings, coming whence they did, did not leave me indifferent. The lofty position to which circumstances had lifted me entailed a considerable share of responsibility in the future destiny of my country. Not to have kept my eyes open, day and night, not to have entered heart and soul into the situation on the eve of the supreme resolution the National Assembly was about to take, would, warned as I was of the consequences that might ensue, have been a terrible neglect of duty on my part. Nevertheless, amidst all those reflections ever present to me, I failed to detect the least cause why my friends should not pursue to the end the glorious enterprise they were resolved to attempt. In reality, and looking at them dispassionately, there was nothing substantial or serious in the prejudices that had been deliberately marshalled against us. No one in France, whether in our own ranks or in those of others (with the exception of some visionaries without the least authority), dreamt of attempting a religious crusade beyond our frontier, or of establishing at home anything resembling the civic domination of the clergy. At a public meeting in Normandy I had given my personal explanation of the matter, and, if the truth must be told, with a kind of scornful assurance, and not a voice had been raised, even from the most advanced ranks of the Right, to attenuate, still less to contradict, the purport of my words. To dissipate that mist, the Comte de Chambord, answering the call of the National Assembly, would but have had to express the same thought, unquestionably his, with the authority due to his rank, and in that dignified language and so distinctly French, he had at his command. All the preoccupations of the friends of order and of peace would have veered round in his favour, considering monarchical stability a better guarantee than could be offered by a Republic raised on the smoking ruins of the Commune. We should have had nothing to confront us but the disguised ill-will and astute threats of one man. To retreat before the supposed mark of his displeasure, before the frown of that Olympian Jupiter, would have been tantamount to declaring that France, abdicating the right to govern herself henceforth, was resigned to submit her national life to the good pleasure of a master, and not to emerge from the shadow of his protectorate. Had we come to this? Had Sedan obliterated to such an extent the memories of Bouvines, Marignan, Rocroy, Denain, Fontenoy, and Austerlitz, as to reduce us to such an avowal of decline and to such a depth of humiliation? I refused to admit that thought. We had just paid sufficiently dear for our independence, we might at least claim to have recovered it. A few months previously, when Herr von Bismarck had given us to understand that, should such circumstances arise, he would not consent to acknowledge M. Gambetta as President of the Republic, I had strongly recommended M. de Gontaut not to let him articulate to the end that pretension to an arrogant right of control and exclusion, but it was certainly not with the intention to allow that stranger, or any other, for that matter, to believe himself entitled to place an interdict on the institution and dynasty which represented to the most eminent degree our greatness in the past, and constituted our greatest hope for its recovery. As for myself, I should have never forgiven myself for attaching to the recollection of such a weakness a name borne before me by more than one generation, which had served, and not altogether without glory, both France and the Monarchy. Never did I feel myself to be so much of a Royalist as on the day I perceived clearly that a German wanted to prevent my being so. One might have never been a Royalist, one could not cease to be one that day. At present, when the passions, then at their height, have calmed down, I feel convinced that every Frenchman will understand me.

Between M. de Gontaut and myself there could be no disagreement of opinion on such a subject. My letters to him, therefore, were not intended to dictate to him words which emanated naturally from his inmost heart as they did from mine; I wrote to him, simply to confirm and to impress on his mind our agreement to that effect at every fresh incident. It was that idea which presided at the conception of the letter I again addressed to him on October 25, and only a few days before the ever-to-be-regretted incident that was to witness the destruction of our common hopes.

"I am constantly thinking of you, and of what your position at Berlin will be while the debate runs its impassioned course here. I have no doubt that the ill-will against any monarchical combination is at its height there. Herr von Bismarck is evidently pursuing it with that instinctive hatred of everything calculated to raise France to her former position, and with that mixture of genuine impatience and simulated dread he displays against everything that may aid the interests of the Catholic Church. Unfortunately, I am much afraid that the French

Republicans, *even the most illustrious and of the most recent standing*, will not hesitate to accept that support which confers so little honour on their cause. All this will make it a difficult time for you (*un quart d'heure difficile à passer*) as well as for us, and you will need all your vigilance and more to detect before it is too late, and to frustrate all the bad tricks they will play us in order to increase our home difficulties. I can only repeat to you what I have already said. When you happen to meet with sincere people, really uneasy at the idea that we are going to set Europe on fire in the interests of the temporal power of the Papacy, try to dispel their uneasiness with valid reasons. You lack no means to convince those whom it is possible to convince. With regard to the others, save your breath, put on the appearance of perfect tranquillity, of being confident of your cause, display neither excitement nor agitation. After all, our territory, take it as you will, is liberated; our debts are paid, and we are no longer at the mercy of a whim. I know how precarious and insecure that independence is with our arsenals empty and our frontier open. But they will, at any rate, have to find new pretexts in order to fasten new quarrels on us. Equally, no doubt, the stronger need never be at a loss for a pretext. Nevertheless, there is still sufficient interest in Europe for an unfortunate nation trying to retrieve her position, the traditions attached to the

Monarchical cause are still sufficiently strong to render provocation on the part of the 'crowned revolutionary' at Varzin practically impossible, as long as we refrain from giving him the opportunity. Take no notice whatsoever of things said or done to annoy you, unless you consider them too serious to be passed over, and do not give Herr von Bismarck the satisfaction of appearing to mind his anger. We have right if not might on our side, and we should show the calmness suitable to the situation which is not without its dignity.'"

I may be permitted to add, that I had by my side, or rather above me, in the attitude of Marshal MacMahon, the model for that dignity which seemed to me to be incumbent, at that critical moment, on all the representatives of France. Owing to a scruple, the nature of which I have pointed out, the Marshal, having promised to the various parties to remain, did not think himself justified to depart from that neutrality and to associate himself personally with the design pursued around him; nevertheless, from the bottom of his heart he was intensely interested in it. He made no secret of his wish for its success, although the result would have entailed the descent from the foremost position he had attained. That, to his thinking, was such an insignificant fact that he seemed not only not to trouble himself about it, but not to perceive, an indifference which did not exist to the same degree with his predecessor. But when informed of the attempt to discredit his advisers by spreading all sorts of rumours against them, he was the first to tell them to take no heed. To those who would endeavour to question our good faith he willingly pledged his reputation of personal loyalty in guarantee of ours. Above all was he convinced of his ability to arrive finally at an understanding with the King of Italy. I do not remember whether it was on that occasion or on a similar one that occurred later on that he said to me—"I will write to Victor Emmanuel; he knows me, we have fought side by side; whatever I say he will believe."

If, unfortunately, M. de Gontaut's answer had not reached me too late to be productive of anything but regrets, I should have had the satisfaction of being able to verify that the line of conduct agreed on between us would produce its effect, even at Berlin. The best course to take in this world is not to yield to intimidation. When a resolution is properly taken, even those who are displeased with it resign themselves to make the best of it, and would fear to show their annoyance by a too conspicuously bad reception. "Very interesting, those forthcoming events in Paris," remarked one of the Prussian ministers to M. de Gontaut. "With France one never knows what will come next. What wonderful resources you have! What vitality!"

And M. de Gontaut sent me at the same time German newspaper articles, which, without reinstating us in their favour, had considerably lowered their tone. His diplomatic colleagues already began to inquire of him with regard to the course the restored Monarchy was likely to adopt, and in such a manner as to show him that each one, looking upon the thing as an accomplished fact, was debating with himself how best to turn it to his own profit. The same impression was communicated to me from London by the Duc Decazes, from Vienna by the Marquis d'Harcourt, and by General Leflô from St. Petersburg, where, it should be said, our relations had never ceased to be cordial.[1]

Hence, I remain convinced, that however many and great the obstacles, owing to the division of parties, might have been at home to the restoration of the Monarchy, no spoke would have been thrown in its wheels from beyond the frontier. Everything would have simply passed off as it did in 1814, with even this advantage to the grand-nephew of Louis XVIII., that the territory being free, and France's ransom paid, he would have resumed in the councils of Europe the place

[1] In the course of that summer of 1873, one of our friends of the Assembly, and a distinguished diplomatist, the Comte de Chandordy, while travelling in Switzerland, where Prince Gortschakoff was spending the season, had at my request paid him a visit, and had found him as kindly disposed as M. de Gontaut had found him the year before. Prince Gortschakoff scarcely noticed the objections with which the Conservative Government was assailed.

occupied by his forebears without owing anything to anybody, and without having to ask them for anything.

*Dis aliter visum.* The Monarchy, alas! was not called upon to undergo the ordeal whence, I feel confident, it would have emerged with credit to its principle and to the welfare of France, as it had emerged from similar ones before. And it was not, as I have heard it hinted more than once, the fear of exposing France to serious diplomatic difficulties that prevented the Prince who was naturally chosen to fill the throne, to come to an understanding with the representatives of the parliamentary majority. Nor was it the apprehension of having to make concessions with regard to religious questions that was repugnant to his conscience. No questions of general policy, any more than question of constitutional organization, were raised, still less debated, by him during those parliamentary negotiations which for a little while were believed to have paved the way to a much-desired agreement. The understanding was complete on all points but one—the expediency or rather the possibility of taking away from the French army the standard under which for nearly a century it had fought, conquered, or suffered, and which misfortune had as much endeared to it as glory. That this has been the only, absolutely the only subject on which it seemed impossible to arrive at an agreement has been practically known all along; recently, however, evidence more authentic than any that had been advanced before, namely, that of a confidant and representative of the Comte de Chambord, has removed whatever doubt there may still have existed; and this is a fact of such importance to history, which would have always been more or less reluctant to put faith in it, that the friends of truth cannot be sufficiently grateful to the Marquis de Dreux-Brézé for having rendered them that service, whatever the inaccuracies may be that have crept into other parts of his story.[1]

My letter to M. de Gontaut conveyed, I imagine, the very general impression consequent on the publication of the famous letter from Frohsdorf, which reached us on October 29.

"The letter of M. le Comte de Chambord has

[1] I was all the more pleased to have M. de Brézé's confirmation on a point on which I have always been convinced, notwithstanding the doubt apparently still existing on the subject in the minds of people who ought to have been completely posted up in the events of that time. For instance, M. de Gontaut himself, in the notes that have been communicated to me, states confidently, that among the number of points discussed between the Comte de Chambord and those who intended to propose his restoration to the Assembly was that of *ministerial responsibility*, a provision restricting the royal prerogative which M. le Comte de Chambord could not make up his mind to accept. In M. de Brézé's *Souvenirs, ministerial responsibility*, in common with the other conditions of a parliamentary *régime*, figures among the points granted without discussion by the Comte de Chambord in the note M. Chesnelong[2] had submitted to him at Salsburg, before being brought back to Paris to be communicated to M. Chesnelong's friends.—AUTHOR.

[2] M. Chesnelong has given a full account of all this in a very recent work, *La Campagne Monarchique d'Octobre* 1873, E. Plon, Nourrit et Cie., Paris, 1895.—TRANS.

caused all the parties unanimously to abandon any idea of the present restoration of the Monarchy. Consternation reigns in the camp of all decent people,[1] for the success was as good as certain. We ought to be thankful that we have in this emergency a man like the Marshal around whom we can group ourselves."

As at the same time I was urgently requesting M. de Gontaut to come to Paris in order to take his part in the important resolutions of the Assembly in view of this unforeseen situation, he could neither watch the impression produced at Berlin by this change of scene, nor inform me in writing of it. Hence I have to recall to mind our conversations to enable me to state that at the first moment a feeling of surprise, mingled with apprehension, dominated every other. The effect seemed so disproportionate to the cause that people had great difficulty to understand the scruple which had stopped the Comte de Chambord midway. The military chiefs, above all, knowing as they did the effect of symbols and outward emblems on the imagination of an army, and alive to the risk of upsetting its moral conditions, those chiefs did not disguise their astonishment. "Why," said Moltke to M. de Gontaut,

---

[1] The author writes "*honnêtes gens*," but he evidently uses the term in the sense in which it was used during the seventeenth and eighteenth centuries in France, when the adjective "*honnête*" did not only imply honesty, but "good form," familiarity with the usages of good society, etc., etc.—TRANS.

when the question was discussed in his presence, "why should the King of France be more difficult than our Emperor, who, while reserving his own ensign for his palace, has left the German tricolour to his troops?" It was exactly the same remark Manteuffel had made to one of my friends one day, at a dinner party at M. Thiers'. "That brave French army which I have learned to appreciate so highly should not be deprived of its standard," he said. "It will be sufficient for the King to display his own colours on his helmet."

Others who were watching the crisis, and who were equally impressed, asked themselves whether the disappointment of the Conservatives would not result in bringing the Republican minority of the Assembly back to power amidst a gust of reaction which, even if M. Thiers were replaced at its head, could not fail to place that Assembly at the mercy of the revolutionary party; and they (the spectators) expressed their opinion, not without a certain show of impatience, that France always went from one extreme and from one danger to another. When, therefore, the news spread that the Assembly had secured to Marshal MacMahon a prolongation of his presidential power for seven years, there was a general feeling of satisfaction. This solution was neither the Monarchy which had inspired a kind of mistrust, nor the advent of M. Gambetta, or some one like him, and of whom people were afraid. The solution, assuredly the best one for the moment, although insufficient and precarious, inasmuch as it, while insuring tranquillity for the present, offered no like guarantee for the future, answered perhaps all the better to the degree and the character of the interest others took in us. It would seem that that sentiment showed itself in the terms in which the Prussian Under-Secretary of State assured our *chargé d'affaires*, M. le Marquis de Savye, "that his Government viewed with satisfaction the powers conferred upon the President of the Republic, on which it looked as a new guarantee for the prosperity of France, which, together with the maintenance of the harmony and the friendly relations of the Republic with the foreign powers, constituted its most ardent wish." Twice in that little speech had the word "Republic" been uttered with evident gusto.

The ministerial changes that followed on the re-constituting of the Marshal's powers involved no change to me; at any rate, not for some months to come, during which I remained at the head of the Cabinet; after which, for various reasons, the portfolio of Foreign Affairs devolved on my old friend, the Duc Decazes. I am free to admit that I felt some regret at having to abandon the functions and attributes which had once more placed me amidst surroundings where

I had spent my youth, and in the centre of grand interests, the study of which had always exercised a great fascination over me, and constitutes even to-day in my retirement my favourite occupation. Nevertheless, I was the first to acknowledge that I had been most usefully replaced, and that they could not have hit upon a better substitute. I had been too much mixed up with ardent struggles, I had aroused too much enmity and prejudice on all sides, to remain in power very long in an Assembly the divisions of which I unfortunately knew too well; and I fostered no illusion in that respect. On the morrow of crises such as those through which I had just passed, the foreign policy of a nation wants conducting on a basis of continuity and sequence. The Duc Decazes, who had been less mixed up with our dissensions than I, was enabled to represent France worthily for four years without the need of recanting any of his convictions. His credit for having wielded that power is none the less because of the facility with which he did this, in spite of the oscillations and backsliding of our home policy. During that time he mapped out a line which his successors had only to follow. It is a service for which one cannot be too grateful to his memory. I knew, moreover, how well prepared he was for the task he had to accomplish, by reason of the exceedingly great pliancy of mind, his charm and grace of manner, his skill in managing men, for I had seen him at work during the years we had spent together in the diplomatic career. When M. de Gontaut expressed to me his affectionate regret at the termination of our short collaboration, I was enabled to assure him that he would lose nothing by the change, and he must have seen since then that I was not mistaken.

# III

# THE EPISCOPAL CHARGES AND THE CRISIS OF 1875

# THE EPISCOPAL CHARGES AND THE CRISIS OF 1875

I

NEITHER the ambassador nor his new minister were to enjoy for any length the kind of calm that had succeeded the check to the Monarchy, and the ill-disguised satisfaction of Herr von Bismarck thereat. For if it was not in our power to be Royalists actually and actively, we still remained—M. Decazes, as well as M. de Gontaut and myself—reported Clericals, and that was quite enough to make us unworthy of any confidence or consideration on the part of the inventor of the *Kulturkampf*. His irritation against everything pertaining to the Catholic Church was even going to be pushed to its height by a startling manifestation of religious zeal a very few days after the constitution of the new Ministry.

The occasion or the pretext for it was a cry of pain and indignation uttered by Pius IX. in his captivity against the odious and hourly increasing rigorous treatment to which the Church was subjected in Germany. That eloquent wail was dragged from the generous Pontiff by an attempt which plainly brought to light the scandalous reality of the situation. A prince of the Church, Cardinal Ledochowski, Archbishop of Posen, at first sentenced to two years detention and an enormous fine, was moreover deprived of his spiritual powers by a lay tribunal which had arrogated to itself the right to depose him, a proceeding as contemptible as it was ridiculous, 'and which, in subjecting the whole of the inner life of the Church to the disciplinary power of the State, was but the strict application of the new legislation. An Encyclical denounced to the Christian and civilized world that attempt against the sacred rights of conscience, in terms the just severity of which was not questioned by the sincere organs of Liberal opinion. It was but natural that the bishops, to whom the pontifical document was addressed, finding themselves threatened in the independent discharge of their ministrations, should have made themselves the echo of their spiritual head's voice; it was a duty which those who, like the bishops in England and in Belgium, had the unrestricted liberty of speech were the first to recognize and to discharge conspicuously. Several French bishops, impelled by the same feelings, and having even fewer motives to show any consideration to the German despotism, yielded to the temptation of following the others' example, and the only reproach against them was that they had taken no time to reflect that their condition was, unfortunately, not the same. If, moreover, in the pastoral letters to which they gave publicity their patriotic feeling added some sharpness to the expression of their faith, if here and there their language seemed more or less impregnated with the bitterness still brimming over in every French and Christian heart, if all this were true, then, conscientiously speaking, it could not be accounted as a crime to them. But those who had to bear the burden of the day had the right to remind them of the reserve imposed by a situation as yet indifferently consolidated, and of which only they who bore the burden could estimate the danger. The Church assuredly commanded no one to forget the obligations due to one's country, and the first of those obligations was not to expose the country, by provoking language, to acts of reprisal which might re-open her wounds, that were still smarting and but barely healed.

In more than one instance the Prussian Government at Berlin or the German ambassador in Paris had shown great sensitiveness to far less harsh things said in the French Press, hence we fully expected that blame dispensed from such high quarters would not pass without protest. It was pretty certain that Count Arnim in particular would feel seriously hurt at it, for that ambassador was at that moment more irritable than ever, probably by reason of the foreboding of his near downfall. He complained of everything, and equally held the French ministers responsible for everything; one day it was the rudeness of a lady who declined to sit next to him at dinner at the Marshal's, the next, the severe appreciations enumerated in the course of the Bazaine trial with regard to the conduct of the Prussian generals during the war. Hence, and as a matter of course, came he to complain of the episcopal charges. M. Decazes was prepared for his visit, and was able to answer him that he had already devised measures to stop a course of polemics, the awkwardness of which had been felt beforehand. And, in fact, a circular from the Minister of Public Worship, M. de Fourtou, had requested the bishops not to renew attacks *calculated to arouse the susceptibility of neighbouring governments.* That document, couched in a sad but firm tone, was not to be published officially. It was not to our interest to establish beyond a doubt the fact that what was allowed to pass elsewhere without objection we did not consider ourselves in a position to tolerate at home. But the Press easily got wind of it, and M. de Gontaut was obliged, as it were, to read the document to the Prussian Minister for Foreign Affairs, Herr von Bülow, who showed his appreciation of what we had done. And as, after all, the prelates who had received the notice concurred in the suitability of it, we might cherish the hope that the trouble caused by the noisy incident would quickly be forgotten, as had been the case with several analogous disagreements.

Herr von Bismarck was, however, not of the same mind; the pontifical allocution, the echo of which placed him, as it were, without the pale of public opinion, had wounded him to the quick. Whatever his belief in and worship of material force, his political sense warned him not to despise the action of the highest moral power; the fact is proved by his subsequent conduct, when retracing his steps and emerging from the error of ways into which he had flung himself, he endeavoured, more or less, to obtain the absolution of Pius IX.'s censures by public homage to Leo XIII. But at that particular moment, in his impatience at being struck by a power which he was at a loss to reach, it was on something nearer to hand and on us that, to use a vulgar expression, he tried to vent his ill-humour. Are we to believe, as some competent judges were inclined to believe, that having found a grievance against France which might be invested with a semblance of justice, he would not lightly relax his hold of it, but rather keep it carefully in reserve by means of a prolonged discussion, in order to utilize it in case of need—that is, if his home difficulties became so urgent as to compel him to provide a diversion from them beyond the frontier? Be this as it may, when Herr von Bülow informed him of M. de Gontaut's communication, he showed his displeasure at his minister's having been satisfied with so little. Contrary to his habit of personally communicating as seldom as possible with the ambassadors, he sent word to M. de Gontaut to come and see him. He received him very coldly, and assumed at once a very decided tone. "The German Government," he said, "does not share your opinion that the circular of M. de Fourtou is a sufficient satisfaction, it requires something more than that. It is not sufficient to warn the bishops; they must be punished; that is the only way in which you can prove that you have no share in the insults we receive from them, and that you repudiate your responsibility with regard to them. Do not be induced into any error," he added; "it is a question affecting our security. Your bishops foment the revolt in the Empire, and that is what we will not tolerate. In particular is this the case with the Bishop of Nancy," he remarked, with still greater emphasis, "whose jurisdiction is as yet a mixed one, and extends to the territories recently annexed. If you allow those proceedings to continue, it will be you who will have made war inevitable, and we will make war before the Clerical party, possessing itself of the power, declares it in the name of the persecuted Catholic religion. That is why," he went on, in a frank tone he had not adopted before, "that is why your projects of monarchical restoration never pleased me. I had my suspicions as to the influence your Clericals would bring to bear on the Comte de Chambord." M. de Gontaut having pointed out to him that, as far as he knew, there was no means of penal repression with regard to bishops who had only made use of the common liberty in France as others had done elsewhere, Herr von Bismarck retorted: "You make a mistake, you have two means at your disposal; you can bring them before the Council of State on a writ of appeal against the abuse of their functions ('Appel comme d'Abus'),[1] or else you can cite them before the ordinary courts for having insulted a foreign monarch; and if you refuse to avail yourselves of that right,

---

[1] The word "*abus*" (abuse) signified for a long while and in a special sense the attempts of ecclesiastics against the jurisdiction and rights of laymen. The appeal to the lay authorities against those encroachments was called "Appel comme d'Abus." The "Appel comme d'Abus" was, above all in France, the resistance of the civic authorities against the encroachments of the ecclesiastical powers. The "Appel comme d'Abus" first became common in the fourteenth century. The law of the 18th Germinal of the year X. (April 8, 1802), still in operation at the present day, designates as "*abus*" by ecclesiastics: (1) Usurpation or excessive use of power; (2) Infraction of the laws and rules of the State; (3) Infraction of the French canonical laws, attempts against the liberties, franchises, and customs of the Gallican Church; (4) All enterprises or proceedings which in the exercise of religion may compromise the honour of citizens, arbitrarily trouble their freedom of conscience, degenerate into oppression against them, and cause public injury or scandal. Ecclesiastics have the same means of redress against a civic functionary troubling them in the exercise of their religion. The Council of State adjudicates in those matters, but it can only decide whether there has been abuse or not; it cannot inflict any penal judgment.—TRANS.

your law also grants that right to the representative of the insulted sovereign, and we will avail ourselves directly of it." In face of a decision which appeared as irrevocable as the language in which it was expressed was calm, discussion was out of the question, and M. de Gontaut had no alternative but to take his leave with the positive declaration of Herr von Bismarck ringing in his ears that the minimum of reparation the Prussian Government would accept would be the citation before the Council of State of the Bishop of Nancy, whose language was deemed more violent and more offensive than that of any one else.

Moreover, Herr von Bismarck took care that the conversation should not remain a secret very long. M. de Gontaut had barely had time to dispatch his account of it to Paris when a paper, whose source of inspiration was a secret to no one, published an article on the same theme, and in terms absolutely identical with those he had heard from the lips of the Chancellor.

"The moment France identifies herself with Rome," said the *Nord-Deutsche Zeitung*,[1] "she becomes our sworn enemy. The peace of the world becomes impossible with France subject to the pontifical theocracy." And the Chancellor himself very openly used language the meaning of which was still less ambiguous. "I am not

[1] The author has *l'Allemagne du Nord*, which would mean *Nord-Deutschland*, and to my knowledge there is no paper of that name. —TRANS.

the ememy of France," he said, in a sufficiently loud tone to be overheard by hearers on whom he imposed no secret; "I have proved it well enough by inducing the Emperor to accept the proposal of M. Thiers with regard to the anticipated evacuation; but I declare that, should France support the Catholics in Germany, I shall not wait until she be ready. That will be in two years; before then I shall seize a favourable opportunity." And a few days later, in the rostrum of the Reichstag itself, he took the opportunity, although the subject under discussion did not lend itself to it, to speak of a possible war with us as a contingency of which he had forecast the most minute chances. "I have been reproached," he said, "with having made use in 1866 of the Hungarian deserters against Austria; I have merely availed myself of the rights of warfare; and if one day we found ourselves involved in a war with France whose chief then might be Henri, Comte de Chambord, we should have no cause for complaint if they constituted a pontifical legion with the Catholics of South Germany, incited to desert by the bishops who preach disobedience to the laws." Those alarming rumours soon became sufficiently general for the Empress to refer to them. One day at a Court dinner she came up unaffectedly to M. de Gontaut, and reminded him of their conversation of a few months previously.

"I warned you that your troubles were not at

an end," she said; "and that there were even graver difficulties in store for you than those you had gone through in the past. Was I right?" "Yes, Madame," replied M. de Gontaut; "and your Majesty's words have recurred to me more than once." "Are you not treated as you ought to be?" she added, with a kind of uncomfortable though interested tone, glancing in the direction of Bismarck in another part of the room. "As far as that goes, yes. There is never a want of politeness, but the reality is very sad and very difficult." M. de Gontaut was speaking in a low tone of voice. "Do you think people are listening?" asked the Empress, somewhat eagerly. "No, I do not think so, but we might be overheard;" and in a few words M. de Gontaut explained to her the new subject of the dispute.

At that time I was still M. de Decazes' colleague, and he was kind enough to communicate to me the dispatches he received. The conversation of Herr von Bismarck was, as a matter of course, the subject of a consultation between us, in which we were free to confess to one another that we felt even more embarrassed than uneasy. Though M. de Gontaut was assuredly correct in alleging a want of legal power which, as we shall see directly, was real, he had not been able to close Herr von Bismarck's mouth completely with regard to his pretensions; and the latter, by invoking against the bishops whom he accused by the administrative procedure of the "Appel comme d'Abus," showed himself an expert adept of our new parliamentary Gallicanism. In reading again the dissertation he sent to Count Arnim in support of his demand, I cannot help being even struck by the likeness of his argument to that we hear daily (once not later than a few weeks ago) unfolded in the rostrum of the Chamber by the Republican organs.[1] It is the same convenient forgetfulness, or rather the same denial of the spiritual independence of the Church, the same refusal to recognize the new moral conditions and changes brought to bear upon ancient legislation by the introduction of the liberty of the Press and of worship into the laws of nations. The bishops receive a money stipend from the State; whatever be the origin of that remuneration, that fact alone makes them functionaries of the State like every other category of functionaries; as such they are bound to obey the Government, which in that way becomes responsible for all their acts; and it was in virtue of that title that Herr von Bismarck asked us to bring them to justice by taking administrative action against them. The lawyers at Herr von Bismarck's elbow had not less carefully read him his lesson on the practical bearing of Articles 12 of the law

[1] That dissertation may be found in the volume entitled *Antécédents du procès d'Arnim*, pp. 117—153 (the French version of the *Vorgeschichten* already mentioned). Count Arnim was accused of not having supported the claim of his chief with sufficient energy. He had no difficulty in refuting that accusation.

of May 19, 1819, and 7 of the law of March 22, 1822, both of which provided a judicial way to foreign sovereigns and their representatives for obtaining redress for insults and offences of which they believed themselves entitled to complain. In that rather complete enumeration of all the weapons at our possible disposal against the clergy there was, however, one the absence of which from the list may well cause our surprise to-day, because the practical application of it has since then become as common as it is convenient. Not a word was said to us about withholding the stipend of the incriminated bishops. Could it be that the most assiduous search had failed to bring to light either a legal foundation or even a precedent sufficiently recent to be remembered for that method of "taming" dignitaries holding episcopal rank? In any case, that omission will no doubt appear extremely regrettable to our Republican priests; it would have provided a precedent emanating from an authority which they might have quoted with as much honour as profit.

The most cursory examination was sufficient to show us that neither of the two means between which Herr von Bismarck had told M. de Gontaut to choose for his (Bismarck's) expected satisfaction was for us honourably practicable. We were in no way disposed to drag from the discredit into which it had then justly fallen the superannuated procedure of the "Appel comme d'Abus," of which the constitutional Monarchy had made but sparing use, to which the second Empire had only resorted once, and which had emerged from each ordeal riddled with biting epigrams. In its right place, perhaps, in a social organization where the Church, enjoying certain powers in temporal matters, might be suspected of abusing those powers, and where the State professing a religion might, to a certain point, pretend to some competence in spiritual matters; but the "Appel comme d'Abus" has no longer any appreciable meaning in a purely lay society, the very principle of which emancipates it from all threats on the part of religious authority. A verdict which has neither a moral value, nor entails a material consequence, is nothing but a puerile vexation, the only effect of which is to secure a noisy publicity to facts at which it pretends to tilt. I doubt whether the high-minded and serious-minded men constituting the Council of State would have lent themselves, even at our request, to the touching-up of the old scenery of that comedy. They would have been bound, as it were, to tell us that the most severe censure of the acts of a foreign government did not come within any of the cases provided for by the organic clauses, inasmuch as such appreciation could neither be construed into *an excess of power*, nor into *a contravention of the laws of the State*, and least of all into *an attempt to raise trouble in men's consciences*.[1] As for the idea of resorting to the ordinary tribunals under the provisions of the press-laws, the proposal to adopt such a remedy could assuredly not have been serious, inasmuch as the remedy would have been worse than the disease. What French magistrate or Council would have consented to bring bishops, his own countrymen, to the criminal's dock (*sur le banc où siègent les malfaiteurs*) to allay the susceptibilities of the Chancellor of the German Empire? If one could have been found to play that sorry part, one dreads to contemplate the storm of abuse he would have raised among the audience the moment he opened his lips, and the kind of reply he would have had from the opposing counsel. Where is the jury that would have listened to or even have admitted the claimant's arguments? The alleged offence would have been withdrawn from the judicial arena, but embittered, envenomed, magnified a hundredfold by the conspicuousness of the debate, the noise of the Press, and the unanimity of the acquittal. The result was such a foregone conclusion as to lead to the belief that Herr von Bismarck, who must have foreseen the result, was not far from fostering a hope to that effect.

[1] I had serious thoughts of reducing all this to the phraseology of the Ecclesiastical Courts. But after I had found the seemingly English equivalents, I came to the conclusion that the ordinary reader would fail to understand them, inasmuch as I did not understand them myself. It would have been the blind leading the blind.—TRANS.

We were therefore practically reduced to expressing to Herr von Bismarck the regret at not being able to comply with any of his desires. How would he have received that answer? It was difficult to foretell. Admitting (and I am inclined to that belief) that from the outset he had somewhat elevated his voice in order to intimidate us, and that he would in reality have hesitated to resort to the extreme measures with which he had threatened us in vindication of a grievance, which, after all, consisted of words only; admitting all this, yet the least we could expect from his wounded self-love was the taking of one of those steps which, on more than one occasion, he was about to take; namely, the recall of his ambassador and the breaking-off of diplomatic relations. This would have led to a strained and violent (? *violente*) situation, especially dangerous between two neighbouring nations, who were daily engaged in settling delicate matters, and would have held suspended over them, like a Damoclean sword, the imminent risk of more declared hostility. Meanwhile, all this meant, as far as Prussia was concerned, a great encouragement to the eager designs of the military party; in Europe it meant a feeling of alarm experienced by all, no matter what their interests; in France a check to the progress of reviving public prosperity, and lastly, what perhaps concerned us still more, the arousing of a very general feeling of disapproval of the ministers of religion, who, forsaking their mission of peace, would in that way have sown trouble around themselves, and perhaps have let loose the storm.

Such an effect, in itself very deplorable, would have caused nowhere more regret than in Rome, and to the Holy Father himself, who—as we know from our ambassador, M. de Corcelle, who was a great favourite with him[1]—took a heartfelt share in all our difficulties. Actuated by an altogether fatherly feeling towards France, Pius IX. was in no way desirous to see the uphill task of our re-establishment compromised by manifestations doomed to remain barren in favour of a cause which, unfortunately, we were no longer in a position to serve.[2]

---

[1] M. Claude-François Tircuy de Corcelle must not be confounded with M. le Baron Chaudron de Courcel, the present French ambassador in London, who, I believe, is a Gallican, and probably entertains a different view of the ecclesiastical policy of France from that of his almost-namesake.—TRANS.

[2] I take this opportunity to remind the reader that the conduct of Pius IX. to the French Government was, in point of delicacy and disinterestedness, beyond all praise. He never gave a greater proof of that feeling than when we were obliged to recall from its station at Civita-Vecchia the *Orénoque*, which had been dispatched thither in order to provide him with a retreat in the event of his security being threatened at Rome. In taking that praiseworthy precaution M. Thiers had neglected to inform the Government of Victor Emmanuel, which, amidst the confusion of its taking possession of the Holy City, would probably have offered no objection to any of M. Thiers' wishes. Nevertheless the presence of a war vessel ("a vessel flying the military flag," says the author) in a port without the authority of the power to which that port belonged was (the moment the kingdom of Italy was recognized) in such evident contradiction with the elementary rules of the law of nations as

That was the condition of affairs, and it will be admitted that it gave already sufficient food for serious consideration, the more in that this time there was not, as in the case of the obstacles that had confronted our monarchical hopes, a capital interest at stake, I mean an interest affecting the national security and greatness, which have to be defended at any cost. An incident which we had not the slightest reason to expect suddenly imparted to the crisis an altogether acute character. I have already said that most of the bishops had paid a deferential attention to the advice of the Minister of Public Worship, and acknowledged the moderation of his tone and the gravity of his appreciations. The saint-like Archbishop of Paris, Cardinal Guibert, though one of those who had plunged headlong into the controversy, had not only preached but given them the example to that effect. Hence there had been silence in that direction for more than a month, when that silence was suddenly broken by a pastoral letter from one of the bishops in the South of France,

to make the indefinite prolongation of that presence practically impossible. No objection was taken, however, while M. Thiers remained in power, but the moment he had been replaced by the Conservatives, the journals of the Left made it a point to raise the question, and they themselves urged the Italian Government (which had probably not thought of it) to demand the withdrawal of the *Orénoque*. As a matter of course, as soon as the demand was preferred we could but comply with it. Nothing could compare with the touching resignation with which Pius IX.—without addressing to France the faintest reproach—heard of the disappearance of that last proof of France's powerless sympathy.

which missive was, unfortunately, couched in terms closely resembling those which had already caused so much excitement. The worthy prelate, in his distant see, had certainly not calculated the effect that would attend his step beyond the Rhine; but, contrary to his intention, it was, nevertheless, considering the situation, nothing less than a challenge flung in Herr von Bismarck's face,[1] the consequences of which it was impossible to calculate, in the event of our being accused of complicity. An ultimatum, an altogether direct one this time, might come to us at the arrival of the next messenger. Unless we wished to be confronted by the alternative of submitting to it, or to decline doing so, we had but a few hours to take the initiative.

I do not know who in this emergency suggested to M. Decazes an expedient which, I think, no one will blame him for having eagerly caught at, seeing the narrow strait in which he found himself. Only one Conservative paper, *l'Univers*, had reproduced the pastoral letter; all the others, warned at the outset by us, had ignored the matter of their own accord. It was to indict, not the bishop, but the paper, under the exceptional powers we still enjoyed by the "state of siege" proclaimed

---

[1] The author says, "par le visage de M. de Bismarck." I have translated it according to his probable meaning, but the preposition "*par*" is rarely used in that sense now-a-days. We must remember, though, that M. le Duc de Broglie is a member of the Académie Française, and has the authority of Voltaire for using the preposition in that sense.—TRANS.

in Paris during the war, kept up by the Commune, and which M. Thiers during his two years of administration had not withdrawn. That same evening *l'Univers* was suspended for two months for having published a document *which might cause political difficulties*.

I will willingly admit that the subterfuge was the reverse of heroic; I comforted myself for having given my sanction to it with the thought that there was nothing very heroic either about those who, warned of a grave peril, practically exposed their country to all the consequences of it when they themselves ran no risk whatever. Compared to the trouble they might have caused the penalty was light.[1]

[1] I can well conceive that to-day, the imminence of the danger being over, those who have lost the recollection of it should tax us with timidity; but I confess to having been surprised, and even inclined to smile, when I read in the Correspondence of the celebrated editor of *l'Univers*, M. Louis Veuillot, posthumously published since then, that the measure against his paper was taken, in concert with the Prussian Government, by Catholics formerly on the staff of *le Correspondant* out of sheer resentment at their former quarrels with *l'Univers*. I doubt whether self-importance ever led a man of parts to a supposition so utterly removed from—I will not say the truth, but the probability. It would have required a marvellous love of memory and cool-headedness still to have recollected, after the storms we had weathered and those that threatened at that moment, the former dissensions between certain Catholics on the delicate applications and extreme consequences of their common faith. So far as I was concerned, M. Veuillot's person was the thing furthest from my thought in that interview with M. Decazes. That of Herr von Bismarck worried me a little more. Besides, I cannot help thinking that in his inmost soul M. Veuillot never bore us a deep grudge for having made a martyr of him at such a trifling cost to himself. Moreover, M. Veuillot's

The next question was, what Herr von Bismarck thought of all this? It would appear that he felt somewhat inclined not to show himself satisfied, and I also think that he felt some regret at having to forego the startling demonstration of his power on which he had counted, for the first thing he did was to write to Count Arnim—" There is, as far as I can see, no necessity to give *l'Univers* a gratuitous advertisement by representing its suppression as in accordance with our wishes."[1] But this is not the only instance of the Scriptural saying being verified—"ye thought evil against me, *but* God meant it unto good." It was the noise he had made about his grievances—in reality of no importance—that prevented his insisting upon a more complete reparation. His threatening declarations had produced a fictitious state of uneasiness and excitement, the prolongation of which was irksome to all sincere friends of peace in Europe. When they saw a way out of the situation, there was a general feeling of relief at being let off with nothing more than the alarm. M. Decazes having, moreover, taken the opportunity to state in answer to an interpellation on the relations between France and Italy, that he

---

friends, and they were many in the Assembly, were not quite so susceptible as he, for they had made up their minds to interpellate us, but they gave up the idea when we informed them of our reasons, and pointed out the awkwardness of having to state those reasons publicly.

[1] *Antécédents du procès d'Arnim*, p. 151.

was assiduously labouring for the maintenance of peace by removing all misunderstandings and *preventing all conflicts, and that he would also defend France against all regrettable agitation, no matter whence it came*, the general approval that greeted his prudent language everywhere showed Herr von Bismarck that he would be neither understood nor followed should he show himself more difficult. Graciously or not, satisfied or dissatisfied, he declared himself satisfied. But the incident once at an end, the impression left was not favourable to him. Unstable situations like that to which Europe was committed after so many successive commotions, and to which she will probably stand committed for a long while to come, have this peculiar characteristic; they cause public opinion to veer round very easily, and to consult uneasily, now that point of the horizon, then the other, according to the fear as to whence the alarm signal may come. That was what Herr von Bismarck had not sufficiently foreseen. None of the imaginary designs with which he had credited Monarchical and Catholic France had been realized, but the relentless hostility he nursed against the religion of more than half of Europe, and of at least a third of his own countrymen, had engendered more serious perils than those designs themselves. Henceforward it became a question of who should try his hardest not to be involved in the difficulties he created for himself.

"I shall not follow him into that path," said the Emperor of Austria himself to our ambassador. "He wished to drag us into his unfortunate religious campaign," said Prince Gortschakoff to General Leflô; "but we formally declared to him that we would not join him, but we remain friends all the same." Queen Victoria expressed herself to the same effect to the Emperor in a private letter, the existence of which was known, though its contents were not, her ambassador having allowed the secret of it to leak out. "What does this man want?" said one of M. de Gontaut's diplomatic colleagues to him. Until then he had been on the most cordial footing with Bismarck, while during and even after the war he had shown himself the reverse of favourable to France. "What does this man want?" he repeated. "The powers will have to come to an understanding one day to put a stop to his encroachments on the liberty of others." To have noted that sentiment before having to appeal to it in the much graver crisis which was to burst forth very soon was at any rate useful, and as such the bad quarrel he had tried to fasten on us was not altogether to be regretted.

## II

During one of those fits of real or simulated passion to which Herr von Bismarck had yielded in order to justify the overbearing persistency of his claims, a sufficiently significant phrase had, as we have seen, dropped from his lips. "If France does not get rid of her pontifical policy, I'll not wait to declare war on her till she is ready, and that will be in two years."

That sentence alone suffices to show what eager attention and accuracy of information were brought to bear from Berlin on the progress of the reorganization of our army. For among all the suspicious observers who exercised that surveillance on us, Herr von Bismarck was far from being the most ostensibly concerned with regard to the use we should make of our strength when we had recovered it. The most constant solicitude about this was shown in military circles. There, the usual wind-up to all conversations was to the effect that, as we must be without a doubt resolved to seek the revenge for our defeats as soon as our strength would enable us to pretend to it, it would be as foolish as imprudent on the part of Germany to wait for, instead of forestalling, our convenience in that respect. Viewed from that point, every scrap of news in our papers, with reference to the completion of our lines of defence, the perfecting of our armaments, the instructing of our young officers into the latest improvements in modern tactics, became the subject of impassioned comment, which in the shape of warnings or threats reached the ears of M. de Gontaut. "Could we not manage to talk a little less of our experiments with small arms, cannon, army corps—in one word, of all the elements of our military reorganization?" he wrote. Then he hastened to add—"And to talk less of them would not mean to concern ourselves less with them." The advice was unquestionably sensible, but apart from the difficulty of getting the Press, on which one cannot impose silence at will, to follow it, there was one spot where, and there were certain times when, the observance of silence would have been impossible; and that was in the rostrum of the Assembly, when a law of a similar character to that on the recruitment of the army, and quite as important as the other, came on for debate—namely, the law regulating the constitution of the *cadres* of the active army; or, after having decided the number and the nature of the soldiers with the colours, we also had to decide by whom and in what manner they should be commanded.

We have already seen how important a factor

the first of these two capital laws, namely, that on the recruitment, had been in the negotiations we had engaged in for the liberation of the territory; one point in particular had nearly caused the miscarriage of the whole, viz. the intention of the Assembly to impose compulsory and personal military service on every Frenchman. If it had persisted in that demand, from which the whole weight of M. Thiers' authority was scarcely sufficient to make it deviate, our deliverance, as we also saw, would have been indefinitely adjourned. Similarly, in the new law there was a provision apparently more inoffensive than the other, and which, during the first stages of the debate, passed unperceived; but which, exciting as it did the public mind in Germany, might have been fraught with a much graver consequence, and have compromised the security and independence we had but just recovered. That provision dealt with the increase of the number of battalions of which each infantry regiment was to consist. The Government and the Commission had fixed the number at three, the Assembly increased it to four. I was present at the sitting in which the improvised amendment, involving the introduction of that fourth battalion, was adopted, and I even watched the debate with an altogether particular interest, because the career of some young officers with whom I was on terms of personal friendship depended largely on it. I am therefore enabled to state distinctly the motive of that resolution, adopted somewhat hurriedly, and to which the minister, after having opposed it, was obliged to give way. The increase of the number of *chefs de bataillon* (majors) would relieve the block among the subalterns caused by the too numerous promotions during the war, and provide an easier and more elastic form of hierarchical advancement. That was in reality our main idea; all other, and especially the intention to increase the numerical strength of our effective troops by a prevarication or subterfuge, was altogether foreign to the majority to which I belonged. The proof whereof is, that when the minister, in order to re-establish his disturbed financial equilibrium, proposed in his turn to reduce the number of companies of which the new battalions should consist from six to four, which was the original number, that mode of compensation met with no opposition whatever, although, all things told, the result of the two modifications combined was to reduce rather than increase the real strength of the fighting unit.

But that did not matter in the least. Whether well understood or the reverse, the moment the measure, commented on by more or less sincere interpreters, became known, there was a blaze along the whole of the line and in all the ranks of the German Press; a general cry arose: the

Assembly in a burst of patriotic impatience had with one stroke of the pen increased the numerical strength of the best part of the French army, viz. the infantry, by at least one-fourth. This increase did not respond to any requirement for the country's better defence, seeing that neither the Marshal nor his ministers had thought of it, hence it evidently meant preparation for a premeditated and not far distant attack. The fourth battalion, the recollection of which had slipped the minds of many of us after having voted it, became the signal for the expected battle to which (the signal) no patriotic German could remain deaf, unless he was positively bereft of hearing.

Such was the theme developed simultaneously, and with a kind of emulation, by all the organs of publicity known to receive their inspiration from official quarters, such as the *Nord-Deutsche Zeitung*, the *Frankfurter Zeitung*, the *Post* of Berlin, etc., etc. The last-named paper especially boasted a writer who gave unrestricted flight to his fancy, and who one day penned a sensational article with the threatening heading—" Is there a prospect of war?" And in order to justify the cry of alarm, he felt himself bound to do something more than merely cast suspicion on our military laws. In order to aggravate their character he, with great glee, no doubt, but with affected terror, traced a connection between them and another measure of much greater importance which the Assembly had passed at the same time, and which, however, did not seem capable of presenting the slightest appearance of bellicose intent even to the most malevolently-disposed perspicuity.

Through a coincidence, in fact, to which no one had paid the least attention, the promulgation of the new law on the *cadres* had been preceded by a few days by that of the law entitled, "*La loi dite des pouvoirs publics*,"[1] which by the feeble majority of a few votes had just provided the Republican form of government with a regular constitution (law on the public powers, February 25, 1875; law on the "*cadres*," March 28). I have endeavoured to explain in its proper place how the transaction between the discouraged Monarchists and the Republicans who had imbibed wisdom had been effected, a transaction whence sprang the somewhat hybrid Republican expedient under which we live up to the present day. People may continue to comment on, to explain, to condemn, or to justify in various ways, and for many a year to come, the *rapprochement* brought about in that manner between political men who were divided on the previous day, and who were to be still more divided the day after; but no historian will be able to evolve from that *rapprochement* the shadow of a thought, still less of a threat, calculated to cause the faintest anxiety

[1] Literally "a law regulating the public powers;" practically, a set of constitutional laws—a constitution.—TRANS.

to the most suspicious neighbour or the most timorous friend of peace. It was the impromptu result of an absolutely inner evolution which, it may be boldly affirmed, was swayed by no consideration, nor even by a retrospective thought of foreign policy.

That, however, was not the opinion, or at any rate not the supposition, of the German writer. In his opinion the only motive that could have led the two opposing parties to a fusion was the design to present a combined face to a common enemy. No Royalists could have become Republican, and no Republicans could have adopted institutions that had more than one trait of resemblance, except to prepare themselves by mutual sacrifices, to quench a thirst equally parching in both for national vengeance and retrieval. The Assembly before its separation wished to have the signal honour to preside itself at the revenge, and to recover the whole of the territory it had been compelled to cede at its birth to Germany. It was in order to deliver that supreme attack that the newly-constituted Republic grouped on the same ministerial benches M. Buffet and M. Dufaure, M. Léon Say and M. Decazes.

Equally the paper did not fail to point out that the most active agents in the operation just concluded were political men known for their fidelity to the memory of the House of Orleans. And the princes of that family, soldiers heart and soul, were generally honoured with the reputation of having suffered as much as, if not more than any other from the spectacle of France's humiliation, and credited with aspiring to the glory of contributing to lift her out of that position; an honour which, as is equally well known, brought upon them the particular displeasure of Herr von Bismarck. Thus, all the signs of a combined plan were patent; the constitutional law had had the effect of closing up the ranks of the aggressors, and of preparing leaders for them; the military law doubled the potentiality of their means of attack. It was Germany's duty to be on her guard.

To what degree were we justified in believing that the fiction, composed with such evident gusto, had been inspired by the *entourage* of the Chancellor? That question can never be answered positively, considering that every bad case may be denied, and the issue of the movement thus provoked did not finally turn out to the advantage of those that had provoked it. But inasmuch as the gist of the story, if not all its details, was reproduced with a touching unanimity though with different shadings by all the habitual interpreters of the master's thoughts, it was sufficiently clear that a real or assumed belief in it was certain to please. Hence no one doubted that this paper war had received its original impulse, at any rate indirectly, from high quarters. The extravagance and agitated tone which marked that polemical outburst did not seem, moreover, to be out of keeping with the state of mind, or rather with the state of nerves, of the Chancellor, as observed by those who came into personal contact with him. His ever irascible temperament was particularly high-strung at that moment. His generally fretful and quarrelsome humour had passed from the chronic to the acute state, which might be accounted for by the series of successive disappointments his policy had experienced. But moderately satisfied with the to him insufficient reparation he had obtained from us for the wounds inflicted by papal or episcopal censure, he had sought for a more complete one, first at Brussels, then at Rome. In several haughtily-worded notes he had claimed from the Belgian Government certain modifications of their Press-laws, which would admit of the repression of the attacks against him in which the Catholics indulged. He had brought pressure to bear on the Italian Government to raise obstacles to the publication of documents emanating from the Vatican of which he saw fit to complain. The ministers of King Leopold had nobly refused to pass any measure derogatory to the liberty of the Press sanctioned by their Constitution, and threatened to have recourse, if violence were offered to them, to the support of the Powers that had guaranteed the neutrality of Belgium. Victor Emmanuel, in order to oppose a like refusal, entrenched himself behind "the law of guarantees," which was a condition of his establishment at Rome, and by which his Government had pledged itself not to interfere with the communications to the Church from its head. The dissension was complete, for even Spain contributed to fill the cup of the Chancellor's miscalculations. Indeed, the Spanish Republic as well as ours had for the time being found an unexpected auxiliary in the founder of the new Empire. But in that instance the game had not been successful, inasmuch as the advent of Alfonso XII. had been accomplished in spite of his efforts, and in spite of the official support he had lent at the eleventh hour to the ephemeral dictatorship of General Serrano. Intensely disgusted at having lost the scent on so many different tracks, he gave way to fits of impatience, and had even days of discouragement. He talked of resignation and retirement, a usual form of sulks, as is well known, with men who believe themselves necessary, and who, spoilt by Dame Fortune, deem it a piece of impertinence on her part not to exempt them from all untoward complications. Being in such a frame of mind, it was but natural that he should endeavour to make a show with the power that was left to him by trying to terrify those whom he felt certain could offer no resistance. He indulged in threats against France which, caught up and repeated by his confidants, were, perhaps, canvassed in a more serious spirit than he intended, but which, nevertheless, were powerful encouragements to the bellicose aspirations of those around him.

Besides, the threats were not always confined to words; there were also official acts, and in particular one very important one, which could not have been carried out without superior consent, and which, by the comments to which it gave rise, was eminently calculated to increase the general trouble. An Imperial Order (in Council), foreseen by no one, suddenly stopped the exportation of horses from Germany. The publicly alleged motive for this interruption of one of the most active and profitable traffics of the Empire was the necessity of preventing the too numerous purchases of the French Minister for War; contracts, it was said, had been made for more than ten thousand cattle expected in France. This altogether extraordinary purchase of cavalry-remounts seemed to be the completion of our equally unjustified increase of our line regiments. To put a stop to the former appeared, therefore, a measure of national security, and the German Press did not fail to testify its approval noisily.

The alarm thus propagated by all the echoes of the Press, as well as by military circles, rapidly spread through the whole of Germany, and principally to the smaller courts, which foresaw with terror the day when their aid would be once more required. The most clear-sighted and generally prudent minds were affected by what was rapidly developing into a genuinely contagious emotion. For instance, the Prince Imperial in passing through Munich appeared to be in a state of violent agitation. He seemed "all in a heap" (*tout ébouriffé*), wrote our consular agent in that capital. It was the English *chargé d'affaires* who had to take the defence of France, and to assure the Prince that there was not a word of truth in all the plans imputed to us. There was, nevertheless, and as a consequence of that visit, a meeting of all the superior officers at the Ministry of War to discuss the situation.

M. de Gontaut was in Paris on a few months' leave of absence when the rumbling of the storm was beginning to be heard. M. Decazes recommended him to return to his post without delay. On the day fixed for his departure, he met in the lobbies of the Assembly with a personage of importance among the Republican party, one of those whom the new constitution brought nearer to power. "How do we stand with Germany?" asked M. Ernest Picard. "We must not allow our confidence to be carried away by our fear," replied M. de Gontaut. "There are, nevertheless, two things for which I cannot answer; namely, for your discretion in Paris, and for the nerves of Herr von Bismarck." Very shortly after his arrival in Berlin, he had to face his duty of trying to dispel the suspicions of the Imperial Government, by submitting the natural and perfectly sincere explanations of the facts that had given rise to those suspicions. But though the demonstration was not difficult, the incriminated measures being in reality thoroughly inoffensive, his task was, for all that, one of the most difficult he had to discharge in the course of his mission.

In fact, the most elementary experience of diplomatic matters tends to show, that even in the ordinary relations of two States bordering on one another, no dissension could be more grave and more easily productive of conflict than one bearing on the purport, nature, and character of their armaments. When a difference of that kind arises, and grows embittered, it is really not susceptible of any pacific solution whatever. The right of every nation to constitute and to dispose of her military forces at her own will, to spread them according to her own convenience over the various points of her territory, is a condition of her independence, and a sovereign prerogative, which in principle she cannot and must not allow to be questioned by anybody, and the pretension to hinder or criticize which she must ever be entitled to resent. Yet, in point of fact, this or that manner of exercising that right, this or that increase of troops responding to no need of surveillance or defence, this or that unwarranted concentration of troops on a particular frontier, all this may denote hostile intentions; and in such a case, the neighbour, finding himself threatened, has no doubt the right, in order not to be taken unawares, to demand the explanation of and justification for those movements. The discussion raised under such conditions bears on a point of fact always susceptible of being contested; it is purely a question of proportion, of expediency, and, above all, of good faith. If there be a want of sincerity on either or both sides, if one of the parties refuses to supply the explanations demanded, or if the other, after having obtained them, persists in his unfounded anxiety, two rights, or if one likes two pretensions, stand confronted, between which no agreement is possible. How many wars during the last two centuries have been due to such an origin or such a pretext?

The question that awaited M. de Gontaut was, then, one of those the treatment of which by an ambassador, under no matter what circumstances and in no matter what country, is always fraught with the gravest danger. But to the representative of France at Berlin the ordeal presented a particular character of gravity. Could he fail to remember that the debate was going to be shifted at once to the very ground on which ten years before Austria had found herself on the eve of Sadowa? Was it not because the Vienna Cabinet failed to account to Herr von Bismarck's satisfaction for the dislocation of troops, real or false, supposed to have taken place on the Bohemian frontier, that it found itself compelled to reply at less than a twenty-four hours' notice to a challenge which Austria's armies proved unable to meet? It would even appear that this manner of believing, or pretending to believe, herself threatened, in order to justify an abrupt commencement of hostilities, had become an hereditary and traditional method with the sovereigns of the House of Brandenburg. For it was that employed by the Great Frederick before engaging with Maria-Theresa on the struggle that had set Europe on fire for seven years; and Herr von Bismarck, in order to compel Francis Joseph's appearance on the tented field, had only in those circumstances, as in several others, to follow the example of the hero whom he had taken as a model. In both cases the demand for an explanation on the nature of the armaments had only preceded by a few days, and as a simple matter of form, the overture of hostilities. That twofold recollection was a sufficiently instructive warning to remind M. de Gontaut of the trap or yawning chasm that might be hidden behind the interrogatory he had to undergo.

To what extent was he to accept it, in what terms was he to reply to it? There was a rock to steer clear of here. Among the number of conditions a vanquished nation may be compelled to endure in the days of distress and despair, there was one (and the most humiliating of all) which we might well have fancied to be lying at our door; it was that imposed conspicuously and deliberately by victorious Napoleon on crushed Prussia; nevertheless, by a fortunate omission that condition had been spared to us. No limitation, in the shape of a maximum figure, had been imposed on us with regard to our military forces. No restriction whatsoever had been stipulated with regard to their nature, their distribution, and their use; we remained free to be armed as we liked.

Truly, Herr von Bismarck pretended now and again that at Versailles M. Thiers had promised him that the new Government would not raise the number of "effective" troops beyond that of Napoleon III. But if such a sentence had been uttered at all, it had to be looked upon as a mere bit of conversation dictated by the circumstances of the moment, and which constituted no promise for the future, and at best only pledged the speaker. According to the letter of our treaty, we had no rights nor obligations with regard to Germany other than those that regulate the neighbourly relations between two adjacent States. It was essentially important not to allow any others to be created by a practice which would have soon degenerated into a prescriptive right. Any explanations that were either too accommodating, too eager, above all too much tinged with emotion, would have added *de facto* a clause and an additional rigour to the Treaty of Frankfort, by appearing to recognize as legitimate a kind of control over our military condition.

M. de Gontaut got through this pass with the tact and skill particularly his own. In an interview with the Minister for Foreign Affairs he was bound, as it were, to present the distorted facts in their true light; but he volunteered the statement in a natural, candid—I might almost say, unconcerned—tone which was neither that of an inferior who has to give an account, nor that of an accused person trying to justify himself. Besides, the truth came to light by itself; the vote for the Fourth Battalion explaining itself by what was recorded in writing beforehand, *i. e.* during the incidents of the discussion that had preceded it; and the purchase of horses having been made, not on account of the French Minister for War, but on that of dealers accustomed to trade in that way with Germany, and whose transactions during that year did not exceed the ordinary average. In short, the Minister who at the beginning of the interview had shown signs of listlessness submitted easily enough to the evidence. He admitted that if, in fact, there had been some uneasiness at the measures taken in France, that uneasiness was really unfounded, and when M. de Gontaut assured him with some show of warmth that during the visit he had just paid to France, and being of the peaceful disposition he was, he had neither met with a single person nor heard a single word that was not in harmony with his own feelings in that respect, the Minister showed neither signs of incredulity nor of doubt; and the interview was brought to an end by regrets expressed in common on the injury an imprudent, ignorant, and often interested Press did to the public peace. M. de Gontaut soon perceived that Herr von Bülow had not kept his satisfactory impressions to himself, for a few days later the Emperor, on meeting M. de Gontaut at some gala reception, showed himself more gracious than ever to him, and on the French military *attaché*, Prince de Polignac, paying his respects, he said to him in a loud voice, so as to be heard by every one: "They wished to sow trouble between us, but that is done with."

A proof of good-will from such high quarters was assuredly of great weight; M. de Gontaut, however, did not think it sufficient to justify his full confidence. The Emperor had evidently been inspired in his utterance by Herr von Bülow, and the recollection of what had occurred with reference to the episcopal charges had taught the ambassador that the Chancellor was not always so easily satisfied as his minister, and did not scruple to return to the charge on certain matters, even on those which were apparently definitely settled.

It was, therefore, more in sorrow than in surprise that he noticed after that not one of the alarming symptoms had absolutely vanished.

The tone of the Press, which had become more mild for a moment, very soon resumed its bitterness; there was the same constant eagerness to admit and to spread all items of news which, by distorting our intentions, might arouse the susceptibility of public opinion in Germany. The denials Herr von Bülow had promised to have inserted in the official journals, on points the untruth of which he had admitted, were only given in a partial and inadequate form; the stories that went the round of military centres, not excepting those that emanated from the General Grand-Staff, always maintained their character of affected anxiety, of impatience, and provocation. But the truly significant fact was that, especially among his colleagues of the Corps Diplomatique (before whom assuredly people spoke more unrestrictedly than when he was present), M. de Gontaut could not help noticing the most lively preoccupation. The English, Russian, and even Austrian ambassadors, although the latter was ever the most reserved, vied with one another in impressing on M. de Gontaut's mind the necessity of his recommending increased caution and prudence. "Do not go away," said one of them to him, in answer to his expressed intention of his leaving Berlin for a few days; "do not go away, there is no saying what may happen in your absence." The language of M. van Nothomb, the Belgian Minister, and the dean ("doyen") of the diplomatic agents, was most explicit of all; and he, moreover, was considered an authority, because he had resided for many years at the Prussian Court, and in the differences that had recently arisen with his Government had had occasion to come into contact with the Chancellor more than any of the others, and been enabled to appreciate the state of the latter's temper.

A conversation M. van Nothomb had had, first with the Chancellor then with Marshal von Moltke, and the substance of which he communicated to M. de Gontaut, was by no means reassuring. "France," Herr von Bismarck had said, "will be unable to sustain for any length of time the financial burden entailed by her military re-organization; she will be compelled to reduce her armaments or to make war; she stands inevitably committed to an act of madness or to an act of inconsequence."

And the Marshal, after having developed the same theme, had observed: "They may say what they like; I look at facts only. A battalion may mean a thousand men; a hundred and forty-four battalions mean, therefore, a hundred and forty-four thousand men France has just added to her army. It means the offensive within a short delay, and we ought not to wait for it."

Another conversation, if not more significant, at least more original and characteristic, contributed to open M. de Gontaut's eyes to the fact that the peril had not been averted, notwithstanding the official assurances that had been given to him. That conversation has become public property to such an extent, and in consequence of the discussions and contradictions to which it gave rise, that to give it *verbatim*, as M. de Gontaut reported it while he was under the influence of the emotion it had caused him, is not violating any professional or private secret, but, on the contrary, rendering a service to history.

At a dinner at the English ambassador's, M. de Gontaut met with a Prussian diplomatist of high rank, Herr von Radowitz, who had occupied an important post at the Ministry for Foreign Affairs, and was credited with enjoying the confidence of Herr von Bismarck. Herr von Radowitz had just returned from St. Petersburg, whither, notwithstanding his already official appointment to the Court of Athens, he had been sent as *chargé d'affaires*, in the absence of the ambassador on leave. There seemed to be no proportion between his acknowledged diplomatic merit and the insignificant mission and employment *ad interim* which he had accepted; besides, it is not customary anywhere to give to an ambassador on leave a substitute occupying a rank pretty nearly equal to his own. Every one had made that remark, and naturally arrived at the conclusion that in reality Herr von Radowitz's temporary translation to St. Petersburg, devoid of reason as it seemed, was intended to disguise a confidential mission. What was the nature of the communication Herr von Radowitz had been charged with for the Czar? There was no light on the subject, and people went on commenting and surmising to no purpose. As a matter of course, M. de Gontaut was not behindhand, and succeeded no better than the others in getting to the bottom of the secret. But he suspected (and he saw later on that he had been right) that a step intended to promote more intimate relations between the two Imperial Courts could bode but little good to us. It made him all the more anxious to ascertain the opinion of this interesting fellow-guest, with whom he was so unexpectedly brought into contact, on the subject that occupied every one's mind.

Hence he plunged spontaneously into matters by talking about the unfounded anxiety the Press had aroused, and of his own satisfaction at having been enabled to dispel them from Herr von Bülow's mind. "I am aware of it," said Herr von Radowitz, "and I know that the Chancellor was equally satisfied with the report of the interview the minister addressed to him. But you are bound to admit that there was cause to be surprised at the impromptu increase of your regiments, while we were not favoured with an explanation on the subject. You gave it, and it seems to have been considered sufficient." Then he added, in a somewhat pointed manner: "If I were not authorized to say this, I should hold my tongue."

Practically this was investing beforehand with an official character everything he believed himself justified in saying. M. de Gontaut, therefore, thought it advisable to repeat most of the considerations he had developed before Herr von Bülow, so as to allow his interlocutor to give to each of the considerations reviewed his mark of approval. The perfectly correct conduct of the French Government and its irreproachable attitude having been acknowledged by Herr von Radowitz, M. de Gontaut went on: "But why, then, those constant provocations of the Press," he said, "when it would be so easy for you to put a stop to them?"

"That would not be so easy as you appear to imagine," replied Herr von Radowitz; "those papers, and especially the *Nord-Deutsche Zeitung*, enjoy a considerable importance, and if there were an attempt to direct them in a way that did not suit them, it might lead to an interpellation in the Chamber, and to lively debates. And that direction itself on the part of the Government, is it as easy as you think? You probably have no conception of what we are told constantly in the name of those parties that constitute the majority.

'You feel assured, maybe, with regard to the present, but what about the future? Can you answer for that?' or else, 'Can you make sure that France, having recovered her prosperity and re-organized her military forces, will not be in a position to conclude those alliances which she is not in a position to conclude to-day, and that the resentment she harbours as a matter of course on account of the two provinces that have been taken from her will not inevitably impel her to declare war upon Germany? And if meanwhile we had allowed France to recover, to prosper, and to resume her old position, should we not have everything to fear from her? And if the thirst for revenge be the inmost thought of France (and one cannot see how it could be otherwise), why wait to attack her until she have contracted alliances?' In common fairness you are bound to admit, philosophically, politically, and even from a Christian point of view, that those deductions are not without foundation, and that such preoccupations may prove a safe guide to Germany."

M. de Gontaut had sufficient control over himself to restrain his indignation at this naïve exposition of such a strange theory; nevertheless, he replied with some show of animation: "You admit then," he said, "that our policy is sensible, moderate, and beyond reproach. You have at this moment not the least cause to harass us or to declare war upon us. And yet that does not satisfy you. And because you foresee that at some future period you may have some cause for uneasiness against us you have not at present, you devise measures to attack us. But may I ask you to consider carefully whither such a doctrine would lead, if generally practised? The world would not have peace for a single day, and war would not cease to afflict the whole of the globe. What they tell you with regard to us may be equally conceived with regard to all the other Powers. To-day, for instance, you are at peace with Russia; nevertheless, you may have reasons to fear that she will trouble you at some future period; and that, in your opinion, would constitute a reason for attacking her?"

"Oh," interrupted Herr von Radowitz, "that would not be the same thing. Why should we think about making war on Russia, with whom we have never ceased to entertain excellent relations? Such is not the case with France. We have been too often at war with her, and two hundred and fifty years ago she ravaged the Palatinate and wrested Alsace from Germany."

M. de Gontaut declined to go back into history so far as that, and reminded his interlocutor with a smile that if that mode of historical retrospection was admissible, France might also claim to have some grievances against Germany, whence in times of old had come to her all the invasions of barbarians. "And," he added, "I may be allowed to say, seeing that you referred to Christian motives, that the acts to which you have referred just now would be the reverse of Christian."

The interview, which had lasted for more than an hour, could of course not proceed in that tone, and Herr von Radowitz himself brought it to an end by some flattering remarks to M. de Gontaut personally, assuring him that no one was more fit than he to promote the maintenance of friendly relations between the two countries, and that he had full confidence in the pacific assurances a man of his stamp would give.

"But," he concluded, in a somewhat sceptical tone, "you are giving me those assurances for this year; would you be equally ready to give them for the next?"

"Yes," replied M. de Gontaut emphatically.

As a matter of course, M. de Gontaut did not fail to inform his colleagues of a doctrine likely to interest them all, and the novelty of which was its least merit. That manner of eliminating the elements of good faith from the intercourse of nations, of keeping them constantly on the verge of hostilities by reducing to a dead letter the obligations imposed by treaties, did not commend itself to many. Some, in fact, refused to look at the matter in a serious light, or, considering the assurances given sufficient for the day thereof, were inclined to let the future take care of itself. Herr von Radowitz, moreover, had the reputation of being somewhat intemperate of speech, especially after a good dinner. "All the more reason," replied M. de Gontaut, "to let none of his words fall upon deaf ears, inasmuch as, on the spur of the moment, he may say something he would have better left unsaid."

However, before M. de Gontaut was many days older, he gathered from pretty sure quarters positive information as to the nature of the mission that same Herr von Radowitz had just accomplished at St. Petersburg, and on the plans Herr von Bismarck must have confided to the trusty envoy charged with that mission. True, the information came from a Russian lady, but she happened to be in a position to know many things, seeing that her husband filled the office of a chamberlain after having been an ambassador, and that her father had been for a long while one of the Czar's Ministers. According to her, Bismarck's proposals might be summed up as follows. That Russia should allow him to do what he considered essential to the security of the German Empire, and Germany would allow her to do in the East what he (Russia) deemed necessary to her interests. In one word, they were to share and share alike. Unrestricted liberty for Germany in the West, equally unrestricted liberty for Russia in the East. It was, in different words, the bargain proposed by Napoleon I. to Alexander I. at Tilsitt. But, instead of accepting the proposal, Russia had pretended not to understand what Germany was driving at. For the moment, then, the plan had miscarried. But it might be taken up afresh at any moment, and it accorded but too well with the order of ideas developed by Herr von Radowitz. It was in order to have an absolutely free hand with regard to France that Alexander II.'s attention was sought to be diverted to Asia.[1]

Having been warned in so many ways that the horizon was by no means clear, M. de Gontaut had to seize every opportunity of meeting with Herr von Bülow, in order to watch carefully the changes that might occur in the ministerial atmosphere, and in a little while he was bound

[1] The particulars of the character of Herr von Radowitz's mission to St. Petersburg were confirmed at that selfsame moment by Leflô, in accordance with the general opinion prevailing in diplomatic circles at St. Petersburg. As a matter of course, the facts have been denied by Herr von Bismarck and his defenders, and it was on that occasion that Herr von Bismarck expressed himself so severely with reference to Herr von Radowitz. "He has never been my confidant," he said; "he has inherited from his father the deplorable habit in a diplomatist to talk too much, and to blurt out everything after his third glass."

[The author does not give his authority for this statement, but I have an idea that it is to be found in Mr. Beatty-Kingston's translation of *Unser Reichskanzler*, by Dr. Moritz Busch (Macmillan, 1884), and the reader more particularly interested in that special phase of the attempted bribing of Russia had better read pp. 267-70 of the first volume of that work, taking care, however, to take Busch's statements with several grains of salt.—TRANS.]

to confess to himself that the minister's language became less explicit and more reserved than it had been in their first interview. "He was obscure, vague, very reticent, and shifty in his language," wrote M. de Gontaut. Finally, the Minister hinted at a conversation the German ambassador in Paris, Prince Hohenlohe, was supposed to have had with M. Decazes, the purport of which conversation was somewhat of a puzzle to M. de Gontaut, who had no knowledge of the fact. He had not long to wait for the explanation.

Pondering the threatening conversation of Herr von Radowitz, the Duc Decazes had made up his mind with as much discernment as promptitude. There was nothing to show that the confidant had not echoed the thoughts of his master, he certainly did not evolve them from his own imagination. Under the cloak of apparent satisfaction with the actual state of things, no promise of any kind had been given; on the contrary, France was to be left in fear with regard to the future. The utmost she could count upon was two years of respite, and it would have been foolish to trust even to that. M. Decazes, therefore, did not hesitate for a moment to communicate the very text of M. de Gontaut's dispatch to our representatives with such governments as might be supposed to take a direct and personal interest in European politics. In a confidential circular he pointed out to his diplomatic agents the advisability of careful attention to the reflections suggested by the document, and of losing no opportunity to lay stress on the peril to the common peace involved in the strange thesis that seemed to gain ground in the councils of the new Empire. There was some credit due to M. Decazes for having lost no time in taking that step, which was in many quarters considered a hasty one, and criticized for a moment as a tendency to show a somewhat exaggerated fear with regard to language which, after all, lacked an official character. The sequel soon showed that this very salutary precaution was in no way premature. The ground, moreover, was already everywhere prepared for that kind of warning, as I have had occasion to point out before. The imperious arrogance of Herr von Bismarck, as characterized in his latest acts; the haughty pressure he had endeavoured to bring to bear on Germany, the idea he had frequently expressed of claiming international legislation against the Press that offended him, had caused a general feeling of impatience with regard to him. The yoke was getting heavier each day. The idea that the troubles he had caused for himself at home impelled him to seek a diversion to them outside, was also generally entertained. Our *chargé d'affaires* in London, M. Gavard, had occasion to notice that this apprehension was strongly felt by the English Minister, Lord Derby, who fancied, though, that Austria was fated to experience the first blows. But the Queen of the Netherlands, that very distinguished princess whose salutary warnings Napoleon III. had made the mistake to neglect, sent privately for our Minister, M. Target, for whom she cherished a great esteem, and assured him that she fully shared all M. Decazes' fears, which were, moreover, confirmed by her own information on the subject. "Everything is going wrong at Berlin," she said. All she added was that the Emperor of Russia, with whom she kept up a private correspondence, would soon pay his annual visit to his uncle at Ems, and that she counted on his presence there to intervene favourably at the decisive hour.

Truly it was in that direction that our clear-sighted Minister for Foreign Affairs had already cast his glances. Inasmuch as there was at St. Petersburg a monarch who had several times declared that not only did he not wish for an enfeebled France, but that he wished her to be strong, on condition of her being wise, it was but natural to appeal to his judgment. Hence, several weeks before, when disquieting but as yet vague rumours began to circulate, General Leflô, returning to his post after a leave of absence, had been instructed by Marshal MacMahon himself to acquaint the Czar with the feeling of fear generally prevailing. The ambassador met with the same friendly disposition so often shown to him; but it was argued that France was too prone perhaps to take the alarm, that she attached too much importance to rumours propagated by the Press, was inclined to believe too implicitly in the evil designs of Bismarck, to which in any case Emperor Wilhelm would not lend himself.

"Make your mind easy," the Czar said to him; "if you were seriously threatened, you would know it quickly enough. And," he added, after a few moments of hesitation, which gave the greater weight to his guarantee, "you would know it through me."[1]

That, assuredly, was a promise, but with regard to a future which the Czar persistently believed to be far distant. M. Decazes proposed to himself to obtain its renewal in a manner to secure its timely and effective accomplishment, no matter how quickly events might succeed one another, and to that effect dispatched to General Leflô a

---

[1] See, for all the particulars of that interview, and those that followed with Prince Gortschakoff, the dispatch of General Leflô, published in the *Figaro* of May 24, 1887.

[I have a much more minute account of that transaction than the article in the *Figaro* referred to, but my notes are dated July 1884. It is impossible to give them here, and my recollection as to their source is somewhat vague. They were, however, evidently taken for the purpose of showing the possibility of a Russo-Franco *entente* which has since then been more or less established, and the impossibility of an Anglo-French alliance which is being advocated to-day.—TRANS.]

confidential letter under the same cover with that of his general circular.

"The strange doctrine developed by Herr von Radowitz," said the dispatch, "is one of those calculated to fill with the intensest indignation the straightforward and honest conscience of that great sovereign, and it is but in accordance with his usual dignity to treat it as it deserves to be treated. If I am not as confident as Prince Gortschakoff would wish me to be, it is not because I am in doubt with regard to the support his sovereign would lend us against the spread of baneful tendencies, any more than with regard to the efficacy of his influence, *if it were exercised in time*. But it is just because his will to maintain peace is well known in Berlin, it is because they know that he would energetically protest against any perverse designs, it is just because of all this that I cannot divest myself of the fear that those designs will be carefully hidden from him, and that one day they will make up their minds to confront him with an accomplished fact. I should have that fear no longer, and my security would be absolute the day his Majesty would declare that he would look on a surprise as on an insult, and *that he would not permit such an iniquity to pass*. One word like that would simply insure the peace of the world, and it would be worthy of Emperor Alexander to utter it. His Majesty has deigned to tell you that in the day of danger we would be warned, and warned by him. . . . But if he himself were not warned in time, his Majesty would be obliged to understand and to acknowledge that he also had been deceived and taken by surprise, and that, as it were, he had been made the involuntary accomplice of the trap laid for us, and I, moreover, wish to be certain that his Majesty would avenge what practically would constitute an insult to himself, and shield with his sword those who trusted to his aid."

General Leflô himself has told us that being instructed to read some extracts from this eloquent letter to Prince Gortschakoff, the latter asked to see the whole of it, and also the various documents that might have inspired it. He afterwards asked that the whole of the documents might remain in his hands, in order to place them in their integrity before the Emperor. "The Emperor must be made acquainted with the whole of the truth," he said. "I know my master, and he will appreciate your step."

One single line—that which referred to the drawing of the sword—seemed to have stopped him for a moment. "That is rather strong," he had said; "never mind, leave it as it is. We shall not draw the sword; there will be no need; we shall be able to manage without." And two days later he sent back the documents that had been entrusted to him with the following lines: "General, the Emperor has this morning handed me the documents you confided to me; he has instructed me to thank you for this proof of confidence. His Majesty has added that he would confirm to you *vivâ voce* everything he had said through me." And a few days after that, the General, having had the opportunity of approaching the Emperor in order to pay his respects before the sovereign's departure for Berlin, gave the following account of the interview—

"His Majesty was loud in his praise of the calmness and prudence of M. de Gontaut at the exposition of the very strange theories of Herr von Radowitz; and as I ventured to remark on that subject to what aberrations and mental excess a blind passion was apt to lead, his Majesty said emphatically: 'A blind passion is the mildest term for it! But all this, I trust, will subside. In any case you know what I told you, and I will keep my promise. *Au revoir;* be sure that I will remember, and I hope there will be no surprise.'"

From all this it will be gathered that there had been no time to lose if the ambassador had to apply to the Emperor personally for that reassuring guarantee, for there would have been no means of running after the sovereign when once he had started on his journey. But M. Decazes had special reasons to congratulate himself on his hurry when, having received, during the evening of May 4, General Leflô's telegram giving an account of the Imperial interview, he was told next morning, *i. e.* on May 5, that Prince Hohenlohe, the Ambassador of Germany, was waiting to see him.

That visit was altogether unexpected. Prince Hohenlohe, being about to absent himself from Paris for some time, had already taken his leave, and was supposed to be *en route* for the last twenty-four hours. He was supposed to have gone with his mind at rest, inasmuch as he had stated more than once that, thanks to the explanations tendered by M. de Gontaut, and confirmed by his own information, all the clouds that had darkened the minds of his Government had been dispelled. The day of his departure and his unexpected re-appearance were therefore calculated to surprise, and the nature of the message of which he was the bearer did not tend to diminish that feeling.

"I have been apprised by Herr von Bülow," he began, in a somewhat embarrassed tone, "that M. de Gontaut, in the reports he addressed to you, has shown himself too optimistic. Herr von Bülow is not quite so satisfied with the explanations of the French Government with regard to its armaments as M. de Gontaut would have wished you to believe. He finds it difficult to believe that the law on the *cadres* has been passed for the sole purpose of securing the promotion of a few captains, and he thinks it more consistent with ordinary caution to count on your application of your military laws to the fullest extent they are capable of being extended. Herr von Bülow himself believes that France harbours no hostile intentions, and has faith in your pacific intentions, but the German Grand-Staff persists in the belief that the final aim of your military organization is a war with Germany. Another grievance which is causing a good deal of uneasiness at Berlin is your accumulation in the strong rooms of the Bank of six hundred millions of notes withdrawn from circulation; they seem to constitute a veritable war-fund. In short," he concluded, " no appeasement will be possible while the French papers shall continue to denounce the intentions of Germany."

Prince Hohenlohe added that he was not instructed to make this communication, which only appeared to have been addressed to him for his private information, and because he did not seem to attach sufficient importance to France's armaments.

A cool head is the first and foremost qualification of the diplomatist as well as of the soldier. M. Decazes was not lacking in that qualification, seeing that he took advantage at once of the alleged non-official character of the communication to receive it in silence and without as much as wincing. While accompanying Prince Hohenlohe to the door, he only said : "*Au revoir;* we'll talk of all this when you come back." We may take it for granted, though, that he would have had greater difficulty in remaining perfectly placid if at that moment he had not had in his pocket an assurance that henceforward France would not stand alone in the resentment he himself felt at the contemptible attempt at a surprise.

Everything, in fact, was "passing strange" in the language to which he had just been obliged to listen. It was the direct contradiction of all the assurances that had emanated successively from the lips of the Minister, of the Emperor himself, then of the Ambassador, and finally of the Chancellor through the intermediary of a spokesman who had professed himself specially authorized to that effect. For what reason and to what end did they give themselves the lie in that way? What new fact had cropped up to justify the re-opening of the discussion after they declared it to be closed? All this was very puzzling.

There was one supposition, though, which it was difficult to admit; namely, that Prince Hohenlohe should have spoken as he did without being, not only authorized, but specially invited to do so by a superior authority. There are certain commissions one does not undertake without being obliged. If Herr von Bülow had only communicated his personal feelings to his ambassador, the latter had no motive whatsoever to pour out in his turn their confidential particulars into the heart of the French Minister for Foreign Affairs. Such effusions are not customary in diplomacy, in the conduct of which it is always fair to assume that an indiscretion is committed with an ulterior purpose. And inasmuch as at that very moment Count Arnim was being indicted and stood in jeopardy of losing his head for no other reason than because he had failed to please his chief, it was highly improbable that Count Arnim's successor would take on his own account an initiative that might complicate matters. Such a step would have constituted an infraction of discipline analogous to that of a sentry on duty firing without orders.

Equally inadmissible was it that Herr von Bismarck merely intended to put the French Government on its guard, and to confine himself to a simple warning without taking further action. Did it stand to reason that, having denounced the armaments of France as a future peril to Germany, he would be content to fold his arms, to allow France to complete those armaments unhindered, and await their completion with the alternative of offering a tardy opposition? When had he been known to be satisfied with empty threats, to speak without acting? No. Prince Hohenlohe's step, if spontaneously taken, would have been a heedless and unpardonable blunder on his part, but if ordered without an ulterior purpose it would have denoted a still more incredible absence of tact on the part of a statesman who was only taxed with an absence of scruple.

Absolutely there remained but one possible explanation, and it was that adopted by M. Decazes—as, I imagine, it would have been adopted by every man of sense in his position; namely, that the non-official protest against our excessive armament was but the prelude and the preparation for an official summons to reduce. That was the logical and therefore necessary consequence of the step. Admitting this to be the case, was M. Decazes mistaken in assuming that on the day such a demand would be forthcoming, and would have to be submitted to France and the Assembly, it would prove the signal for an appeal to arms? I think I may take it upon myself, in this instance, to answer for him, and I feel confident that not one of my colleagues of those days will care to contradict me when I say that the Minister who would have proposed to us to modify a single one of our military laws in compliance with a request to that effect by Germany would not have been allowed to finish the sentence in the tribune. The consequences of such reception would have been patent to every one of us. We were better aware of the terrible chances of another war than any one; we knew better than any one how empty were the *cadres*, of which we had just mapped out the lines; and there was not one of us but who had a brother, a son, or a friend whom the vote we should have been bound to give might not send into captivity or to his death. But that would not have mattered. To have accepted the control of our military conditions at the hands of our victor of yesterday, who was so obviously interested in maintaining us in a permanently weak state, would have been consenting to remain in subjection for an indefinite period. Anything was better than to submit tamely to conditions. I am inclined to think that—with the exception of Herr von Bismarck, to whom our humiliation without firing a shot would perhaps have appeared preferable—all the firebrands of the German Grand-Staff did us the justice to count upon a resistance which would have satisfied their impatience to resume the campaign. But although M. Decazes was prepared to accept that prospect as resolutely as any of us, he experienced nevertheless a feeling of emotion, which I defy any man of heart not to feel when he knows that the fate of his country, and perhaps the lives of a million of men, may depend on a word of his. He was still under the influence of that emotion (according to the narrative of one of his personal friends) when the Ambassador of Russia, Prince Orloff, with whom he was on most intimate terms, came to see him.

"But what, after all, shall you do if you are attacked at a moment's notice?" asked the Prince, when his friend had told him everything. "What shall we do? We shall retreat behind the Loire; that is where we will concentrate our army, and we shall wait and see if Europe will stand tamely by and allow a defenceless nation to be invaded and devastated without a reason."

In spite of all this, there was not the slightest trace of his temporary excitement in the instructions he dispatched to M. de Gontaut, informing him of the step taken by Prince Hohenlohe, and of the consequences that seemed unavoidable. On the contrary, an exceedingly well-written dispatch went into all the possible explanations of that unforeseen re-appearance, after which M. Decazes dwelt on the only admissible one. He even carried his conscientious examination of matters to the length of seriously discussing the alarm that had been expressed to him on the score of the accumulation of available securities in the coffers of the Bank, and he pointed out in sober earnest the strange nature of that mistake, not a single bank-note having been withdrawn from circulation except on payment of its equal value in coin, which would diminish instead of increasing the resources of the Treasury in the event of war breaking out. Concluding from all this that an impending summons to disarm might be looked for, he instructed M. de Gontaut to decline all conversation on the subject if such a proposal were broached, "inasmuch as," he was to say, "no instructions could have been given to him in view of a demand which was neither based on any clause of the treaty nor justified by any fact." This would enable him to gain the necessary time until the arrival of the Russian sovereign and his Chancellor; and M. Decazes forwarded under the same cover the exact text of the promises given to General Leflô in order to enable M. de Gontaut to claim their fulfilment. The main thing was to prevent all discussion and interchanging of notes while waiting for an intervention which, confronted with an already accomplished fact and aroused self-pride, might prove either less efficacious or more hesitating.

But it was not enough to open Russia's eyes only—the whole of Europe, governments as well as peoples, must alike be warned at that moment, when a threat might be suspended over any of them. We might this time, and above all, usefully invoke English public opinion, the ill-will of which in 1870 had been almost as fatal to us as Russian neutrality. The idea of this had already presented itself to our excellent *chargé d'affaires*, M. Gavard, who on receiving a telegram informing him in a few words of Prince Hohenlohe's conversation, had, without express instructions to that effect and of his own accord, immediately repaired to Lord Derby's. " I spoke," he said, "impelled by a feeling of emotion which was by no means feigned, for I imagined that there was immediate danger."[1] The effect was completed and insured by an article in next day's *Times*, which exposed the seriousness of the situation, and imputed the whole of the blame for it to the German military party, whose intentions it showed up.

The theories enunciated by Herr von Radowitz were also exactly reproduced and generously combated in it, and the anonymous writer wound up with the following stirring peroration:— " Those theories imperil everything that still remains intact of that moral force called the right of nations. That consideration ought assuredly to awaken Europe from her indifference, and remind her of that scarcely flattering but ingenious recommendation of the peasant-woman who, on leaving her children by themselves at home, said to them: 'If anything should happen to you, don't cry "stop thief." No one would come, because you alone would stand in danger of being robbed. But if you want the neighbours to come to you, shout "fire," for a fire might set the whole village ablaze.'"

The effect was deep and instantaneous; it was like a flash of lightning tearing the clouds asunder. Whence came the flash of light? M. Decazes had always been credited with having had a hand in its production; as a matter of course he has always

[1] Charles Gavard, *Un Diplomate à Londres Lettres et Notes*, p. 242.

denied the flattering imputation. And, in fact, the *Times* correspondent, whom every one in Paris knew, was sufficiently well-informed and endowed with sufficient political sense to have spoken without inspiration.

Nevertheless, there was, even in Paris, a spot, more or less assiduously frequented by the diplomatic world, where the reality of the crisis was called in doubt; namely, M. Thiers' drawing-room. M. Thiers, from a foible sufficiently common with eminent men who feel themselves stricken with age, did not like and almost usually made it a point to depreciate his successors, whom, justly perhaps, he refused to consider his equals. Moreover, he failed to perceive that time, which glided past him without impairing his brilliant faculties, also brought to light, and by his side, in the case of others, the developments due to maturity and experience; nevertheless, the man of fifty or thereabouts was persistently regarded by him as a beardless politician.

From that point of view, then, M. Decazes was simply a diplomatic novice, and did not cease to incur M. Thiers' censure. In the present instance M. Thiers made merry over his exaggerated fears; he would have willingly reproached him with want of tact in not having succeeded in worming himself into the good graces of Herr von Bismarck. Those remarks tended to produce a bad effect, reproduced as they were in the dispatches of all the foreign representatives who had had the good taste to continue their visits to the late President of the Republic, and treat him with the same regard as when he was in power. M. Decazes, therefore, considered it advisable to put an end to those comments, and through the intermediary of one of our mutual friends, Count de Bourgoiny, he placed before that enlightened though ill-disposed judge the most significant of the documents in his possession. M. Thiers opened his eyes very wide, gracefully bowed to the evidence submitted to him by acknowledging the difficulty of the situation, and sent to M. Decazes the assurance that he had to fear no opposition in the Assembly either from him or from his friends. He volunteered to say the same to Prince Orloff, in order to impress upon the Czar and his advisers that Russia's siding with France would evoke the unanimous gratitude of all parties.

Truly, nothing could be more deserving of honour than such conduct, and the justified trust of M. Decazes in M. Thiers' patriotism redounded to his own credit. But what was, perhaps, less correct and at the same time less generous, was the subsequent demeanour of some of M. Thiers' friends in their efforts to misrepresent this very natural proceeding on the part of two sterling (*bons*) Frenchmen. According to them, it was

M. Decazes who, at a loss how to get out of the difficulty, came in a state of great excitement to throw himself upon the reputation of wisdom M. Thiers had maintained with the Courts of Europe. The inexperienced helmsman was said to have abandoned for some hours, and during the storm, the helm to the old pilot. The simple comparison of a few dates would suffice to show the ridiculous falsehood of that story. I do not pretend to say what might, or would have been, the result of M. Thiers' conversation with the Russian Ambassador if it had occurred in time; a support of that kind would unquestionably have been of real use. But, as it happened, the game was won, and conviction carried to the mind of the Czar before the news of it had time to transpire, even in Russia.[1]

Everything had been prepared, then, to cause

---

[1] Strangely enough, this little story, based upon a curiously disfigured fact, was repeated with great assurance by a Republican candidate at an election contested by me. I was compelled to give it an absolute denial, based upon the formal evidence to that effect of M. Decazes himself. Since then, that candidate, having become a Deputy, has figured among the twelve or thirteen Ministers for Foreign Affairs that have succeeded M. Decazes, and has therefore been enabled to convince himself personally that he was misinformed. The only trace of M. Thiers' intervention which I could find in M. de Gontaut's correspondence was a remark of the Emperor of Russia, expressing his pleasure that a *rapprochement* was taking place between M. Thiers and Marshal MacMahon. M. de Gontaut, not having understood the meaning of that remark, asked M. Decazes for an explanation of the sentence, and the Minister told him everything that had occurred between him and M. Thiers.

the summons to disarm, if it did come to us, to be received with a sentiment of moral reproof as unanimous as it would have been energetic, and it was even because of that that it did not come. There is no better parry, nor a surer, than that which absolutely forestalls the thrust. Certain is it, however, that at the very moment when the natural conclusion of so many reiterated threats was expected, there was an unforeseen and simultaneous retrograde movement along the whole of the line, political as well as military. The Press was the first to give the signal, just as heretofore it had been the first to open the attack on the morning of May 10; hence, on the day the Emperor of Russia was to arrive in Berlin, there appeared in the *Nord-Deutsche Zeitung* an article expressing deep surprise at the uneasiness prevailing throughout Europe, seeing that between the German and French Governments THERE HAD NOT CROPPED UP THE SLIGHTEST INCIDENT CALCULATED TO CAUSE ANXIETY: the big characters of the latter part of the sentence are not mine. And in order that nothing might be wanting to this audacious perversion of the truth, the same paper mentioned, in proof of its assertion, the departure of Prince Hohenlohe, who assuredly would not have left his post if there had not been a perfect understanding between the two Governments. Of course there was not a word of the poisoned arrow the ambassador had shot before leaving. As a sequel to those statements, the ingenuousness of which raised a smile, there came a bitter protest against the article in the *Times*, in which an unknown writer had thought fit to slander the innocent intentions of the Empire and the Chancellor. Then, immediately after the Emperor's arrival, Prince Gortschakoff was the first to come and see M. de Gontaut. "You have been very uneasy; you may set your mind at rest," he said. "The Emperor, who wishes to see you, will give you even a more positive assurance. Bismarck has shown himself to be animated by the most pacific intentions. He gave his word that the relations with France were never better."

What had happened then? The truth soon transpired. Alexander had been forestalled by a few days by his ambassador in London, Count Schouvaloff, who, returning to his post, had taken Berlin *en route*, and acquainted the Chancellor as well as Emperor Wilhelm with the very firm resolves of his sovereign. He warned him (says a writer, who must have been very well informed) to be careful as to what he was going to do, and assured him that if he would not believe him, others would soon follow in whom he would be obliged to put faith. Thinking himself fortunate, perhaps, to have been warned in time, Herr von Bismarck deemed it prudent to be guided by that pointed advice, the rather that the old Emperor, who had probably not clearly understood the direction in which he was being led, showed himself very determined not to advance another step. In the interval a dispatch from London, couched in the sense M. Gavard had already announced, had come just in time to turn the movement of conversion that had already begun into a complete reversal of tactics. According to the same writer, Herr von Bismarck publicly, and with imperturbable audacity, maintained that the whole of the noise had been caused by Stock Exchange speculators "bearing" the market, and by the intrigues of the Clericals.[1]

[1] Extracted from an article in the *Edinburgh Review* (for October 1879), entitled "Germany since the Treaty of Frankfort." The author of this book, an authority assuredly, thinks that the writer of the article must have had access directly or indirectly to the official documents bearing on the question. Absolute want of time has prevented my comparing my re-translation from the French with the original text, and also my perusal of the whole; I feel pretty certain, though, of not having made any important mistake, either with regard to the spirit or the wording. Yet, with all due deference to both the author of the book and the author of the article, I cannot wholly agree with their estimate of the Emperor's share in the matter. The late Emperor Wilhelm was not gifted perhaps with the spirit of initiative, nor was he very prompt to take a decision; but, powerful as Bismarck was, Wilhelm would not have allowed him either to inaugurate or to pursue a policy like that discussed above without his (Wilhelm's) sanction, and without his being informed day by day—nay, hour by hour—of the incidents due to that policy. Wilhelm was not the man to be led in any direction blindfolded, and Bismarck knew this but too well. "He spares me no shocks" (literally, he does not forget to stir me up), said Bismarck to one of M. de Gontaut's successors, M. de Saint-Vallier, the same who had the French Embassy in the Pariser Platz rebuilt at a cost of £24,000; "he spares me no shocks; and I should be all the better without those little letters in his own hand-

From that moment, all the clouds being dispelled, the situation, as a matter of course, became less strained. The interview between the Czar and M. de Gontaut took place at the Russian Embassy. It lasted a good while, and was as thorough as it was cordial. The sovereign, in rising to intimate that the conversation was at an end, summed up the whole by the following words, uttered solemnly and with deep emotion: "Peace is necessary to the world; every one has quite enough to do to look after his own business at home. Count on me, and set your mind at rest. Convey to Marshal MacMahon the assurance of my esteem for him personally and my sincere wishes for the consolidation of his Government. I trust that our relations may become more and more cordial. We have many interests in common; we must remain united."

But the strangest thing of all was this—not a single syllable seemed to have been uttered, either

---

writing which he does me the honour to write." Wilhelm was not quite so straightforward as many people seem to think. Queen Victoria had a proof of that in 1866, when, being on the eve of declaring war against Austria, he sent word to her that peace was assured. It is an open secret that her Majesty was by no means pleased with this instance of dissimulation. Here is another proof of Wilhelm's duplicity: "Pray do not forget that the King *is supposed to be ignorant of all this*," wrote Bismarck to Prim, when he wished to revive the Hohenzollern candidature for the throne of Spain. In fact, Wilhelm I. often reminds one of that Scotch parson who, having heard a ribald song, refused to sully his lips with it, but proposed to his congregation that his clerk should whistle it to them.—TRANS.

in the conversations between the two Emperors, or in those between their Ministers, about those ill-fated armaments of France that had caused so much noise. Prince Gortschakoff told M. de Gontaut without the least reserve that in his conversations with Bismarck he (Gortschakoff) had pointedly referred more than once to the right of every State to organize its military resources at its own will and pleasure, and that to this reiterated remark on his part his interlocutor had opposed neither objection nor reservation with regard to special cases; nay more, that he had shown neither a mark of dissent nor a sign of confusion. Nor had there been the slightest reference to the unusual scene at the Quai d'Orsay, although that reckless step would assume a still stranger complexion if considered as null and void and not followed up. Finally, even Prince Hohenlohe received instructions to pretend to have forgotten that unfortunate bit of business, for, on his return to Paris, he had to come to one of the Marshal's receptions and assure him that he came back as a messenger of peace, of which his sovereign intended to remain the vigilant and strict guardian.

Neither M. Decazes nor M. de Gontaut were bound to remind people of what they were evidently determined to forget. M. de Gontaut was all the more disposed to preserve silence with regard to the whole of the latest incident, inasmuch as he had had barely time to acquaint himself with the particulars. The letter setting forth those particulars having preceded by but a few hours the effect produced by the presence of the Emperor of Russia, M. de Gontaut was, as a matter of course, absolved from worrying himself with the matter. It was owing to this that a fact which gave the real key-note to the situation has remained practically unknown, and was scarcely mentioned, a few years later on, in the retrospective polemics in the German Press on the real character of that short-lived crisis.[1] It is, nevertheless, the contrast between the solemnity of the act and the inaneness of its result which the officious apologists of Herr von Bismarck will never be able to explain satisfactorily. They can only exculpate his intentions by inculpating his intelligence, and the latter attempt will convince no one. Either the words M. Decazes heard from the German ambassador's lips were void of sense, or else they were the premonitory signs

[1] It was, in fact, four years later that, in consequence of an article published in the *Figaro* in October 1879, a controversy was started in the German papers on the subject of the so-called crisis of 1875. All the journals supposed to have been inspired by Herr von Bismarck maintained that the designs with which he was taxed were only so many fabrications meant to serve as a pretext to the French and Russian Governments to account for their *rapprochement*. I do not intend to enter into the details of those respective discussions that gave rise to insulting remarks about M. Decazes and Prince Gortschakoff. I maintain the alternative I suggested. Either the step which Herr von Bismarck instructed Prince Hohenlohe to take was a solemn farce, or it was the preface to a summons which would have entailed war, for compliance with it would have been assuredly declined.

of a storm which would have broken forth on the morrow if we had not been in a position to arrest it. This was pointed out in covert terms, though with a precision essentially British, by the English minister, Lord Derby, when interpellated in Parliament on the part England had played under his guidance in a game in which the general peace was at stake. "*It had been said,*" Lord Derby informed his hearers, "*by personages of the highest position and authority,*[1] *that, in order to avoid a war, it became necessary that France should interrupt her armaments, and there was reason to fear that the first step would be a formal demand by Germany to France to discontinue her armaments. If that step had been taken, it would have been difficult to maintain peace.*"

### III.

Thus ended, as it were in smoke, the strong commotion by which the whole of the political world had been stirred for six weeks. No trace of it

---

[1] Who were those persons of such high authority and position whom Lord Derby designated as having given him that salutary warning? It was generally believed that his words pointed to a direct intervention on the part of the German ambassador in London, Count Münster, who, it was said, had been instructed to express himself in the same sense to the Foreign Office with Prince Hohenlohe in Paris. But that fact, affirmed by the whole of the European Press, has been positively denied by Herr von Bismarck and by Count Münster himself. We are, then, left to suppose that Lord Derby simply wished to allude to the step taken by Prince Hohenlohe, and brought to Lord Derby's knowledge by M. Gavard.

remained anywhere except in the mind of Herr von Bismarck, but there it was deep and lasting. For the first time in his career, and on the very stage he ruled despotically, he had appeared before an ironical audience, been convicted of duplicity and want of power. In vain did he multiply his denials with affected superciliousness; he read the signs of a malicious incredulity on the faces of all who surrounded him, especially in the political and diplomatic world. His displeasure was great, and during the first hours vented itself in bitter terms, aiming at the highest in station. To begin with, there was Lord Derby's speech, which was of a nature to exasperate him, and to which he replied in his accredited paper by a denial couched in such violent terms as to border on insult. But it was especially against the Russian Minister that he refrained with difficulty from giving vent to his irritation, even in public. He accused him of having seized, nay manufactured, the opportunity to afford his master a sensational entrance on the political stage by having cast him for the part of arbiter of peace—when that peace was in no way threatened.

"Humour him," said Prince Gortschakoff to M. de Gontaut, and seemingly impressed by the state of mind of the Chancellor; "humour him, he is in a sombre mood and in a nervous state, and is constantly railing us on the *Quos Ego* of Virgil, which he says we pronounced before the storm had arisen. Do not show yourself too satisfied before him."

The advice was full of wisdom, but Prince Gortschakoff would have done better perhaps to have been guided by it himself, and not to have shown his own feeling of triumph too ostensibly. That is, if we are to judge by another and rather strange Press incident which made even a good deal of noise at that moment, and which even to this day is rather variously interpreted by those who narrate it. At the moment of the Czar's departure from Berlin for Ems, the Stuttgart papers published a telegraphic dispatch, addressed in the Emperor's name by his Chancellor to the Emperor's sister, the Queen of Würtemberg. It was written in French, and not in cipher, and ran as follows: "The hot-headed one of Berlin gives formal assurances of peace." The astonishment was universal, and, in fact, it would have been difficult to conceive anything less diplomatic than this almost offensive epithet alluding to the foremost statesman of Germany; but what appeared stranger still was the want of caution which had sanctioned, nay, seemed to have invited its publicity. The irritation of the Press devoted to Herr von Bismarck was great, and not without cause. A sufficiently natural and altogether credible explanation has, however, been given to a proceeding so utterly out of the usual course; it was simply a mistake in the translation of the telegraphic signs. The telegram, written with the ordinary abbreviations, said: "I carry away with me from Berlin formal assurances of peace."[1] An accent placed on the last letter of the word "*emporte*" had transformed an altogether inoffensive tense of a verb into an ugly-sounding adjective, and as the message itself contained only useful news, it was but equally natural that no steps should have been taken to prevent the indiscretion of the telegraphist. That no doubt was also the explanation that disarmed Herr von Bismarck's susceptibility, which, without such rectification, would assuredly not have been with-

---

[1] The explanation I beg to give here of that telegram, which has remained famous, and which strongly aroused the anger of the German Press, is, I have been assured, that of the Würtemberg journalist who published the telegram first.—AUTHOR.

[For the better understanding of the reader I give the telegrams in French.

The telegram supposed to have been sent: "J'emporte de Berlin assurances formelles de paix."

The telegram as it was transcribed and published in the papers: "L'emporté de Berlin donne des assurances formelles de paix."

It will be seen at once that there is a discrepancy of two words between the telegram supposed to have been sent by Gortschakoff and the one alleged to have been received; and even if we allow for the absence of the word "*des*" in the former for the purpose of abbreviation, there is still the word "*donne*" to be accounted for. Of course, the Russian Chancellor could not have been guilty of sending such a message, nevertheless the presumption was strong against him. The error might be much more easily accounted for by the fact that the telegraphic operator who received the message was probably a Würtemberger, and Würtembergers have never been particularly partial either to Bismarck or his *régime*. I, however, should not like to take the responsibility of such an explanation.—TRANS.]

out cause. But those mishaps are always awkward, for the simple reason that they would probably not impose upon people but for a corresponding foundation of truth. And even when the error was explained, Herr von Bismarck could not have felt inordinately flattered with a portrait in which people fancied that they could detect a certain likeness to the original.

There was, however, one thing to be genuinely and seriously feared, namely, that Herr von Bismarck, taking advantage of the influence he usually exercised over his sovereign, would endeavour to make the latter share his dissatisfaction. Would he not attempt to persuade him that he had been drawn into a trap, and that both threats of war and pacific intervention were only parts of a comedy arranged beforehand in which the most telling *rôle* had not fallen to his master? Emperor Wilhelm's annoyance at having been duped in that way might lead to fresh complications in a situation but barely consolidated. If a similar attempt was made to embitter the mind and prick the self-esteem of the aged sovereign it met with no success. Having reached the limits allotted to the life of man, he was too much surfeited with glory, he felt too keenly the need of rest that comes with advancing years, to be easily moved by trivial susceptibilities. His confidence in his nephew seemed in no way shaken, and the disappointed statesman was perforce obliged to champ his bit silently (*de ronger son frein en silence* [1]) : and to borrow from the Latin poet, as he did—"to hide within his inmost soul the resentment of his insult," but with the determined intention to vent it later on, which he did after three years, when a Congress at Berlin brought the two Chancellors side by side. On that day the German considered himself free to take his revenge by riddling the Russian with darts, which, though still covered with quasi-friendly veneer, did put an end for a long while to the friendly relations of the two Empires.

Meanwhile, instead of the grand culprits whom he had to acknowledge himself powerless to reach, there was one of less power whom he fancied to be within his reach and at his mercy; and that one, whose offence originated in less exalted spheres, and which (the offence) was therefore all the more galling to him, had to pay for all the others. That was M. de Gontaut. If, in fact, it could be shown that the whole of this business was the result of a plot hatched between Russia and France, then M. de Gontaut, placed as he was in the very centre whence the movement started, must have been one of the principal artisans of it. In that respect, Herr von Bismarck was not altogether on the wrong track, and his anger

[1] *Anglicé*—"to brood over his disappointment in silence."—TRANS.

made him clear-sighted. It was, in truth, M. de Gontaut, who, by lending an attentive and intelligent ear to all the rumours circulated around him, by refusing to be lulled to sleep with official denials, by his tact in listening to and inviting confidential and instructive communications, had given the alarm, subsequently transmitted from Paris to St. Petersburg. It was, above all, the conversation between M. de Gontaut and Herr von Radowitz, the graphic and faithful narrative of which, placed in the nick of time before the Czar, had led to the Imperial veto at the crucial hour. It was then, in reality, M. de Gontaut who had prepared the piece of ordnance the unexpected play of which had disabled the Prussian batteries, and Herr von Bismarck had as much cause to bear him a grudge for it as France has to this day to be grateful for it to his memory.

M. de Gontaut fostered no illusions with regard to the means at the disposal of the Chancellor, and of which he liked to make use for the purpose of avenging his wounded pride, or to rid himself of some one to whom he objected. In default of any other experiment, that made on me during my short-lived tenancy of the Ministry for Foreign Affairs ought to have taught him all he wanted. He was, therefore, not in the least surprised to see that very obliging Press which had blown hot and cold, preached war and peace with the same docility during the crisis, turn on a given day on him, place him, as it were, on the stool of repentance (*le mettre en quelque sorte sur la sellette*[1]), in order to pursue him with its attacks, and in a little while with its invectives. M. de Gontaut was executed in due form. The whole of his life,—past and present, public and private, —all his family and social relations were sifted with a like libellous bitterness, and with a marvellous *ensemble* and that perfect accord of the most diverse instruments, which accord, at every fresh evolution, attested the unity of direction. Among many insignificant or commonplace grievances preferred against him, and the expression of which was often trivial, there was one, which, repeated with persistence, sufficiently indicated the origin and the aim of that polemical controversy intended to injure him. M. de Gontaut was represented as having profited by his relations with the Court

---

[1] The French "stool of repentance," a cross between the English pillory and the Scotch cutty-stool, was a kind of wooden seat set up in the Criminal Courts, and on which they placed the accused to undergo his last interrogatory when the conclusions of the counsel for the prosecution (which might be either the king's procurator or the procurator-fiscal) went against him with regard to the application of capital punishment or at least of penal corporal punishment. The "stool of repentance" implied moral degradation, and it was for that reason that its use was limited to persons accused of crimes entailing corporal punishment. A person accused of lesser crimes underwent his last interrogatory standing behind the seats allotted to the members of the bar. (*Ordonnance Criminelle de* 1670, Titre IV. Art. 21.) The "stool of repentance" was abolished by an edict of Louis XVI., May 1, 1788, which edict was confirmed by the Constituent Assembly, Nov. 3, 1789.—TRANS.

and the sympathy of the German Catholics to convert his embassy into a centre of intrigue and hostility against the policy of the Chancellor. The consequence was a most natural one. Germany could not stand tamely by and watch the agent of a foreign and always inimical power becoming the head and soul of an opposing coterie with impunity. The recall of M. de Gontaut was therefore a question of dignity with the Empire, nay, almost a question of public security. Herr von Bismarck owed it to himself to insist on that recall. In fact it was soon said that he was sure to obtain it, and even was already in a position to designate M. de Gontaut's successor. He had, it was added, made choice of M. Thiers as the only one among French men of politics who understood the situation, and with whom he could get along comfortably.

Nothing is more contrary to the customs of international courtesy which constitute the bond between civilized States than personal attacks on a distinctly-named ambassador in active service. Even in those countries where the Press enjoys an almost unrestricted freedom, only organs of the lowest stamp and blind to all notions of decency would infringe the law of politeness to such an extent. On the part of a disciplined Press, strictly obedient to orders like that of Germany, that conduct became a veritable scandal, and M. de Gontaut's colleagues, rallying round him to protest against an insult that affected them all, did not hide their dissatisfaction. But what neither they nor any one else could have surmised, was the fact that Herr von Bismarck —finding, no doubt, that the execution he had instigated was coming too slowly—made it a point to bestir himself in the matter. On no theory, in fact, but that of his desire to make M. de Gontaut's stay in Berlin impossible can one explain the Chancellor's attitude towards him the first time he was,. as it were, obliged to receive him after the annoyance and disgust the ambassador was accused of having caused him. The turn he at once gave to the conversation was such that if the dialogue had been carried on both sides with the same disregard of courtesy and mutual respect, the two interlocutors, after having parted in that way, could have never met one another again.

At the date of that first interview, December 31, 1875, several months had already gone by since the exciting period of the past spring. Herr von Bismarck himself had taken advantage of his frequent absences during the summer, spent at his own home in the country, or at some watering-place, to avoid the visits M. de Gontaut had at various times endeavoured to pay to him. Their relations had been simply confined to the leaving of cards.

It would have been easy, therefore, to avoid all

allusion to a past the recollection of which was gradually being effaced, and M. de Gontaut endeavoured to set the example in that respect by expressing his satisfaction that at the opening of the year there was no subject likely to produce a disagreement between the two countries. "I am glad you think so, and still more glad to hear you say it," remarked Herr von Bismarck abruptly. "You are no longer under the impression, then, that I wish to recommence the war and set the whole of Europe on fire?" And having once started, he entered without transition upon a long and entirely uncalled-for apology of the whole of his conduct, which at that moment no one called in question. The evident aim of this gratuitous justification was to shift the responsibility of the trouble that had been imputed to him from the outset (that was the stereotyped theme) on to the shoulders of the Stock Exchange agitators and Clericals, and to attribute to them, above all, the false news sent from Paris to St. Petersburg.

"It is from France, I know, that Orloff gave the signal for the alarm," he said; "and you yourself," he added, looking fixedly at M. de Gontaut, who was seated opposite him, "you yourself went to St. Petersburg last year to tell them that I wanted another war."

Surprised, but in no way troubled by this personal attack, M. de Gontaut replied: "No, it was not last year that I went to St. Petersburg;

it is two years and two months ago that I stayed there for a little while."

"Your memory is playing you false; it was last year."

M. de Gontaut had no difficulty in proving that his interlocutor and not he was mistaken. Having been silenced on that point, Herr von Bismarck did not even trouble himself to apologize for the persistent and scarcely polite manner in which he maintained his error.

That strange incident would have been sufficient in itself to convince M. de Gontaut that the Chancellor meant to provoke a personal discussion which would probably have become very animated, and the account of which, left—in the absence of all witnesses—to the Chancellor's own discretion, would assuredly have shifted all the wrongs on to the ambassador's shoulders. The latter, therefore, took the prudent precaution to let the avalanche of words, which, moreover, nothing could have stopped, pass by, and to reply to it as briefly as possible, simply confining himself to a mild defence of the reproaches preferred against him, and to rectify misrepresented facts avoiding all the while everything in the shape of recriminations which he might have easily made clinching and triumphant, but which by embittering the discussion might have led exactly to the goal aimed at. He contained himself sufficiently to contest none of the proofs the Chancellor advanced as to his own moderation. He offered no objections to protestations like the following one—

"If people refuse to believe in my pacific protestations, it will be useless for me to continue them. Virtue is really no good in this world."

"There is this much to be gained by it," replied M. de Gontaut, smiling; "one's own conscience is at peace."

Owing to that prudent attitude the interview came to an end without an apparent rupture, and M. de Gontaut, on reaching home, after that very heated interview, could write to M. Decazes: "I believe that he was very vexed at my reserved attitude. I scarcely expected that my interview with him would at once take the turn it did take; but when I saw what was in store for me, I made up my mind to say as little as possible, lest I should play into his own hand. I felt that if I attempted to discuss with him, I should perhaps have great difficulty in containing myself, and might probably be carried further than I meant to go. I also understood more clearly, maybe, than I ever understood it before, the extent of my responsibility and the necessity of suffering personally rather than compromise the interests of my country and my Government. That was the thought, my dear friend, which enabled me to keep my patience during a painful and almost offensive interview. I could not have resigned myself to it except under such considerations. The position is not an agreeable one, but one must put up with it as long as possible. As far as I am concerned, I have made up my mind to provide myself with a double stock of patience and caution until the day the Marshal shall think fit to relieve the sentry on duty."

The provocations having remained unanswered, and the insinuations apparently not understood, Herr von Bismarck had to make up his mind to speak frankly, and to gain his end by proceeding discreetly. Prince Hohenlohe was instructed once more to communicate to M. Decazes a letter from Herr von Bülow, the writing of which had probably been as much against the grain on the latter's part as the reading of it was productive of visible discomfort to the reader. The recall of M. de Gontaut was requested in formal terms. The reasons alleged in support of this demand were neither serious nor clearly defined; but the bitterness of language was evidently intended to make up for the insufficiency of motive. It was a downright indictment incriminating the smallest act of all the members, even the humblest, of the French Embassy. Everybody there, according to the epistle, was conspiring against the Empire, from the Consul-Secretary,[1] who lived on a footing

[1] In French *Chancellier du Consulat*. Every French consulate of importance has attached to it a *chancellier*, who is appointed by the President of the Republic. He is the secretary, cashier,

of the closest intimacy with the correspondents of the French papers most hostile to Germany, to the secretaries and military *attaché* who let their tongues wag too freely, and up to the ambassador himself, who had become the chief of a *camarilla*, fomenting Ministerial intrigues in a sense openly hostile to the Chancellor. The ambassador was also conspiring to procure the Chancellor's disgrace with his sovereign, and, in one word, aimed at reviving the traditions of the Court of Catherine II., but seemed to forget that such attitudes on the part of a diplomatic representative would not be tolerated in this century. Interpolated with this sentence there was an historical reminiscence with reference to Catherine II.'s Court, the aptness of which reminiscence was not perfectly clear. Then the letter went on to say that English Ministers would never suffer an ambassador to keep up relations with parties hostile to the Cabinet constituted by the Queen.[1] In short, Herr von Bülow declared

---

keeper of the archives, notary, librarian, clerk (in the meaning of the term "clerk of the court"), and even, if needs be, writ-server to the consulate. A similar *chancellier* is attached to all legations, but in the case of very important embassies, such as that of Berlin, it is often a consul of the first or second class who performs those duties. In my time the French Embassy at Berlin consisted of, besides the ambassador, one secretary of legation first-class, one secretary of legation second-class, four secretaries of legation third-class, one naval *attaché*, one military *attaché*, one consul for the clerical work, and a couple of young *attachés*.—TRANS.

[1] I am not at all certain of that. I fancy English Ministers, unless the thing became too flagrant, would take no notice. At

that he could not continue his diplomatic intercourse with M. de Gontaut.

There is no need to point out that this declaration was not based on any right, or even on any diplomatic usage. If, in virtue of a generally-observed rule of courtesy, a Government, before accrediting an ambassador to a foreign Court, ascertains whether that choice will be agreeable to the Court which is to receive him; when once that agreement has been obtained—and it would require grave motives to have it withheld—there is no means of coming back on that decision. The diplomatic agent, after he had entered upon his duties, would scarcely care to have the duration of his mission limited or threatened at any and every moment through the whims or ill-will of a Power which he may be compelled now and then to contradict or oppose, and which, nevertheless, might have nothing to allege against him except the warm and zealous defence of the interests of the nation whose representative he is. What, indeed, could be more convenient to a Power than to be able to get rid at will of a

---

any rate they took no notice when, about 1881, M. Challemel-Lacour, then ambassador in London, and the late President of the Senate, joined in the Irish agitation, showed his sympathy with the late Mr. Parnell, then in prison, and would scarcely ever discuss any other subject than Irish politics with the late Lord Granville, who on one occasion said: "I should like to know some one who enjoys sufficient authority over M. Challemel-Lacour to tell him in confidence that he may talk politics to me"; by which, of course, his lordship meant other politics than Irish.—TRANS.

negotiator she might consider too cautious, or of an observer whose perspicuity might appear embarrassing to her?

What, in this particular instance, would have been the situation of M. de Gontaut's successor if Herr von Bismarck's haughty and unceremonious dismissal of M. de Gontaut himself had been accepted? Warned beforehand that he was only an ambassador on tolerance, and that he would have to vacate the place the moment he ceased to please, the documents such an ambassador would have handed to the sovereign would not have been credentials, but a kind of declaration of homage of a vassal to his liege lord. It would have been (to apply the historical reminiscence referred to by Herr von Bismarck more pertinently than he did) the exact case of the ambassador of mutilated Poland to the Court of Catherine. All that M. Decazes had to do, then, was simply not to appear to admit, or even to understand, the pretension, the motives for which he was, nevertheless, bound to refute.

His task was made particularly easy by the vague character of what he called "a tendency suit" (an attempt to establish a precedent); in other words, of a more or less cleverly dovetailed collection of trivial facts, not one of which would stand the test of serious examination, and some of which referred to subordinate agents who had already left Berlin.

As for the reproaches addressed to M. de Gontaut, not a single proof was forthcoming, and it would, indeed, have been particularly awkward to use greater precision, inasmuch as the relations at which Herr von Bismarck took offence were principally, as every one knew, the intimate relations of the Empress and the Princesses with the Gontaut family; truly a singular grievance, and which an ambassador of the Empire could not express in too clear terms with any regard to decency. As for the German Catholics belonging to the Parliament, in spite of the assertions of some of the papers, and notwithstanding M. de Gontaut's esteem for their character and admiration for their talent, he had carefully abstained from associating with them; a reserve rendered all the easier, moreover, by the attitude of those Catholics themselves, who were anxious, as I have already had occasion to remark, to avoid the faintest shadow of entertaining relations with the alien, as much on account of their patriotic scruples as from precaution not to compromise their popularity. M. Decazes even expressed himself with ironical finesse on the subject.

"We have no intention to mix ourselves up with your home affairs; we know that if we were suspected of taking too great an interest in them, it would be the means to attenuate rather than aggravate your difficulties." Finally, he concluded by saying very emphatically: "It is but just to

M. de Gontaut to say that without him we should not have been able to place our relations on the footing they are to-day."

Then, in order to remove all expectation of a different answer, he declined the offer of a copy of the document that had just been read to him. He merely promised to inform Marshal Mac-Mahon of everything he had just read. In a question of dignity and honour the Marshal's sentiments precluded all shadow of a doubt. "Patience, my poor friend," wrote M. Decazes to M. de Gontaut, giving him an account of the conversation.

We have seen that M. de Gontaut had laid in a stock of that virtue which was not yet exhausted. Nevertheless, he already foresaw the day when it would be exhausted,—in other words, the day when he would no longer feel himself backed up by the sincere and unreserved confidence of his Government. If, from that point of view, the accord of feelings that had never ceased to reign between M. Decazes and himself left him no doubt, he was not quite so confident with regard to the change that was going on at that very moment in the home condition of France. The National Assembly had been dissolved,[1] and the elections for the Chamber intended to replace it put the Conservatives in the minority. In the new Cabinet, of which M.

[1] On December 30, 1875, by its own vote, as it were.—TRANS.

Dufaure became the head, M. Decazes was the only one left of the preceding administration. He kept the portfolio of Foreign Affairs, for no other reason than because Marshal MacMahon, from a very praiseworthy feeling of caution, wished to shield France's foreign policy from the hazards of Ministerial instability. But would not M. Decazes' colleagues, not one of whom thought like him, be disposed to consider that the declared hostility of Herr von Bismarck was calculated to try the temper of the new-born Republic too much?

The German papers, which did not cease to tilt against M. de Gontaut, welcomed at the same time, and often in the same issue, the advent of the Republican party with most auspicious signs of good-will, and inserted with loud praise the electoral addresses of M. Gambetta. Would those who had the power to-day remain insensible for any length of time to this difference of treatment?

Already, in the department of Lower-Pyrenees which had just elected M. de Gontaut to the Senate, his opponents had accused him of having compromised and of continuing to compromise, in virtue of his Clericalism, the good relations with Germany, and pretended to substantiate their imputation by the evidence of MM. Thiers and de Rémusat, without, I feel convinced, being in the least authorized to do so. The *Journal des*

*Débats*, the most moderate of all the organs of the French Republicans which supported the new Ministry, had, without contesting the eminent merits of M. de Gontaut, insinuated more than once that he would be better suited to another post. M. de Gontaut considered it only consistent with his dignity not to let those insinuations and verbal stabs pass unnoticed, and a candid explanation on the subject with M. Decazes was the easier, inasmuch as those stabs both in character and origin aimed at the Minister as well as at his Ambassador.

"Tell me candidly, my dear friend," he wrote to him, "if your new colleagues have confidence in me? If I should happen to inspire the least mistrust, I have no desire to remain here; I do not care to be an ambassador at all costs. Attacked as I am already by the Chancellor and the German Press, if in addition to this the Government of my own country has no confidence in me, you will easily understand that, as a man of honour and conscience, I must not retain an unbearable position."

Being ready to admit the hypothesis that Bismarck threatened to annul his bargain, and refused to promise the renewal of his good-will unless the recall he had demanded was granted, M. de Gontaut wrote a few days later: "That man will not forgive me for the service I have been able to render to my country with honour, thanks be to God, and assuredly there is nothing in that either to astonish or to stop me. But having failed to reach me, that he should vent his spleen on France and try to embitter the relations of the two countries, that would be almost monstrous. As for myself personally, my dear friend, on no consideration will I allow myself to become the pretended or real cause for evil relations between Germany and France; and on the day when you acquire the certainty of what at present seems to me only a possibility, I would beg of you, and if you will permit the expression, I would command you to tell me so without mincing words, and my resignation will be forthcoming very quickly."

# IV

# THE EASTERN QUESTION AND THE BERLIN MEMORANDUM—THE ELECTIONS OF 1877—THE RESIGNATION

# THE EASTERN QUESTION AND THE BERLIN MEMORANDUM—THE ELECTIONS OF 1877—THE RESIGNATION

## I

AFTER the demand for M. de Gontaut's recall, politely but clearly shelved by Marshal MacMahon and M. Decazes, the ambassador's position at Berlin continued to be strangely delicate and peculiar. Herr von Bismarck's dislike was shown to him more and more brutally every day by all the organs of the Press which received their orders from the Imperial Chancellerie. It did not prevent his becoming the object of daily-increasing good-will on the part of the whole of political society, of the royal family—including, besides the Empress, the Prince and Princess Royal—and not even excepting the Emperor himself, who never pronounced M. de Gontaut's name without adding to it the following expression—the highest proof, perhaps, he was enabled to give of his esteem : " He is an honest man and a perfect gentleman." This contrast was too evident to remain unnoticed by the public, even if it had not suited Herr von Bismarck to draw attention to it in Parliament.

By a bold display of omnipotence he showed that he would not shrink from pointing that contrast even there. At the first opportunity afforded to him to explain to the Reichstag his attitude with regard to the bellicose humours of the previous year, he resumed his apologia with all the old arguments, affirming, moreover, that the Emperor at his age, being anxious to avoid quarrels, would not have consented to engage in a war without an adequate motive, and that, besides, such a war could not have been declared without contracting a loan of five or six millions of marks; which loan would certainly not have been granted to him in order to perpetrate the "colossal piece of idiotcy" of preventing the possible attacks of France in the future. "That would have been," he went on, "the opinion of diplomatists who, through lack of experience, have drawn their knowledge from disreputable sources, and of highly-placed personages yielding to drawing-room cabals, too ignorant of affairs to form a solid judgment, and also animated by too little kindness for the establishment of the Empire." Herr von Windthorst having taken up the parable to point out that it was the Press which had spread those alarms, and that when a certain portion of the Press spoke, the source whence it drew its inspiration—nay, whence it drew even its substance—left no matter for doubt, Herr von Bismarck retorted that this intervention of a Catholic in no way surprised him, the highly-placed personages to whom he had alluded being famed for their sympathy with the Centre rather than with the policy of the Government. If M. de Gontaut had no difficulty in recognizing a portrait of himself in the description of "diplomatists who fish in troubled waters," the Empress, whose repugnance for the policy in connection with the *Kulturkampf* was well known, found herself just as clearly designated, and it was no doubt in order to reply to this public provocation that she showed herself more gracious than ever to M. de Gontaut on the occasion of a ball at the French Embassy on the following day, and which ball she honoured with her presence.

For how long could those strained relations, which brought trouble even in the Imperial household, have continued without snapping? What would have happened if some serious difference had cropped up afresh between France and Germany? All this it would have been impossible to determine even then, for an unforeseen diversion abruptly ended the situation. It so happened that at that very moment Berlin ceased to be the exclusive stage for the discussion of the question in connection with the powerful interests of the European policy; and a new series of events was being unfolded, in which no doubt the two countries respectively had still an active part to play, but which were no longer placed in direct conflict.

Every one knows, and there is no need for me to recall how, in the course of the year 1875, an insurrectionary movement broke out in the provinces of Bosnia and the Herzegovina. Considered of small importance at the outset, it gradually provided the opportunity for the display of a feeling of violent irritation on the part of the whole of the Christian populations still subject to the domination of the Porte against the tyrannical and arbitrary *régime* of which they were the victims. It soon became evident that if some kind of satisfaction was not afforded to their just grievances, the uprising would become general on the shores of the Lower Danube, as well as at the foot of the Balkans, and one that the Turkish forces by themselves would have considerable difficulty in suppressing.

It was, moreover, certain that the provinces recently freed from the yoke of the Porte, like Servia and Roumania, would not remain callous to the sufferings of the oppressed, whose lot they had shared for a long while; and Russia herself soon gave the world to understand that she also could not for ever remain deaf to the cries of agony of her co-religionists. Hence, it was the existence of the Ottoman Empire, the integral territorial condition of which has always been considered as one of the bases of the law of European nations, which might be at stake. And that everlasting Eastern question, the primary cause of so many bloody struggles, bade fair to be revived once more in a threatening and acute form. If the conflagration was allowed to rage unchecked in those countries containing so much inflammable material, no one could predict either its extent or the destruction it might cause.

It was but natural that the Powers which have been in the habit of considering themselves the guardians of the decaying Porte, and who in its days of trouble lavish not altogether disinterested consolation and advice on it—it was but natural that they should endeavour to obtain from it administrative measures calculated to alleviate the sufferings and to satisfy the claims of its subjects quivering with fear and excitement. Preliminary communications were started, both to prepare the Porte to set on foot the reform deemed necessary, and to settle in concert with the Powers themselves the programme of the measures they intended to propose to it. It was a long and complicated negotiation, mainly carried on at Constantinople itself, but which had, nevertheless, to be pursued simultaneously in nearly all the capitals of Europe. M. de Gontaut's personal share in these negotiations was, as a rule, but slight, inasmuch as he could only watch the phases of them from a long distance, and because the subject, in virtue of its far-spreading importance, did not come within the active sphere of an embassy. Nevertheless, Berlin, which has always been a much-frequented "half-way meeting-place" for the interchange of diplomatic communications, became more than ever, and owing to the preponderant influence of the new Empire, a centre whither converged all the information of a more or less important character. It was, therefore, no small gain to France to have stationed there beforehand a very attentive and intelligent spectator, who, seated in the first row, had no need to hold all the wires of the piece to enable him to detect the mechanism of the various springs at work, and to master the passions as well as the motives of all the actors. The most cursory perusal of his dispatches suffices to appreciate the superior tact and judgment he brought to bear upon his part of a mere observer, which is neither the least delicate nor the least precious part of the profession. The perusal of those dispatches shows, furthermore, how his task was facilitated by the friendly and confidential relations he had previously established with his colleagues of all nations, English, Russians, Austrians, Belgians, and even Ottomans, who kept him posted in everything that happened, without even mistrusting his discretion or doubting his word. Equally easy is it to note at every page the beneficent influence he exercises around, in virtue of his counsels always breathing the spirit of prudence and conciliation.

There even arose one particular occasion when

he was, as a matter of course, called upon to put himself forward, and enabled to co-operate with M. Decazes in the cautious policy the latter had adopted, and the outlines of which he had more than once explained in the Chamber. The real difficulty of the situation (as will have been understood already) lay not so much in inducing the Porte to follow the counsel that would be given to it by the unanimous European Powers, as to establish the basis for that common action in concert with the counsellors themselves. It is a peculiar and at the same time most difficult feature of the Eastern question that it is comparatively easy for those interested in it to agree while the question is being left to rest, but the moment it shows signs of stirring, each one concerned in it, having his own interests to guard, his clients to protect, his views with regard to the future to pursue, divergencies do not fail to crop up, and the conduct with regard to it is no longer looked at in the same light either in London or Vienna, at St. Petersburg or Paris. The danger, then, was to avoid quarrelling with each other, while trying to come to an agreement with regard to the means to influence the Porte. Such a division would not only deprive the peaceful counsels of Europe of all authority, but might lead to fresh complications of more extensive bearing. Allies, after all, never lose sight of the fact that they are rivals, and it has occurred before then that while closing up the ranks too tightly, in order to march "together," the would-be allies had found their elbows sticking into each other's sides, and had come to blows themselves.

As for France, the condition to which fortune had reduced her made her line of conduct very easy, or, to speak correctly, she could only follow one line. We had but one interest to guard; viz. to prevent all conflict in which the as yet badly-mended imperfection of our military forces would have prevented us from taking the least part. Prudence commanded us above all to remain neutral, but lest such neutrality should try the patience of the nation too much, and also impair her future prestige, we were bound to prevent around us an aggravated state of dissent which, whatever its issue, would do us no good. Very sensible general instructions recommended, therefore, to our agents to show themselves favourable (even without disputing too much over the conditions) to any and every arrangement which, while maintaining the union between the great Powers, would permit them to make the whole weight of their common intervention felt at Constantinople. To begin by agreeing with one another, then to speak and to act together, that was the counsel we wished to give to every one; it was, moreover, the advice dictated by reason and humanity. Owing nothing to, and asking nothing from, anybody, we were in a better position than the others to gain a hearing for that advice.

For a moment it seemed as if that result was about to be attained. After a few attempts to feel their way and fruitless efforts at conciliation both at Constantinople, at Vienna, and on the scene of the insurgent provinces themselves, the Chancellors of the German, Austrian, and Russian Empires, having met at Berlin, succeeded in agreeing upon a Memorandum containing the demands, or rather the summons, to be addressed to the Porte, and submitted their document to England, France, and Italy. The terms of this Note were distinctly severe.

In addition to the demand for reforms of a general character, such as guarantees for religious liberty, the just distribution and the regular application of the taxes, there were others more painful, perhaps, to a sovereign threatened in his authority. The Sultan had to grant an armistice of two months to the rebels, and to promise them an indemnity for the barbarous acts which the Turkish forces, under the pretext of suppression, had committed. Moreover, if at the expiration of the delay indicated, order had not been restored, the Powers announced their intention to devise more efficacious measures to check the evil. The extreme severity of these conditions was explained, nay justified, by the daily-increasing gravity of the news from the East. Owing to the state of terrible excitement equally shared by the Mussulman and Christian populations, everything on Turkish territory was rapidly going from bad to worse, even in the countries which till then had taken no share in the revolt; and it looked as if before long there would be security nowhere and for nobody. At Salonica, for instance, in a bloody riot, in consequence of the abduction of a Christian girl, two European consuls, namely, the French and the German, had lost their lives.

The emotion caused by facts of that nature was so widespread, and the demand for prompt action had become so obviously necessary, that not one of the three ambassadors to whom the Memorandum was handed, to be transmitted to their respective Governments, seemed to doubt the latter's quick assent to it. The most clearly-expressed approval was that of the English ambassador, who refused to admit the possibility of hesitation. He felt himself authorized by the general character of Lord Derby's policy, to guarantee the acceptance of the Memorandum. As for M. de Gontaut, who had instructions to practise as well as to preach a mutual understanding, he saw no reason to deviate from it when he was naturally impelled to it. M. Decazes, like himself, considered this an opportunity for meeting on common ground too precious to be lost. He has been accused of, and has even reproached himself with, having been too eager to seize that opportunity. But it is not just to appreciate the fitness of a political act without looking at the awkwardness a contrary conduct might perhaps have entailed, and the invitation of the authors of the Memorandum was couched in such pressing terms that a refusal, or even a delay, might have discouraged them. The signature of France, then, was sent by the return of the messenger. There was no reason to apprehend any difficulty on the part of Italy, and, in fact, there was none. But to everybody's surprise, which, however, was nowhere greater than at the British Embassy in Berlin, England alone abstained from following the general example. She was evidently afraid that the humiliation inflicted on the Porte would be conducive to the increase of an influence at which she looked with suspicion. It is well known that all political men in England, and especially the Conservatives, who were in power then, are always haunted by the threatening shadow of Russia looming over Constantinople. In short, the Disraeli Cabinet considered the Note too pressing, and refused to subscribe to the threats conveyed in its conclusion. A threatening pressure was exactly what constituted the merit of the Memorandum in the opinion of its authors; the moment it failed to command unanimous consent, the whole effect would be compromised.

Result: a very awkward position for those who had signed it, and, it must be admitted, more awkward for France than for any other Power. The whole aspect of the affair was, in truth, entirely changed the moment the fact which should have been instrumental in bringing about the concert only served to emphasize the division. The Porte, which might perhaps have been intimidated had its protectors been unanimous, was going to score a victory over their dissensions, and would probably be encouraged in maintaining a resistance which was already practically forced upon it by the fanaticism of the faithful. Would it do to use means of coercion, and would England, which dissuaded their use, look on with indifference? Would she not devise an obstacle to their use? Hence, in that case, instead of the peace that had been assiduously sought for, there would be the impending risk of arousing the spectre of war. And even supposing that the danger was neither so grave nor so immediate as all that, Europe was, nevertheless, divided henceforth into two camps, and which of these two was France going to join? Was her place very clearly defined in that in which Germany seemed to command? Was it in order to take up a position there that she would have to cast to the winds that moral neutrality which constituted almost a guarantee for her material one? Thus the situation became sufficiently painful for M. de Gontaut, forced as he was to abandon the impartial and conciliatory attitude that had been enjoined upon him. Truly the situation was even more disagreeable for the English ambassador, thrown over as it were by his chiefs, and the involuntary author of his colleagues' disappointment; but this was, after all, but cold comfort to M. de Gontaut.

It was the "unexpected" that put every one's embarrassment to an end; the "unexpected" is a powerful factor in all human affairs, and nowhere does it play a more important part than in the East. It was on May 30 that the Berlin Memorandum, with its signatures incomplete and its effect discounted beforehand, ought to have been communicated at Constantinople. But on that day, Sultan Abdul-Aziz, who was to receive it from the hands of the ambassadors, abandoned his throne, and four days later he had ceased to live. He was overthrown by a palace-revolution, the promoters of which placed one of his nephews on the throne under the title of Murad V.

A new sovereign is always lavish of fine promises. As soon as he was seated on the throne, Murad did not fail to announce that he was going to realize spontaneously all the reforms the Powers proposed to demand with regard to the general administration of his Empire; and although neither he, who was but little known, nor his *entourage*, entirely composed of fanatical sectaries, inspired the least confidence for the realization of such a high-sounding programme, it was felt that the least one could do was to grant him the necessary respite before taking it for granted that he would not even make an attempt in that direction. The "handing" of the Memorandum was therefore postponed to a future but indefinite time, and the delay, in order to make the proof a loyal one, could not be less than a few months. But there are times when months count as years, and when the events change under our very eyes within the space of a day, not to say an hour. The adjournment of a measure under such conditions practically means the abandonment. In a very little while the Berlin Memorandum had ceased to be spoken of, because having become either insufficient or inapplicable on more than one point, it would have answered no longer to the necessities of the situation or to the feelings of those who had inspired it.

The whole of the question being opened afresh, as it were, the French Minister could apply himself once more to the loyal but ungrateful task he had imposed on himself, *i.e.* to take up anew the strands of the broken accord, and to discover on the constantly-shifting ground a point that might serve as a new centre of union. The chief thing was to influence England, for it was she who had left the line traced out for common action, it was she who had to be converted from the personal interest that had induced her to stand aloof, to considerations for the general interest, and therefore of a more lofty character. I doubt whether he would have succeeded if Turkey herself had not aided in that conversion by a terrible and gory sermon. Its humour indulged and its hands left free by the hesitations of Europe and the protection it fancied it had secured in London, the Ottoman Ministry, instead of paying attention to the promised reform, flung upon the revolted provinces, and even upon those which, like Bulgaria, had until then only protested in words, wild hordes, recruited from the lowest strata of Islam, and the unspeakable excesses and fiendish conduct of which made even English opinion recoil with horror. The indignation caused by those outrages, or "Bulgarian atrocities" as they were called then, was turned to account by the incomparable eloquence of the leader of the Liberal Opposition, Mr. Gladstone, in such a manner as to make it impossible for the Conservative Cabinet to take the presumed authors of those foul deeds under its protection. "I am compelled to admit," said one of the English Ministers on a visit to Paris to me, "I am compelled to admit that the Turks have not proved very creditable clients to us, and that we shall not be able to defend them very long." And he as good as concluded that, to save them from being ruined completely, it would have been better, perhaps, to have resorted to measures of deserved severity, which, their principle being admitted at the outset, might have been directed and tempered in their application by friendly hands.

But while on that side there were visible signs of a tendency to a *rapprochement*, were there not, on the other, symptoms of an impending withdrawal in the opposite direction, and in a manner that might prove irreparable? The odious spectacle afforded by Turkish agents caused a disgust in England that impelled her to a better understanding with the Powers. Was not that same feeling of disgust in Russia apt to arouse a generous and boiling impatience it might be difficult to keep within bounds? At every fresh misdeed on the part of Turkey, a general cry resounded throughout the orthodox Empire, which cry penetrated to and was re-echoed in the councils of the Czar, and impelled him to rush by himself to the defence of religion, justice, and humanity, without counting on evidently laggard allies. The Russian army, already massed on the Ottoman frontier, was burning to cross it.

Again M. Decazes had recourse to M. de Gontaut to prevent extremities that might, once more, have compromised everything. The Czar and his Chancellor were, as usual, to spend the summer season at Ems. M. de Gontaut might meet them there without stirring from home, as it were, and without incurring the suspicion of having come after them. There is no need to remind the reader that a friendly intercourse of a few weeks in a watering-place may lend itself to frequent and confidential conversation. M. de Gontaut was to seize the opportunity of those daily gatherings to preach patience. It was not an easy task. At the outset, the recollections of the previous year invested M. de Gontaut's intercourse with his august visitors with a particularly friendly and effusive character. But when, having come to the question of the day, he ventured to utter a few sentences counselling calmness and moderation—when, especially in M. Decazes' name, he considered himself justified in submitting one or two propositions which, more moderate in form than those of the Berlin Memorandum, might have facilitated a return to the *entente* with the Cabinet of St. James', then the aspect of the scene changed, and the extremely friendly feeling made room for visible signs of displeasure. Astonishment was expressed that France should show such cool unconcern for the interests of Russia, which coolness, it was not denied, was apt to cause surprise and even disappointment after the service Russia had rendered to her. Russia had expected a little more tenacity of memory on France's part. Russia also did not fail to remind France that her signature, transmitted by M. de Gontaut himself, still figured at the bottom of that Memorandum, which had not been withdrawn, but only suspended, out of confidence, which had turned out to be singularly misplaced, in Turkey's projects of reform. Such being the case, they—M. de Gontaut as well as his Minister—stood still committed to an active policy the mode of which, though not the principle, might be susceptible of alteration, and from which they were no longer free to depart.

The subject gave rise to lively discussions, revealing on the sovereign's part a feeling of wounded self-love which might have been easily embittered by the slightest want of tact or the slightest incautious word on the part of the ambassador. M. de Gontaut was sufficiently fortunate to be able to pour balm into those wounds by never departing from an attitude of moderation which was not altogether devoid of art. His principal and constant argument was to remind his interlocutors that the greater the isolation of the Porte, the smaller its hopes of finding support, the easier would be the overthrow of its resistance whether moral or material. But in his attempts to prevent the discussions from becoming embittered M. de Gontaut derived his greatest aid from the confidence his word inspired, from the certainty felt by his interlocutors that there were no mental provisos hidden behind the intentions he expressed, and that he would not have condescended either to serve or to second underhand any other views than those of which he had made himself the interpreter.

Thanks to that assurance the end of that

stormy season was reached in comparative peace; and the time having arrived when it was no longer possible for any one to hope or to wait for any beneficial change in the East, it was England herself who felt the necessity for getting out of the equivocal position in which she had placed herself, and took the initiative in proposing a Conference at Constantinople between the representatives of the Powers. This was practically coming back—though somewhat late—to the ground for a common understanding which France had never deserted, and to which she had never ceased to invite everybody, she herself waiting for them there all the while. It is not detracting from the merits of M. Decazes to affirm that nothing aided him more efficiently in the attainment of the aim he had so constantly pursued, than the confidential conversations of M. de Gontaut with the two Emperors during the latter weeks.

I say the two Emperors, for the Emperor of Germany had also frequently been to Ems, and made a third at those interviews. He brought back from them—and did not scruple to say so very openly—a feeling of complete satisfaction both with regard to the policy of France and the attitude of her representative. "We are united with France," he remarked on several occasions, "and I trust that we shall remain united in a task of conciliation and peace." He was lavish in his praise of M. de Gontaut. "He is the best ambassador we could possibly have, and I verily believe," he added, laughing, "that if they wished to take him away, I should make it a *casus belli.*" And when people ventured to point out that Herr von Bismarck did not share that answer, he answered: "I am aware of it, and it seems incredible to me. I have told him many a time that we shall never have any one better, and I have also told him that he did not see the ambassadors often enough, and, for that reason, did not judge them properly." To which he replied, "that it was not worth while seeing them, because they always had something disagreeable to say about us. But they are only doing their business; an ambassador is not appointed to say nothing but what is good of the country in which he is on duty."

At every Court there are always a number of officious and spiteful listeners ready to report to those in power remarks calculated to annoy or worry them. Herr von Bismarck, therefore, was not left in ignorance of the Emperor's expressed satisfaction with M. de Gontaut, and his irritation increased in consequence, without prompting him, though, to modify the manifestation of it, so confident was he of the strength of his position. The conversations at Ems, above all, did not fail to cause him an annoyance which he was at no pains to hide. And the papers followed suit in representing this confidential intercourse with the Imperial personages as a new proof of the ambassador's tendency to extend his influence beyond his regular attributes. They even formulated the theory that Ems being without the centre of his diplomatic relations, his right to direct his embassy from there was open to question.[1]

In order to convey an accurate and thorough idea of the complexity of the situation, we ought to add that Herr von Bismarck's feeling of annoyance was not solely due to M. de Gontaut's conduct personally; he was just as dissatisfied with the line of conciliation and peace advocated by the French Government, of which M. de Gontaut was the organ, and with which line of conduct, though not daring to oppose it, he had no intention whatsoever to associate himself.

It may be remembered that of all the enigmatical and obscure attitudes during the first phase of the Eastern question, Herr von Bismarck's attitude was the most enigmatical and obscure; and his explanations in the Reichstag

---

[1] This objection, which the German ambassador in Paris was really instructed to point out to M. Decazes, was all the more unwarranted, inasmuch as M. de Gontaut, whenever he absented himself from Berlin, left secretaries to act for him in whom he had implicit trust. Those secretaries were respectively, during the first period of his mission the Marquis de Sarye, and during the latter period M. Victor Tiby. But the one and the other were excellent agents, who kept M. de Gontaut informed of the slightest incidents, attended to current affairs with rare intelligence, and with regard to whom, in his correspondence, M. de Gontaut expressed at various times his full satisfaction.

on the subject, given apparently against his will, did not tend to elucidate it, judging by subsequent events. One may, however, affirm with certainty that at the moment he was by no means sorry for the outbreak of the crisis, and that, after all, it was he who at the eleventh hour frustrated all the attempts whence a pacific solution might have issued.

That was the bit of burrowing he pursued assiduously; and the fact of his not pursuing it more openly was not due to his anxiety to avoid the censure of public opinion, for which he cared not one jot, and which, if anything, he liked to defy, but because he feared to alarm by his double-dealing the rectitude and good sense of his sovereign. This difference of tendency between the Monarch and his Minister explains all that struck one as shady, dark, and enigmatical during the negotiations, based upon a policy labelled with their name, and which policy was affected by that want of accord.

Wilhelm, cherishing as he did the recollections of an old family alliance, and grateful, moreover, for the aid his nephew had lent him in 1870, unquestionably showed himself strongly in favour of the hopes entertained by Russia, and sincerely desired the debate, when once it was entered upon, to turn to the benefit of Russia's intended influence in the East. But he sincerely wished to manage in such a way as to obtain that satisfac-

# THE EASTERN QUESTION

tion without Russia or any one else having to resort to the extremity of war, the contagious influence of which he always dreaded both with regard to Europe and his own neighbourhood. His gratitude to M. de Gontaut was due to the latter's efforts to realize that dual wish by working to maintain peace while duly observant of the susceptibilities of Russia. "I have seen and had a great deal too much of war in my life," he said. "At my time of life one wishes to end one's days in peace."

Herr von Bismarck, however, was not swayed by such scruples. Far from it; his main concern, on the contrary, was to provide sufficient occupation for Russia in the East, so as to leave her no inclination to meddle afresh with the affairs of Western Europe, as she just had done to his cost, and in an imperious manner which he resented. A war on the Bosphorus—whether successful or the reverse, whether fraught with complications with England or not—such a war meant the removal of Russia from Germany's path for a long while to come. It meant the *de facto* realization, whether voluntary or enforced, of proposals which Herr von Radowitz had been instructed to make at St. Petersburg, to leave the East to be dealt with by the Czars, and the West by the Hohenzollerns. It had, indeed, been declined, but it would practically have to be accepted when all the Muscovite forces had their hands full on the

Black Sea. Therefore, the conflict, feared by his sovereign, suited the Chancellor marvellously well. And the moment he detected tendencies to a *rapprochement* on the part of the Powers, the moment the chances of a conflict seemed to grow more distant, he had a means ready to hand to revive those chances, to shuffle the cards anew, a thing not very difficult to do in a game so complicated in itself.

That was what he intended to do once more, and with a vengeance, in the Conference assembled in Constantinople at the instance of England, and which Conference had been very reluctantly accepted by Russia. For a short while it seemed as if conciliatory tendencies would prevail. The prudence and moderation of the English plenipotentiary, the Marquis of Salisbury, seconded the views of our plenipotentiaries, MM. de Bourgoing and de Chaudordy; Austria was well-nigh rallying to them, and the Russian Minister, the fiery Ignatieff, almost resigned to them. It was that very moment—no doubt fixed upon beforehand—which the Prussian envoy, who of all men was the most gentle and inoffensive in daily life, and who up to then had been silent, selected to burst forth abruptly, treating all the efforts for peace with almost insulting scorn, and declaring that it was unworthy of great Powers to remain content with mere impotent compromises in the case of such serious questions as these. The effect was sudden and decisive. The stentorian voice was Herr von Bismarck's own, giving a signal for the fight. A few timid denials from Berlin did not suffice to drown the sound. Henceforward all hope of agreement was at an end. Russian ardour and Turkish fanaticism, over-excited to an equal pitch, refused to listen any longer, and a recourse to armed strength became unavoidable. "They are at no pains to hide their joy here," said one of M. de Gontaut's colleagues to him, one who was in a position to gauge Herr von Bismarck's sentiments better than no matter who.

## II.

The war between Turkey and Russia broke out, in fact, in the spring of 1877, and M. de Gontaut, who had conscientiously endeavoured to prevent it, was not to see the end of it. Before fortune, undecided at first, had pronounced between the combatants, he had ceased to represent France at Berlin. He was obliged to relinquish his duties in consequence of a home crisis, the effects of which ought not to have attainted him, inasmuch as no question of foreign policy was involved in it. He was, nevertheless, dragged into it, and under circumstances which invested his retirement with a character of noble, dignified, and natural patriotism, fitly crowning such a well-run course.

It would be absolutely foreign to the subject of this narrative if I entered into the smallest detail with regard to the motives that induced Marshal MacMahon to appoint, on May 16, 1877, a Cabinet, the composition of which was at variance with the views of the majority of the Chamber of Deputies, an appointment which made the dissolution of that Assembly unavoidable. I will, therefore, abstain from all explanation in that respect, the rather that even the attempt to explain would seem premature to me. The act of May 16, 1877, will only be justly appreciated when a greater number of proofs shall have conclusively demonstrated the false, contradictory, and cruelly painful situation in which the Constitutional Law of 1875 seems to have made it its special business to place the Chief whom it gives to the Republic. When a few more Presidents shall have found it impossible to maintain themselves to the end in the exercise of their dignity—and be it remembered that out of the six we have already had, four have been unable to complete the whole of their term of office[1]—it will, perhaps, begin to

[1] In reality there are only three; namely, Thiers, MacMahon, and Casimir-Perier, for Grévy was compelled to resign in consequence of the alleged and not altogether unproven complicity of his son-in-law in the Caffarel scandals; Carnot, of course, does not count—he was murdered. Nevertheless, M. de Broglie is practically right; the divulging of the Caffarel scandals was not due to the virtuous indignation of the legislators of France at the corrupt practices of some of their fellow-legislators, under the auspices of M. Daniel Wilson, but to their wish to overthrow the more moderate Govern-

# THE ELECTIONS OF 1877—THE RESIGNATION

dawn upon people that a Chief of the State cannot be both elective and irresponsible without experiencing strong moral trouble now and then; that is, that he will not care to see himself invested one day with power as the representative of a grand political cause in order to see himself on the morrow debarred from serving that cause, nay, ordered, as it were, to desert and betray that cause. The momentary brilliancy of his position is in too great and painful a contrast with the state of cipher to which he is condemned, and with the impossibility to which he is reduced to come to the aid of some interests which are dear, and must be sacred to him because of his having been chosen to serve them. The purely decorative part left to him, the homage to which he is entitled, and which the masses fond of spectacular show address not to his person but to the memories, and so to speak to the relics, of royalty, of which he represents but the pale reflex—all these constitute but puerile consolations, which are not likely to satisfy for any length of time a man with his heart in the right place, or even a man of taste. A resignation, even if it be brusquely tendered,

---

ment, and thus to embarrass Jules Grévy, who, notwithstanding his culpable indifference to any and everything that did not concern the increase of his private hoard, would probably have been extremely reluctant to tolerate the composition of an advanced Cabinet like that of M. Bourgeois. The whole affair is too long to be worked out in a footnote; one thing is certain, the position of President of the Republic is a curious one.—TRANS.

like that we witnessed recently, is sufficiently explained by those painful conditions of the Presidential power.

Before resorting to that extreme step to which, as we know, Marshal MacMahon was finally reduced, he fancied he had found a means of escape from the painful necessity of leaving the power in the hands of the adversaries of the very Conservatives who had elected him. The obligation to affix his name—the most brilliant ornament of which was its reputation for loyalty—to a programme altogether opposed to his well-known convictions and the promises implied by his advent to power, after a while became unbearable to him. He had the right, subject to the approval and with the co-operation of the Senate, to appeal to the country and to ask her to put an end to this. It was part of his constitutional prerogative, and I have never been able to understand what reproach he could incur for having made use of that right.

But the legal consequence of that perfectly regular procedure was a General Election at very short notice. The struggle could not fail to be violent on the part of a political party threatened with the loss of power which it had enjoyed only for a short time. Those who desired to maintain the home policy of France on the lines which had been pursued by the dissolved majority might have adopted several platforms; they decided to choose one in connection with France's foreign policy. That which they did choose, we are bound to remark, was not conspicuous for its originality, and did not greatly tax their imaginative powers. It was simply, as in the days of the possible restoration of the Monarchy, the resurrection of the theme of Clericalism, and of the danger to the world at large from an aggressive revival of Papal pretensions supported in France by a Conservative majority. The grievance was old-fashioned, and a current of new facts had dispelled the credulity which had ensured its acceptance for a little while. For the space of four years, the foreign policy of the Conservative party, represented during the whole of that time by M. Decazes, had sown no troublous seeds anywhere. No Conservative or even Clerical hand could be detected in agitations, one of the results of which, at that very hour, was a terrible conflict. On the contrary, peace and concord had been preached to all, and in every key and tone. Never had greater guarantees been given for—nay, greater sacrifices been made in the supreme interest of—common peace. Hence, the event of May 16 might have caused some surprise across our borders, it could have caused no anxiety.

M. Decazes was enabled to show proofs of all this during the debate that preceded the dissolution of the Chamber, and, moreover, proofs attested by the foreign Ministers themselves in terms of complete and well-meaning certainty. It was so much time and trouble wasted, the pretended dangers of Clericalism insured to those who galvanized the bogey into life, an advantage—or to be correct, an auxiliary—with which they would on no consideration have parted. The blows struck, on the one hand, at religion and at the Church enabled them to hold out the other to Herr von Bismarck with a just confidence in the eagerness with which he would seize it.

This time, in fact, the union, which during the previous ordeals had only been cautiously shown, was proclaimed without disguise, nay, noisily blazoned forth. Until then, whenever there had been an attempt to drag into our home discussion the fear of or sympathy with the alien, Italy alone was mentioned; we were accused of provoking the hostility of Italy, the fears and uneasiness of which our adversaries pretended to share in virtue of a common origin and memories. Germany appeared only in the background as the protector of the threatened Italian unity, and her battalions were only faintly outlined in that background in order to inspire a mute fear. But in the present case the need for striking well and quickly no longer admitted of such compromise; hence, the main sensation-trick of the electoral polemics—which, as will be remembered, was the announcement disseminated throughout the land of a treaty already signed between Rome and Berlin—and in virtue of which an armed intervention, in which Germany would play the principal part, was being prepared, or better still, was ready to chastise France, in the event of the names issuing from the electoral being of such a nature as to predict a Clerical majority. The whole of the German Press repeated the story without denying it. If there was no absolute treaty, said the *Nord-Deutsche Zeitung* (the inspired journal *par excellence*, too wary and too well-informed to utter a direct lie), there was, at any rate, a settled agreement with regard to it, which would be followed without delay by an interchange of signatures the moment the apprehended event should be realized. It is scarcely necessary to say that the allegation in its milder form was as devoid of foundation as in any other. There was no more an agreement than there was a treaty; one might boldly defy people to produce from no matter what Foreign Office in Europe the slightest trace, at that moment, of as much as a preliminary conversation on the subject. The only agreement seems to have been between the journalists of the two countries interchanging correspondences, the dates as well as the foundations of which were settled beforehand, and, as a rule, in Paris itself. Are we to believe that there was also an agreement between the Republican committees of the Eastern departments and the German functionaries of the annexed provinces, such as customs officers and rangers, who in their daily intercourse with the border populations so openly patronized the lists of the opposition as to induce the belief that they themselves, the German functionaries, had distributed them? In spite of the warnings that had been given to us, I am still reluctant to believe that Frenchmen could have accepted such co-operation, and my belief was only shaken once, namely, when the most celebrated representative of that region, M. Jules Ferry, came, after success had been obtained, to justify the Republicans for having made the threat of a foreign invasion their battle-cry, and thus tacitly admitted the benefit they had derived from it. The only theory on which to account for so damning a declaration, which drew forth murmurs even from the orator's friends, was that of gratitude. I remember perfectly well my turning to the box reserved to the *corps diplomatique*, where the German ambassador sat listening in an affable way, and it was that sight which suggested the idea to me to tell M. Ferry in reply that it was only in the Diets of Poland, on the eve of her dismemberment, that members before voting glanced to the envoys of the Queen[1] or of Frederick to try and see what they thought. M. Gambetta, who spoke after me, more cautious than his colleague,

---

[1] Empress is what the author meant.—TRANS.

# THE ELECTIONS OF 1877—THE RESIGNATION 275

carefully avoided the faintest allusion to the subject.[1]

Anyhow, the electoral victory having been won by such means, it was not surprising that a Cabinet should have been constituted which this time did not include M. Decazes, and that the first resolution of the Cabinet Council was the recall of M. de Gontaut. It would have been very ungracious, in return for such services rendered, to refuse to gratify Herr von Bismarck's oft-expressed desire.

The decision was taken without a moment's loss; the only particle of ceremony with regard to it was that M. de Gontaut's recall was not notified to him in a direct way. He was asked to send in his resignation by intermediaries who did not hide from him that his request was eagerly expected. He had so often offered it to M. Decazes, and had so freely talked with him about it from the point of view of general interest, that the answer claimed from him could cause him neither surprise nor embarrassment as far as he was personally concerned. Nevertheless for a little while he was tempted to refuse it to those who were at such little pains to hide the motive of their eagerness. He considered it very hard to appear to be his own judge, and to yield practically to the attacks which the German Press,

[1] *Journal Officiel*, Report of the Chamber of Deputies, Nov. 15, 1877.

in the elation of its triumph, showered upon him anew and with increased insolence. To defy the new Ministry to revoke him would have been to prove that his conscience was at rest, and that he had not ceased to deserve well of his country for a single day. But it would, at the same time, have been laying too much stress on an act of condescension, the nature of which was easily understood by everybody; and he owed it to himself to be careful of the dignity of France, even when he was relieved of the duty of watching over it. His resignation was conveyed to the new Ministry by his sons, and accepted by means of the telegraph, in the brief and dry fashion peculiar to that kind of communication. Not another word was said, not a recollection bestowed on six years of patriotic service accepted under the most painful circumstances, and gone through amidst trials amid which neither the national honour nor the national interest had been allowed to suffer for a single day. So true was this, that those friends of M. de Gontaut who asked what grievances were alleged against him, were frankly told that there were no grievances. "But," it was added, "Herr von Bismarck could no longer endure him, and we wish to stand well with him."

To a Frenchman the most painful feature of an indifference, so closely akin to ingratitude, was the utterly different impression produced by the same incident on alien and but recently inimical territory, *i.e.* at Berlin. At Herr von Bismarck's there was triumphant joy, loudly expressed by the pamphleteers in his pay; everywhere else there was sincere sorrow, shown in an equally undisguised manner. No sooner had the news of M. de Gontaut's retirement spread, and before it had been officially declared, than the French Embassy was peacefully invaded by a kind of procession, consisting of all M. de Gontaut's diplomatic colleagues, expressing their heartfelt sorrow at losing, in addition to his ever friendly counsels, the daily charming intercourse with a host of the best society, whose home had always been open to them on the most affectionate footing. The first to call was verily the Italian ambassador, anxious to grasp the hand of the man who at that same hour was pointed at by all the papers as the incarnation of Clericalism.

Invited by the Empress to come and see her that same evening at a most private gathering, M. de Gontaut wished to observe to the last the somewhat restrictive correctness of the laws of etiquette, and did not consider himself justified in going thither without having previously and personally informed the Minister of Foreign Affairs of what the latter assuredly knew already.

"Monsieur l'Ambassadeur," said Herr von Bülow to him in a grave tone, and weighing, as it were, every word; "you came here under very delicate circumstances; it was an act of great devotion on your part. The Emperor has already expressed to me, and will repeat to you officially, his indebtedness to you for your constant efforts to maintain good relations with Germany."

The cautious Minister had evidently in his mind both the sentiments of the Emperor and those of the Chancellor, which differed absolutely in every respect. He was anxious, on the one hand, to omit nothing of what the Emperor had commanded him to say; on the other, to add nothing that might displease the Chancellor.

At the Emperor's gathering in the evening, the reception was less formal and more cordial. The moment the Emperor was informed of M. de Gontaut's arrival, he came to the drawing-room. "This is news indeed," he said; "you are going to leave us. This is a great grief to me (*c'est une grande affliction pour moi*). It is to you we owe the good relations with France; yes," he added, taking M. de Gontaut's hands in his, "yes, it is really to you." And the eyes of the old man grew moist with tears. "I have asked Prince Hohenlohe why you are going? The answer was that the Ministry made it a point with the Marshal." Then he suddenly stopped, wishing to say no more, perhaps, or not knowing the motive of that demand.

The Empress was even more sympathetic. "I remember," she said, delicately alluding to a conversation in the past; "I remember your telling me that on your arrival in Germany, the first place you went to was the cathedral at Cologne, and I also know the substance of your prayer."

She could not have told him in a more charming and subtle manner that he might console himself with the thought that his prayer had been heard.

A similar recollection forced itself even more strongly upon M. de Gontaut's mind, when a few days later he was obliged to ascend the palace stair-case in official dress—as he had done six years previously—to hand the Emperor his letters of recall in solemn audience. "I prayed to God then," he writes in a note, written the same day, "to support me in the cruel task I had undertaken. I was enabled to thank Him for having helped me to fulfil it."

He had every reason to think that, when mentally reviewing the work done during those years of labour, he should find nothing for which he could not account openly either to his country or to his conscience. His mission had been divided into two periods of unequal duration, but of equal importance. During the first and shorter period, he had responded to the confidence placed in him by M. Thiers, by giving the latter the most useful support in the task that imposed itself before any other, of acquitting the enormous war indemnity due to the alien, and to free the soil from his presence. M. Thiers, having retired, there yet remained another task, almost equally beset with difficulties, and more ungrateful, perhaps, the principal burden of which weighed above all on the ambassador of France at Berlin; for, as the reader may have gathered from these pages, material deliverance meant by no means complete emancipation. As long as the ranks of our army were not re-organized, as long as we had not repaired the breaches of our line of defence, as long as our frontier was unprovided with walls and soldiers, our freedom, but recently recovered, was ever dependent on a chance or on a whim. That weakness of ours was a secret to nobody, and least of all to our enemies of yesterday; they felt sorely tempted to benefit by it by taking once more the road they knew so well, while it was yet open to them, and to consummate, by striking at the foundations this time, a ruin which they felt sorry for not having completed. That was the avowed design—not even disguised in M. de Gontaut's presence—of the greater part of an eager and battlesome staff surrounding the aged Emperor. If Herr von Bismarck seemed less eager to associate himself with that danger, it was not because he did not share their regret at having left a breath of life in us, but because he considered himself in a position to keep a tight hand over us by means of intimidation and by isolation which would effectually prevent our resuming our rank among the independent nations. But how eagerly would he have clutched at the simplest pretext or at the slightest imprudence on our part to strike at us again. And, in fact, his constantly-recurring and unjustified provocations, his affected alarms, can only be accounted for on the theory of his wish to create such a pretext.

To M. de Gontaut belongs the credit of having afforded *la noble blessée* ("the wounded noble-woman")—as M. Thiers called France—the necessary time to heal her wounds, by having maintained himself on that slippery and defenceless ground in an attitude both firm and calm; consequently, when returning to France, after his recall, he had the satisfaction of being able to say to himself that the days of trial were over, and that he had helped his country to pass through the most difficult of these with safety. For after that crisis of 1875, the trap of which he had so effectually put out of gear, there was an end of all pretension, up to then so openly advanced, to keep us in leading-strings by exercising a jealous watch over the progress of our military re-organization, and by haggling with us in that way for *our* very conditions of existence. Those threats, at which M. Thiers himself was moved, are reduced to silence, and of its organization, as of its development, the French army owes no account except to France herself.

Moreover, material force is not everything;

a vanquished nation also feels the need to re-establish the prestige of her shaken moral weight in the sight of those who saw her fail. Nothing is more apt to make her recover that lost prestige than the dignity of character of those who represent her. Nothing was wanting in that respect in M. de Gontaut, neither elevation of sentiment, nor dignified demeanour in all the relations of life; and he had also the advantage which had by no means been overlooked by M. Thiers, when he appealed to him as being able to bring to the service of government, the principle of which was foreign to him, a patrimony of hereditary honour, recalling the traditions of our most glorious days. It will, therefore, be simple justice to inscribe the name of Élie de Gontaut-Biron in the annals of our deliverance side by side with that of the Statesman who selected him, and the enlightened Minister of whom he was the auxiliary and friend.

THE END.

Richard Clay & Sons, Limited, London & Bungay.

*In One Volume, 8vo, with a Portrait, price* 10/6.

## STUDIES IN DIPLOMACY
### By COUNT BENEDETTI

*The Times*—"Count Benedetti's volume constitutes an important and authentic contribution to the history of a great crisis in the affairs of Europe, and if it does not finally determine the share, responsibility, purposes, and motives of the principal actors in that crisis, it at any rate shows good reason for revising the hasty, and in many cases unjust, judgments which prevailed at the time."

*The Daily News*—"There is a good deal of spicy personal interest in the passages which give Benedetti's version of Bismarck's 'goings on.'"

*The Daily Telegraph*—"Its peeps behind the scenes, which lead up to the most momentous struggle of the century, are of permanent interest."

*The Daily Chronicle*—"A fascinating book."

*The National Observer*—"Read in the light of recent events, this book gains interest, and it throws light on the origin of much that is now agitating men's minds."

*The Literary World*—"The book is interesting because it deals with the inner aspect of continental politics during a critical and momentous episode."

*The Manchester Guardian*—"The book is well worth reading."

*The Liverpool Mercury*—"As a personal vindication these studies are convincing, and much interesting matter is incidentally introduced. We recommend the volume to those who wish to study the history of an important and exciting period."

*The Manchester Courier*—"As a contribution to history the volume is striking and valuable, and the brilliant style and thoughtful generalizations of its essays give it a high place in the diplomatic records of the country."

*The Leeds Mercury*—"The book will be of service to the historian of the future as the testimony of an actor in one of the most critical and momentous episodes of the century."

LONDON: WILLIAM HEINEMANN
21, BEDFORD STREET, W.C.

21 BEDFORD STREET, W.C.

Telegraphic Address,
Sunlocks, London.

A List of
# Mr. William Heinemann's
Publications

November 1895.

*The Books mentioned in this List can be obtained to order by any Bookseller if not in stock, or will be sent by the Publisher on receipt of the published price and postage.*

# REMBRANDT.
## SEVENTEEN OF HIS MASTERPIECES
### FROM THE COLLECTION OF HIS PICTURES IN THE CASSEL GALLERY.

Reproduced in Photogravure by the Berlin Photographic Company.

WITH AN ESSAY

### By FREDERICK WEDMORE.

In large portfolio 27½ inches × 20 inches.

*The first twenty-five impressions of each plate are numbered and signed, and of these only fourteen are for sale in England at the net price of Twenty Guineas the set. The price of the impressions after the first twenty-five is Twelve Guineas net, per set.*

**The TIMES.**—"The renderings have been made with extreme care, and, printed as they are upon peculiarly soft Japanese paper, they recall in a remarkable way the richness and beauty of the originals."

# REMBRANDT:
## HIS LIFE, HIS WORK, AND HIS TIME.

BY

### ÉMILE MICHEL,
*MEMBER OF THE INSTITUTE OF FRANCE.*

TRANSLATED BY

### FLORENCE SIMMONDS.

EDITED AND PREFACED BY

### FREDERICK WEDMORE.

Second Edition, Enlarged, with 76 full-page Plates, and 250 Illustrations in the Text. In One Volume, Gilt top, or in Two Vols., imperial 8vo, £2 2s. net.

\*\*\* A few copies of the EDITION DE LUXE of the FIRST EDITION printed on Japanese vellum with India proof duplicates of the photogravures) are still on sale, price £12 12s. net.

**The TIMES.**—"This very sumptuous and beautiful book has long been expected by all students of Rembrandt, for M. Émile Michel, the chief French authority on the Dutch School of Painting, has been known to be engaged upon it for many years. . . . . Merely to look through the reproductions in M. Michel's book is enough to explain the passionate eagerness with which modern collectors carry on their search after Rembrandt's drawings, and the great prices which are paid for them."

## MASTERPIECES OF GREEK SCULPTURE.

A SERIES OF ESSAYS ON THE HISTORY OF ART.

BY ADOLF FURTWÄNGLER.

Authorised Translation. Edited by EUGÉNIE SELLERS. With 19 full-page and 200 text Illustrations. In One Volume, imperial 8vo, £3 3s. net.

*⁎* Also an *édition de luxe* on Japanese vellum, limited to 50 numbered copies. In Two Volumes, price £10 10s. net.

**The TIMES.**—"In very many ways the translation is an improvement on the original. We sincerely hope it will be read by English students in the Universities and elsewhere."

## A CATALOGUE OF THE MUSEO DEL PRADO AT MADRID.

COMPILED BY E. LAWSON.

With Illustrations. In One Volume, crown 8vo.

[*In preparation.*

## A CATALOGUE OF THE ACCADEMIA DELLE BELLE ARTI AT VENICE.

With Biographical Notices of the Painters and Reproductions of some of their Works.

EDITED BY E. M. KEARY.

Crown 8vo, cloth, 2s. 6d. net; paper, 2s. net.

## THE HOURS OF RAPHAEL, IN OUTLINE.

Together with the Ceiling of the Hall where they were originally painted.

BY MARY E. WILLIAMS.

Folio, cloth, £2 2s. net.

## Literatures of the World.
### EDITED BY
### EDMUND GOSSE.

MR. HEINEMANN begs to announce a Series of Short Histories of Ancient and Modern Literatures of the World, Edited by EDMUND GOSSE.

*The following volumes are projected, and it is probable that they will be the first to appear:—*

### FRENCH LITERATURE.
BY EDWARD DOWDEN, D.C.L., LL.D., Professor of English Literature at the University of Dublin.

### ANCIENT GREEK LITERATURE.
BY GILBERT G. A. MURRAY, M.A., Professor of Greek in the University of Glasgow.

### ENGLISH LITERATURE.
BY THE EDITOR.

### ITALIAN LITERATURE.
BY RICHARD GARNETT, C.B., LL.D., Keeper of Printed Books in the British Museum.

### MODERN SCANDINAVIAN LITERATURE
BY DR. GEORG BRANDES, of Copenhagen.

### JAPANESE LITERATURE.
BY WILLIAM GEORGE ASTON, M.A., C.M.G., late Acting Secretary at the British Legation at Tokio.

### SPANISH LITERATURE.
BY J. FITZMAURICE-KELLY, Member of the Spanish Academy.

# THE WORKS AND LETTERS OF LORD BYRON.

### Edited by W. E. HENLEY.

*A New Edition, to be published in Ten Volumes crown 8vo.*

Also a limited Edition printed on handmade paper.

It is agreed that Byron's Letters, public and private, with their abounding ease and spirit and charm, are among the best in English. It is thought that Byron's poetry has been long, and long enough, neglected, so that we are on the eve of, if not face to face with, a steady reaction in its favour: that, in fact, the true public has had enough of fluent minor lyrists and hide-bound (if superior) sonnetteers, and is disposed, in the natural course of things, to renew its contact with a great English poet, who was also a principal element in the æsthetic evolution of that Modern Europe which we know.

Hence this new Byron, which will present—for the first time since the Seventeen Volumes Edition (1833), long since out of print—a master-writer and a master-influence in decent and persuasive terms.

## ANIMA POETÆ.
### FROM THE UNPUBLISHED NOTE-BOOKS
#### OF
### SAMUEL TAYLOR COLERIDGE.
#### EDITED BY
### ERNEST HARTLEY COLERIDGE.

In One Volume, crown 8vo, 7s. 6d.

The present collection of hitherto unpublished aphorisms, reflections, confessions, and soliloquies, which for want of a better name are entitled *Anima Poetæ*, does not in any way challenge comparison with the *Table Talk*. It is, indeed, essentially different, not only in the sources from which it has been compiled, but in constitution and in aim.

## WILLIAM SHAKESPEARE:
### A CRITICAL STUDY.
### By GEORG BRANDES.

Translated from the Danish by WILLIAM ARCHER.

In Two Volumes, demy 8vo, 30s. [*In preparation.*

Dr. Georg Brandes's "William Shakespeare" may best be called, perhaps, an exhaustive critical biography. Keeping fully abreast of the latest English and German researches and criticism, Dr. Brandes preserves that breadth and sanity of view which is apt to be sacrificed by the mere Shakespearologist. He places the poet in his political and literary environment, and studies each play not as an isolated phenomenon, but as the record of a stage in Shakespeare's spiritual history. Dr. Brandes has achieved German thoroughness without German heaviness, and has produced what must be regarded as a standard work.

## ESSAYS.
### By ARTHUR CHRISTOPHER BENSON,
*of Eton College.*

In One Volume, crown 8vo, buckram, 7s. 6d.

*Contents*: The Ever-Memorable John Hales—A Minute Philosopher—Henry More, the Platonist—Andrew Marvell—Vincent Bourne—Thomas Gray—William Blake—The Poetry of Keble—Elizabeth Barrett Browning—The late Master of Trinity—Henry Bradshaw—Christina Rossetti—The Poetry of Edmund Gosse—Epilogue.

# PARADOXES.

By MAX NORDAU,

Author of "Degeneration," "Conventional Lies of our Civilization," &c.

Translated by J. R. McIlraith.

Demy 8vo, 17s. net.      [*In preparation.*

Nordau himself considers this to be his best work, and, since its first publication in 1884, 23,000 copies have been sold in Germany alone. The title is perhaps a little misleading, but the author chose it simply because in this work he deals with certain psychological problems in a spirit quite unbiassed by the intimidating dictates of schools and uninfluenced by customary views and opinions. The questions treated relate to such matters as Optimism and Pessimism, the Rights of Majorities, Genius and Talent, the Natural History of Love, Evolution in Æsthetics, &c., and the main aim of the author throughout has been to examine commonly accepted truths in such a way as to show their weak points. The result is to demonstrate that even what is accepted as self-evident is often still open to many doubts and difficulties. The whole forms a critical review of modern thought by one of the frankest philosophical speculators of the day.

# CONVENTIONAL LIES OF OUR CIVILIZATION.

By MAX NORDAU,

Author of "Degeneration."

SECOND ENGLISH EDITION. Demy 8vo, 17s. net.

*THE TIMES* (First Notice).—"This is neither a vulgar nor a scandalous book, and it well deserves to have its objects and its value impartially examined. . . . There is no doubt of the model which Dr. Nordau has, consciously or unconsciously, followed. His volume is undoubtedly one which Rousseau might have written if he had lived a century later."

# DEGENERATION.

By MAX NORDAU.

Eighth English Edition. Demy 8vo, 17s. net.

# GENIUS AND DEGENERATION:
## A PSYCHOLOGICAL STUDY.

By Dr. WILLIAM HIRSCH.

With an Introduction by Professor E. MENDEL.

Translated from the Second German Edition

In One Volume, demy 8vo, 10s. net. [*In preparation.*

## THE MEMOIRS AND CORRESPONDENCE
### OF
# ERNEST RENAN.

With a Prefatory Memoir of his Sister HENRIETTE.

Demy 8vo, with Two Portraits in Photogravure, 14s.
*[In preparation.*

## THE MEMOIRS
### OF
# CHARLES GOUNOD.

In One Volume, demy 8vo, with Portrait, 10s. 6d.
*[In preparation.*

# ROBERT, EARL NUGENT:
## A MEMOIR.

### By CLAUD NUGENT.

In One Volume, demy 8vo, with a number of Portraits and other Illustrations. *[In preparation.*

## LETTERS OF
# SAMUEL TAYLOR COLERIDGE.
### EDITED BY ERNEST HARTLEY COLERIDGE.

With 16 Portraits and Illustrations. In Two Volumes, demy 8vo, £1 12s.

By far the greater portion of the Letters comprised in these volumes, and including, among many others, several addressed to Mrs. Coleridge, Southey, Wordsworth, the Rev. George Coleridge, John Thelwall, Thomas Poole, John Murray, and Charles Lamb, are now published for the first time; while, of the Letters previously published, most are to be found only in works long since out of print.

The correspondence is dated from 1785 to 1833, and throws much new light upon the extraordinary character and life of the poet, his eventful youth, his continual struggles against poverty and ill-health, his friendships and his literary career.

## STUDIES IN DIPLOMACY.

### By COUNT BENEDETTI.

Demy 8vo, with a Portrait 10s. 6d.

*[In preparation.*

## A BOOK OF SCOUNDRELS.

### By CHARLES WHIBLEY.

In One Volume, crown 8vo, with a Frontispiece.

*[In preparation.*

In "A Book of Scoundrels" are described the careers and achievements of certain notorious malefactors who have been chosen for their presentment on account of their style and picturesqueness. They are of all ages and several countries, and that variety may not be lacking, Cartouche and Peace, Moll Cutpurse and the Abbé Bruneau come within the same covers. Where it has seemed convenient, the method of Plutarch is followed, and the style and method of two similar scoundrels are contrasted in a "parallel." Jack Shepherd in the stone-room of Newgate, reproduced from an old print, serves as a frontispiece.

## SEVENTEENTH-CENTURY STUDIES.

*A CONTRIBUTION TO THE HISTORY OF ENGLISH POETRY.*

### By EDMUND GOSSE,

Clark Lecturer on English Literature at the University of Cambridge.

A New Edition. Crown 8vo. *[In preparation.*

## UNDERCURRENTS OF THE SECOND EMPIRE.

### By ALBERT D. VANDAM,

Author of "An Englishman in Paris" and "My Paris Note-book."

Demy 8vo, 10s. 6d. *[In preparation.*

## Great Lives and Events.

Uniformly bound in cloth, 6s. each volume.

**A FRIEND OF THE QUEEN.** Marie Antoinette and Count Fersen. From the French of PAUL GAULOT. Two Portraits.

*The Times.*—"M. Gaulot's work tells, with new and authentic details, the romantic story of Count Fersen's devotion to Marie Antoinette, of his share in the celebrated Flight to Varennes and in many other well-known episodes of the unhappy Queen's life."

**THE ROMANCE OF AN EMPRESS.** Catherine II. of Russia. From the French of K. WALISZEWSKI. With a Portrait.

*The Times.*—"This book is based on the confessions of the Empress herself; it gives striking pictures of the condition of the contemporary Russia which she did so much to mould as well as to expand. . . . Few stories in history are more romantic than that of Catherine II. of Russia, with its mysterious incidents and thrilling episodes; few characters present more curious problems."

**THE STORY OF A THRONE.** Catherine II. of Russia. From the French of K. WALISZEWSKI. With a Portrait.

*The World.*—"No novel that ever was written could compete with this historical monograph in absorbing interest."

**NAPOLEON AND THE FAIR SEX.** From the French of FRÉDÉRIC MASSON. With a Portrait.

*The Daily Chronicle.*—"The author shows that this side of Napoleon's life must be understood by those who would realize the manner of man he was."

**ALFRED, LORD TENNYSON.** A Study of His Life and Work. By ARTHUR WAUGH, B.A. Oxon. With Twenty Illustrations from Photographs specially taken for this Work. Five Portraits, and Facsimile of Tennyson's MS.

**MEMOIRS OF THE PRINCE DE JOINVILLE.** Translated from the French by Lady MARY LOYD. With 78 Illustrations from drawings by the Author.

**MY PARIS NOTE-BOOK.** By the Author of "An Englishman in Paris." In One Volume, demy 8vo, price 14s.

**EDMUND AND JULES DE GONCOURT.** Letters and Leaves from their Journals. Selected. In Two Volumes, 8vo, with Eight Portraits, 32s.

**ALEXANDER III. OF RUSSIA.** By CHARLES LOWE, M.A., Author of "Prince Bismarck: an Historical Biography." Crown 8vo, with Portrait in Photogravure, 6s.

*The Athenæum.*—"A most interesting and valuable volume."

*The Academy.*—"Written with great care and strict impartiality."

**PRINCE BISMARCK.** An Historical Biography. By CHARLES LOWE, M.A. With Portraits. Crown 8vo, 6s.

**VILLIERS DE L'ISLE ADAM: His Life and Works.** From the French of VICOMTE ROBERT DU PONTAVICE DE HEUSSEY. By Lady MARY LOYD. With Portrait and Facsimile. Crown 8vo, cloth, 10s. 6d.

**THE LIFE OF HENRIK IBSEN.** By HENRIK JÆGER. Translated by CLARA BELL. With the Verse done into English from the Norwegian Original by EDMUND GOSSE. Crown 8vo, cloth, 6s.

**RECOLLECTIONS OF MIDDLE LIFE.** By FRANCISQUE SARCEY. Translated by E. L. CAREY. In One Volume, 8vo, with Portrait, 10s 6d.

**TWENTY-FIVE YEARS IN THE SECRET SERVICE.** The Recollections of a Spy. By Major HENRI LE CARON. With New Preface. 8vo, boards, price 2s. 6d., or cloth, 3s. 6d.

\*\*\* *The Library Edition, with Portraits and Facsimiles, 8vo, 14s., is still on sale.*

**THE FAMILY LIFE OF HEINRICH HEINE.** Illustrated by one hundred and twenty-two hitherto unpublished letters addressed by him to different members of his family. Edited by his nephew, Baron LUDWIG VON EMBDEN, and translated by CHARLES GODFREY LELAND. In One Volume, 8vo, with 4 Portraits, 12s. 6d.

**RECOLLECTIONS OF COUNT LEO TOLSTOY.** Together with a Letter to the Women of France on the "Kreutzer Sonata." By C. A. BEHRS. Translated from the Russian by C. E. TURNER, English Lecturer in the University of St. Petersburg. In One Volume, 8vo, with Portrait, 10s. 6d.

**QUEEN JOANNA I. OF NAPLES, SICILY, AND JERUSALEM**: Countess of Provence, Forcalquier, and Piedmont. An Essay on her Times. By ST. CLAIR BADDELEY. Imperial 8vo, with numerous Illustrations, 16s.

**CHARLES III. OF NAPLES AND URBAN VI.**; also CECCO D'ASCOLI, Poet, Astrologer, Physican. Two Historical Essays. By ST. CLAIR BADDELEY. With Illustrations, 8vo, cloth, 10s. 6d.

**DE QUINCEY MEMORIALS.** Being Letters and other Records here first Published, with Communications from COLERIDGE, The WORDSWORTHS, HANNAH MORE, PROFESSOR WILSON, and others. Edited with Introduction, Notes, and Narrative, by ALEXANDER H. JAPP LL.D., F.R.S.E. In Two Volumes, demy 8vo, cloth, with Portraits, 30s. net.

**THE LIFE OF PHILIP HENRY GOSSE, F.R.S.** By his Son EDMUND GOSSE, Hon. M.A. Trinity College, Cambridge. 8vo, cloth, with Portrait, price 15s.

**MEMOIRS.** By CHARLES GODFREY LELAND (HANS BREITMANN). Second Edition. In One Volume, 8vo, with Portrait, price 7s. 6d.

**LETTERS OF A BARITONE.** By FRANCIS WALKER. In One Volume, small crown 8vo, 5s.

**CORRECTED IMPRESSIONS.** Essays on Victorian Writers. By GEORGE SAINTSBURY. Crown 8vo, gilt top, 7s. 6d.

**QUESTIONS AT ISSUE.** Essays. By EDMUND GOSSE. Crown 8vo, buckram, gilt top, 7s. 6d.
   *\** *A Limited Edition on Large Paper*, 25s. *net.*

**GOSSIP IN A LIBRARY.** By EDMUND GOSSE, Author of "Northern Studies," &c. Third Edition. Crown 8vo, buckram, gilt top, 7s. 6d.
   *\** *A Limited Edition on Large Paper*, 25s. *net.*

**THE PROSE WORKS OF HEINRICH HEINE.** Translated by CHARLES GODFREY LELAND, M.A., F.R.L.S. (HANS BREITMANN). In Eight Volumes.

The Library Edition, in crown 8vo, cloth, at 5s. per Volume. Each Volume of this edition is sold separately. The Cabinet Edition, in special binding, boxed, price £2 10s. the set. The Large Paper Edition, limited to 50 Numbered Copies, price 15s. per Volume net, will only be supplied to subscribers for the Complete Work.

  I. FLORENTINE NIGHTS, SCHNABELEWOPSKI, THE RABBI OF BACHARACH, and SHAKESPEARE'S MAIDENS AND WOMEN.

  II., III. PICTURES OF TRAVEL. 1823-1828.

  IV. THE SALON. Letters on Art, Music, Popular Life, and Politics.

  V., VI. GERMANY.

  VII., VIII. FRENCH AFFAIRS. Letters from Paris 1832, and Lutetia.

**THE POSTHUMOUS WORKS OF THOMAS DE QUINCEY.** Edited, with Introduction and Notes from the Author's Original MSS., by ALEXANDER H. JAPP, LL D., F.R S.E., &c. Crown 8vo, cloth, 6s. each.

  I. SUSPIRIA DE PROFUNDIS. With other Essays.

  II. CONVERSATION AND COLERIDGE. With other Essays.

**THE CHITRAL CAMPAIGN.** A Narrative of Events in Chitral, Swat, and Bajour. By H. C. THOMSON. With over 50 Illustrations reproduced from Photographs, and important Diagrams and Map. Second Edition in One Volume, demy 8vo, 14s. *net*.

**WITH THE ZHOB FIELD FORCE,** 1890. By Captain CRAWFORD MCFALL, K.O.Y.L.I. In One Volume, demy 8vo, with llustrations, 18s.

*The Morning Post.*—"Written with soldierly frankness and accuracy, and illustrated by a number of sketches which prove Captain McFall to be a draughts man of some deftness and skill."

*The Globe.*—"The volume is an important addition to our knowledge of the Afghan side of the Indian Frontier."

**THE LAND OF THE MUSKEG.** By H. SOMERS SOMERSET. Second Edition. In One Volume, demy 8vo, with Maps and over 100 Illustrations, 280 pp., 14s. *net*.

"This record of Mr. Somerset's expedition into the heart of the Hudson Bay Company's territory, through Alberta, Athabasca, and British Columbia, will be of interest to all lovers of sport and adventure."

**ACTUAL AFRICA;** or, The Coming Continent. A Tour of Exploration. By FRANK VINCENT, Author of "The Land of the White Elephant." With Map and over 100 Illustrations, demy, 8vo, cloth, price 24s.

**COREA, OR CHO-SEN, THE LAND OF THE MORNING CALM.** By A. HENRY SAVAGE-LANDOR With 38 Illustrations from Drawings by the Author, and a Portrait, demy 8vo, 18s.

*The Realm.*—"Mr Landor's book .... is of extreme value, for he has used his eyes, his pen, and his brush to picture scenes and natural characteristics, which in all probability will be vastly modified by the events of the immediate years."

*The Morning Post.*—"The book contains a great deal of matter which is entirely new, and cannot fail to attract considerable attention at the present time, when so little is known about Corea and the Coreans."

**THE LITTLE MANX NATION.** (Lectures delivered at the Royal Institution, 1891.) By HALL CAINE, Author of "The Bondman," "The Scapegoat," &c. Crown 8vo, cloth, 3s. 6d.; paper, 2s. 6d.

**NOTES FOR THE NILE.** Together with a Metrical Rendering of the Hymns of Ancient Egypt and of the Precepts of Ptahhotep (the oldest book in the world). By HARDWICKE D. RAWNSLEY, M.A. Imperial 16mo, cloth, 5s.

**DENMARK:** its History, Topography, Language, Literature, Fine Arts, Social Life, and Finance. Edited by H. WEITEMEYER. Demy 8vo, cloth, with Map, 12s. 6d.

\*\*\* *Dedicated, by permission, to H.R.H. the Princess of Wales.*

**THE REALM OF THE HABSBURGS.** By SIDNEY WHITMAN, Author of "Imperial Germany." In One Volume, crown 8vo, 7s. 6d.

**IMPERIAL GERMANY.** A Critical Study of Fact and Character. By SIDNEY WHITMAN. New Edition, Revised and Enlarged. Crown 8vo, cloth, 2s. 6d.; paper, 2s.

**THE CANADIAN GUIDE-BOOK.** Part I. The Tourist's and Sportsman's Guide to Eastern Canada and Newfoundland, including full descriptions of Routes, Cities, Points of Interest, Summer Resorts, Fishing Places, &c., in Eastern Ontario, The Muskoka District, The St. Lawrence Region, The Lake St. John Country, The Maritime Provinces, Prince Edward Island, and Newfoundland. With an Appendix giving Fish and Game Laws, and Official Lists of Trout and Salmon Rivers and their Lessees. By CHARLES G. D. ROBERTS, Professor of English Literature in King's College, Windsor, N.S. With Maps and many Illustrations. Crown 8vo, limp cloth, 6s.

**THE CANADIAN GUIDE-BOOK.** Part II. WESTERN CANADA. Including the Peninsula and Northern Regions of Ontario, the Canadian Shores of the Great Lakes, the Lake of the Woods Region, Manitoba and "The Great North-West," The Canadian Rocky Mountains and National Park, British Columbia, and Vancouver Island. By ERNEST INGERSOLL. With Maps and many Illustrations. Crown 8vo, limp cloth, 6s.

**THE GUIDE-BOOK TO ALASKA AND THE NORTH-WEST COAST,** including the Shores of Washington, British Columbia, South-Eastern Alaska, the Aleutian and the Seal Islands, the Behring and the Arctic Coasts. By E. R. SCIDMORE. With Maps and many Illustrations. Crown 8vo, limp cloth, 6s.

**THE GENESIS OF THE UNITED STATES.** A Narrative of the Movement in England, 1605-1616, which resulted in the Plantation of North America by Englishmen, disclosing the Contest between England and Spain for the Possession of the Soil now occupied by the United States of America; set forth through a series of Historical Manuscripts now first printed, together with a Re-issue of Rare Contemporaneous Tracts, accompanied by Bibliographical Memoranda, Notes, and Brief Biographies. Collected, Arranged, and Edited by ALEXANDER BROWN, F.R.H.S. With 100 Portraits, Maps, and Plans. In Two Volumes, royal 8vo, buckram, £3 13s. 6d. net.

**IN THE TRACK OF THE SUN.** Readings from the Diary of a Globe-Trotter. By FREDERICK DIODATI THOMPSON. With many Illustrations by Mr. HARRY FENN and from Photographs. In One Volume, 4to, 25s.

**THE GREAT WAR OF** 189—. A Forecast. By Rear-Admiral COLOMB, Col. MAURICE, R.A., Captain MAUDE, ARCHIBALD FORBES, CHARLES LOWE, D. CHRISTIE MURRAY, and F. SCUDAMORE. Second Edition. In One Volume, large 8vo, with numerous Illustrations, 6s.

**THE COMING TERROR.** And other Essays and Letters By ROBERT BUCHANAN. Second Edition. Demy 8vo, cloth, 12s. 6d.

ISRAEL AMONG THE NATIONS. Translated from the French of ANATOLE LEROY-BEAULIEU, Member of the Institute of France. In One Volume, crown 8vo, 7s. 6d.

THE JEW AT HOME. Impressions of a Summer and Autumn Spent with Him in Austria and Russia. By JOSEPH PENNELL, With Illustrations by the Author. 4to, cloth, 5s.

THE NEW EXODUS. A Study of Israel in Russia. By HAROLD FREDERIC. Demy 8vo, Illustrated, 16s.

STUDIES OF RELIGIOUS HISTORY. By ERNEST RENAN, late of the French Academy. In One Volume, 8vo, 7s. 6d.

THE ARBITRATOR'S MANUAL. Under the London Chamber of Arbitration. Being a Practical Treatise on the Power and Duties of an Arbitrator, with the Rules and Procedure of the Court of Arbitration, and the Forms. By JOSEPH SEYMOUR SALAMAN, Author of "Trade Marks," &c. Fcap. 8vo, 3s. 6d.

MANNERS, CUSTOMS, AND OBSERVANCES: Their Origin and Signification. By LEOPOLD WAGNER. Crown 8vo, 6s.

A COMMENTARY ON THE WORKS OF HENRIK IBSEN. By HJALMAR HJORTH BOYESEN, Author of "Goethe and Schiller," "Essays on German Literature," &c. Crown 8vo, cloth, 7s. 6d. net.

THE LABOUR MOVEMENT IN AMERICA. By RICHARD T. ELY, Ph.D., Associate in Political Economy, John Hopkins University. Crown 8vo, cloth, 5s.

THE PASSION PLAY AT OBERAMMERGAU, 1890. By F. W FARRAR, D.D., F.R.S., Dean of Canterbury, &c. &c. 4to, cloth, 2s. 6d.

THE WORD OF THE LORD UPON THE WATERS. Sermons read by His Imperial Majesty the Emperor of Germany, while at Sea on his Voyages to the Land of the Midnight Sun. Composed by Dr. RICHTER, Army Chaplain, and Translated from the German by JOHN R. MCILRAITH. 4to, cloth, 2s. 6d.

THE KINGDOM OF GOD IS WITHIN YOU. Christianity not as a Mystic Religion but as a New Theory of Life. By Count LEO TOLSTOY. Translated from the Russian by CONSTANCE GARNETT. Popular Edition in One Volume, cloth, 2s. 6d.

**THE POCKET IBSEN.** A Collection of some of the Master's best known Dramas, condensed. revised, and slightly rearranged for the benefit of the Earnest Student. By F. ANSTEY, Author of "Vice Versa," "Voces Populi," &c. With Illustrations, reproduced by permission, from *Punch*, and a new Frontispiece, by BERNARD PARTRIDGE. New Edition. 16mo, cloth, 3s. 6d.; or paper, 2s. 6d.

**FROM WISDOM COURT.** By HENRY SETON MERRIMAN and STEPHEN GRAHAM TALLENTYRE. With 30 Illustrations by E. COURBOIN. Crown 8vo, cloth, 3s. 6d.

**THE OLD MAIDS' CLUB.** By I. ZANGWILL, Author of "Children of the Ghetto," &c. Illustrated by F. H. TOWNSEND. Crown 8vo, cloth, 3s. 6d.

**WOMAN—THROUGH A MAN'S EYEGLASS.** By MALCOLM C. SALAMAN. With Illustrations by DUDLEY HARDY. Crown 8vo, cloth, 3s. 6d.

**STORIES OF GOLF.** Collected by WILLIAM KNIGHT and T. T. OLIPHANT. With Rhymes on Golf by various hands; also Shakespeare on Golf, &c. *Enlarged Edition.* Fcap. 8vo, cloth, 2s. 6d.

**THE ROSE:** A Treatise on the Cultivation, History, Family Characteristics, &c., of the various Groups of Roses. With Accurate Description of the Varieties now Generally Grown. By H. B. ELLWANGER. With an Introduction by GEORGE H. ELLWANGER. 12mo, cloth, 5s.

**THE GARDEN'S STORY;** or, Pleasures and Trials of an Amateur Gardener. By G. H. ELLWANGER. With an Introduction by the Rev. C. WOLLEY DOD. 12mo, cloth, with Illustrations, 5s.

**THE GENTLE ART OF MAKING ENEMIES.** As pleasingly exemplified in many instances, wherein the serious ones of this earth, carefully exasperated, have been prettily spurred on to indiscretions and unseemliness, while overcome by an undue sense of right. By J M'NEILL WHISTLER. *A New Edition.* Pott 4to, half cloth, 10s. 6d.

---

## Books for Presentation.

**A BATTLE AND A BOY.** By BLANCHE WILLIS HOWARD. With Thirty-nine Illustrations by A. MAC-NIELL-BARBOUR. Crown 8vo, cloth gilt, 6s.

**THE ATTACK ON THE MILL.** By ÉMILE ZOLA. With Twenty-one Illustrations, and Five exquisitely printed Coloured Plates, from original drawings by E. COURBOIN. In One Volume, 4to, 5s.

**LITTLE JOHANNES.** By F. VAN EEDEN. Translated from the Dutch by CLARA BELL. With an Introduction by ANDREW LANG. In One Volume, 16mo, cloth, silver top, 3s. net.

**GIRLS AND WOMEN.** By E. CHESTER. Pott 8vo, cloth, 2s. 6d., or gilt extra, 3s. 6d.

## Dramatic Literature.

**THE PLAYS OF W. E. HENLEY AND R. L. STEVENSON:** — DEACON BRODIE; BEAU AUSTIN; ADMIRAL GUINEA; MACAIRE. Crown 8vo, cloth. An Edition of 250 copies only, 10s. 6d.

*⁎* Early in 1896 these four plays will be reprinted separately. 16mo, paper cover, 1s. 6d.; or cloth, 2s. 6d.

**LITTLE EYOLF.** A Play in Three Acts. By HENRIK IBSEN. Translated from the Norwegian by WILLIAM ARCHER. Small 4to, cloth, with Portrait, 5s.

**THE MASTER BUILDER.** A Play in Three Acts. By HENRIK IBSEN. Translated from the Norwegian by EDMUND GOSSE and WILLIAM ARCHER. Small 4to, with Portrait, 5s. Popular Edition, paper, 1s. Also a Limited Large Paper Edition, 21s. net.

**HEDDA GABLER:** A Drama in Four Acts. By HENRIK IBSEN. Translated from the Norwegian by EDMUND GOSSE. Small 4to, cloth, with Portrait, 5s. Vaudeville Edition, paper, 1s. Also a Limited Large Paper Edition, 21s. net.

**BRAND:** A Dramatic Poem in Five Acts. By HENRIK IBSEN. Translated in the original metres, with an Introduction and Notes, by C. H. HERFORD. Small 4to, cloth, 7s. 6d.

**HANNELE: A DREAM-POEM.** By GERHART HAUPTMANN. Translated by WILLIAM ARCHER. Small 4to, with Portrait, 5s.

**THE PRINCESSE MALEINE:** A Drama in Five Acts (Translated by GERARD HARRY), and THE INTRUDER: A Drama in One Act. By MAURICE MAETERLINCK. With an Introduction by HALL CAINE, and a Portrait of the Author. Small 4to, cloth, 5s.

**THE FRUITS OF ENLIGHTENMENT:** A Comedy in Four Acts. By Count LYOF TOLSTOY. Translated from the Russian by E. J. DILLON. With Introduction by A. W. PINERO. Small 4to, with Portrait, 5s.

**KING ERIK.** A Tragedy. By EDMUND GOSSE. A Re-issue, with a Critical Introduction by Mr. THEODORE WATTS. Fcap. 8vo, boards, 5s. net.

**THE PIPER OF HAMELIN.** A Fantastic Opera in Two Acts. By ROBERT BUCHANAN. With Illustrations by HUGH THOMSON. 4to, cloth, 2s. 6d. net.

**HYPATIA.** A Play in Four Acts. Founded on CHARLES KINGSLEY'S Novel. By G. STUART OGILVIE. With Frontispiece by J. D. BATTEN. Crown 8vo, cloth, printed in Red and Black, 2s. 6d. net.

**THE DRAMA: ADDRESSES.** By HENRY IRVING. With Portrait by J. McN. WHISTLER. Second Edition. Fcap. 8vo, 3s. 6d.

**SOME INTERESTING FALLACIES OF THE** Modern Stage. An Address delivered to the Playgoers' Club at St. James's Hall, on Sunday, 6th December, 1891. By HERBERT BEERBOHM TREE. Crown 8vo, sewed, 6d. net.

**THE PLAYS OF ARTHUR W. PINERO.** With Introductory Notes by MALCOLM C. SALAMAN. 16mo, paper covers, 1s. 6d.; or cloth, 2s. 6d. each.

I. THE TIMES.
II. THE PROFLIGATE.
III. THE CABINET MINISTER.
IV. THE HOBBY HORSE.
V. LADY BOUNTIFUL.
VI. THE MAGISTRATE.
VII. DANDY DICK.
VIII. SWEET LAVENDER.
IX. THE SCHOOLMISTRESS.
X. THE WEAKER SEX.
XI. THE AMAZONS.

**THE NOTORIOUS MRS. EBBSMITH.** A Drama in Four Acts. By ARTHUR W. PINERO. Small 4to, cloth, 2s. 6d.; paper, 1s. 6d.

**THE SECOND MRS. TANQUERAY.** A Play in Four Acts. By ARTHUR W. PINERO. Small 4to, cloth, with a new Portrait of the Author, 5s. Also Cheap Edition, uniform with "The Notorious Mrs. Ebbsmith." Cloth, 2s. 6d.: paper, 1s. 6d.

**THE BENEFIT OF THE DOUBT.** By ARTHUR W. PINERO. Small 4to, cloth, 2s. 6d.: paper, 1s. 6d. [*In preparation.*

## Poetry.

**FIRDAUSI IN EXILE,** and other Poems. By EDMUND GOSSE. Fcap. 8vo, with Frontispiece, price 3s. 6d. net.

**ON VIOL AND FLUTE.** By EDMUND GOSSE. Fcap. 8vo, with Frontispiece, price 3s. 6d. net.

**IN RUSSET AND SILVER. POEMS.** By EDMUND GOSSE. Author of "Gossip in a Library," &c. Crown 8vo, buckram, gilt top, 6s.

**THE POETRY OF PATHOS AND DELIGHT.** From the Works of COVENTRY PATMORE. Passages selected by ALICE MEYNELL. With a Photogravure Portrait from an Oil Painting by JOHN SARGENT, A.R.A. Fcap. 8vo, 5s.

**A CENTURY OF GERMAN LYRICS.** Translated from the German by KATE FREILIGRATH KROEKER. Fcap. 8vo, rough edges, 3s. 6d.

**LOVE SONGS OF ENGLISH POETS, 1500–1800.** With Notes by RALPH H. CAINE. Fcap. 8vo, rough edges, 3s. 6d.
\*\*\* *Large Paper Edition, limited to 100 Copies, 10s. 6d. net.*

**IVY AND PASSION FLOWER:** Poems. By GERARD BENDALL, Author of "Estelle," &c. &c. 12mo, cloth, 3s. 6d.
*Scotsman.*—"Will be read with pleasure."
*Musical World.*—"The poems are delicate specimens of art, graceful and polished."

**VERSES.** By GERTRUDE HALL. 12mo, cloth, 3s. 6d.
*Manchester Guardian.*—"Will be welcome to every lover of poetry who takes it up."

**IDYLLS OF WOMANHOOD.** By C. AMY DAWSON. Fcap. 8vo, gilt top, 5s.

**TENNYSON'S GRAVE.** By ST. CLAIR BADDELEY. 8vo, paper, 1s.

## Science and Education.

**THE BIOLOGICAL PROBLEM OF TO-DAY:** Preformation or Epigenesis? Authorised Translation from the German of Prof. Dr. OSCAR HERTWIG, of the University of Berlin. By P. CHALMERS MITCHELL, M.A. Oxon. With a Preface by the Translator. Crown 8vo.
*[In preparation.*

**MOVEMENT.** Translated from the French of E. MAREY. By ERIC PRITCHARD, M.A., M.B. Oxon. In One Volume, crown 8vo, with 170 Illustrations, 7s. 6d.

A popular and scientific treatise on movement, dealing chiefly with the locomotion of men, animals, birds, fish, and insects. A large number of the Illustrations are from instantaneous photographs.

**ARABIC AUTHORS:** A Manual of Arabian History and Literature. By F. F. ARBUTHNOT, M.R.A.S., Author of "Early Ideas," "Persian Portraits," &c. 8vo, cloth, 5s.

**THE SPEECH OF MONKEYS.** By Professor R. L. GARNER. Crown 8vo, 7s. 6d.

## Heinemann's Scientific Handbooks.

**MANUAL OF BACTERIOLOGY.** By A. B. GRIFFITHS, Ph.D., F.R.S. (Edin.), F.C.S. Crown 8vo, cloth, Illustrated. 7s. 6d.

*Pharmaceutical Journal.*—"The subject is treated more thoroughly and completely than in any similar work published in this country."

**MANUAL OF ASSAYING GOLD, SILVER, COPPER,** and Lead Ores. By WALTER LEE BROWN, B.Sc. Revised, Corrected, and considerably Enlarged, with a chapter on the Assaying of Fuel, &c. By A. B. GRIFFITHS, Ph.D., F.R.S. (Edin.), F.C.S. Crown 8vo, cloth, Illustrated, 7s. 6d.

*Colliery Guardian.*—"A delightful and fascinating book."

*Financial World.*—"The most complete and practical manual on everything which concerns assaying of all which have come before us."

**GEODESY.** By J. HOWARD GORE. Crown 8vo, cloth, Illustrated, 5s.

*St. James's Gazette.*—"The book may be safely recommended to those who desire to acquire an accurate knowledge of Geodesy."

*Science Gossip.*—"It is the best we could recommend to all geodetic students. It is full and clear, thoroughly accurate, and up to date in all matters of earth-measurements."

**THE PHYSICAL PROPERTIES OF GASES.** By ARTHUR L. KIMBALL, of the Johns Hopkins University. Crown 8vo, cloth, Illustrated, 5s.

*Chemical News.*—"The man of culture who wishes for a general and accurate acquaintance with the physical properties of gases, will find in Mr. Kimball's work just what he requires."

**HEAT AS A FORM OF ENERGY.** By Professor R. H. THURSTON, of Cornell University. Crown 8vo, cloth, Illustrated, 5s.

*Manchester Examiner.*—"Bears out the character of its predecessors for careful and correct statement and deduction under the light of the most recent discoveries."

## The Great Educators.

*A Series of Volumes by Eminent Writers, presenting in their entirety "A Biographical History of Education."*

*The Times.*—"A Series of Monographs on 'The Great Educators' should prove of service to all who concern themselves with the history, theory, and practice of education."

*The Speaker.*—"There is a promising sound about the title of Mr. Heinemann's new series, 'The Great Educators.' It should help to allay the hunger and thirst for knowledge and culture of the vast multitude of young men and maidens which our educational system turns out yearly, provided at least with an appetite for instruction."

Each subject will form a complete volume, crown 8vo, 5s.

*Now ready.*

**ARISTOTLE, and the Ancient Educational Ideals.** By THOMAS DAVIDSON, M.A., LL.D.

*The Times.*—"A very readable sketch of a very interesting subject."

**LOYOLA, and the Educational System of the Jesuits.** By Rev. THOMAS HUGHES, S.J.

**ALCUIN, and the Rise of the Christian Schools.** By Professor ANDREW F. WEST, Ph.D.

**FROEBEL, and Education by Self-Activity.** By H. COURTHOPE BOWEN, M.A.

**ABELARD, and the Origin and Early History of Universities.** By JULES GABRIEL COMPAYRÉ, Professor in the Faculty of Toulouse.

**HERBART AND THE HERBARTIANS.** By Prof. DE GARMO.

*In preparation.*

**ROUSSEAU; and, Education according to Nature.** By PAUL H. HANUS.

**HORACE MANN, and Public Education in the United States.** By NICHOLAS MURRAY BUTLER, Ph.D.

**THOMAS and MATTHEW ARNOLD, and their Influence on Education.** By J. G. FITCH, LL.D., Her Majesty's Inspector of Schools.

**PESTALOZZI; or, the Friend and Student of Children.**

## Forthcoming Fiction.

"THE HOUSE BEAUTIFUL" and "AN AWKWARD AGE." By HENRY JAMES. Crown 8vo, cloth, 6s.

A NEW NOVEL by HENRY JAMES. Crown 8vo.

ILLUMINATION. By HAROLD FREDERIC. Crown 8vo, cloth, 6s.

HERBERT VANLENNERT. By C. F. KEARY. Crown 8vo, cloth, 6s.

A NEW VOLUME by G. S. STREET, the Author of "Episodes" and "Autobiography of a Boy," Crown 8vo.

THE DANCER IN YELLOW. By W. E. NORRIS. Crown 8vo, cloth. 6s.

CORRUPTION. By PERCY WHITE. Crown 8vo, cloth, 6s.

MR. BAILEY MARTIN. By PERCY WHITE. A New Edition, uniform with "Corruption." Crown 8vo, cloth, 6s.

*The Daily Chronicle.*—"His book must be pronounced a well-nigh unqualified triumph. A consistently thought-out piece of work, full of happy touches and abounding in acute observation."

A SELF-DENYING ORDINANCE. By M. HAMILTON. Crown 8vo, cloth, 6s.

THE MALADY OF THE CENTURY. By MAX NORDAU. Crown 8vo, cloth, 6s.

A COMEDY OF SENTIMENT. By MAX NORDAU. Crown 8vo, cloth, 6s.

THE ISLAND OF DOCTOR MOREAU. By H. G. WELLS. In One Volume. Crown 8vo.

STORIES FOR NINON. By ÉMILE ZOLA. Crown 8vo, with a portrait by Will Rothenstein. Cloth, 6s.

THE YEARS THAT THE LOCUST HATH EATEN. By ANNIE E. HOLDSWORTH. Crown 8vo, cloth, 6s.

## Popular 6s. Novels.

**IN HASTE AND AT LEISURE.** By Mrs. LYNN LINTON, Author of "Joshua Davidson," &c. Crown 8vo, cloth, 6s.

**A DRAMA IN DUTCH.** By Z. Z. Crown 8vo, cloth, 6s.

**BENEFITS FORGOT.** By WOLCOTT BALESTIER. A New Edition. Crown 8vo, cloth, 6s.

**A PASTORAL PLAYED OUT.** By M. L. PENDERED. Crown 8vo, cloth, 6s.

**CHIMÆRA.** By F. MABEL ROBINSON, Author of "Mr. Butler's Ward," &c. Crown 8vo, cloth, 6s.

**MISS GRACE OF ALL SOULS'.** By W. EDWARDS TIREBUCK. Crown 8vo, cloth, 6s.

**TRANSITION.** By the Author of "A Superfluous Woman." Crown 8vo, cloth, 6s.

**TERMINATIONS.** By HENRY JAMES. Second Edition. Crown 8vo, cloth, 6s.

**OUT OF DUE SEASON.** By ADELINE SERGEANT. Crown 8vo, cloth, 6s.

**AN IMAGINATIVE MAN.** By ROBERT S. HICHENS. Crown 8vo, cloth, 6s.

**SENTIMENTAL STUDIES.** By HUBERT CRACKANTHORPE. Crown 8vo, cloth, 6s.

**AS OTHERS SAW HIM.** A Retrospect, A.D. 54. In One Volume. Crown 8vo, gilt top, 6s.

Mr. GLADSTONE, writing from Capmartin, says:—"I have read with great and unexpected interest the volume you were so kind as to send me. It brings into series many of the latest acts of our Saviour's earthly life. Unhappily I have no means of judging at the place whether and how far it is sustained by any external authority In such supplemental material as it associates with the Gospels."

The Rev. HUGH PRICE HUGHES writes:—"I am much indebted to you for an early copy of 'As Others saw Him.' I have read the volume with much interest. The writer is evidently learned and devout, and has brought an original mind to the study of the most original of lives. It is an exceedingly striking and suggestive volume. I have read it with much interest and profit, and am personally much indebted to the author."

## Popular 6s. Novels.

**THE EBB-TIDE.** By ROBERT LOUIS STEVENSON and LLOYD OSBOURNE. Crown 8vo, cloth, 6s.

**THE MANXMAN.** By HALL CAINE. Crown 8vo, cloth, 6s.

**THE BONDMAN.** A New Saga. By HALL CAINE. Crown 8vo, cloth, 6s.

**THE SCAPEGOAT.** By HALL CAINE. Author of "The Bondman," &c. Crown 8vo, cloth, 6s.

**ELDER CONKLIN;** and other Stories. By FRANK HARRIS. 8vo, cloth, 6s.

**THE HEAVENLY TWINS.** By SARAH GRAND, Author of "Ideala," &c. Crown 8vo, cloth, 6s.

**IDEALA.** By SARAH GRAND, Author of "The Heavenly Twins." Crown 8vo, cloth, 6s.

**OUR MANIFOLD NATURE.** By SARAH GRAND. With a Portrait of the Author. Crown 8vo, cloth, 6s.

**THE STORY OF A MODERN WOMAN.** By ELLA HEPWORTH DIXON. Crown 8vo, cloth, 6s.

**A SUPERFLUOUS WOMAN.** Crown 8vo, 6s.

**AT THE GATE OF SAMARIA.** By W. J. LOCKE. Crown 8vo, cloth, 6s.

**A DAUGHTER OF THIS WORLD.** By F. BATTERSHALL. Crown 8vo, cloth, 6s.

**A COMEDY OF MASKS.** By ERNEST DOWSON and ARTHUR MOORE. Crown 8vo, cloth, 6s.

**THE JUSTIFICATION OF ANDREW LEBRUN.** By F. BARRETT. Crown 8vo, 6s.

**THE LAST SENTENCE.** By MAXWELL GRAY, Author of "The Silence of Dean Maitland," &c. Crown 8vo, cloth, 6s.

**APPASSIONATA:** A Musician's Story. By ELSA D'ESTERRE KEELING. Crown 8vo, cloth, 6s.

**THE POTTER'S THUMB.** By F. A. STEEL, Author of "From the Five Rivers," &c. Crown 8vo, cloth, 6s.

**FROM THE FIVE RIVERS.** By FLORA ANNIE STEEL. Author of "Miss Stuart's Legacy." Crown 8vo, cloth, 6s.

**RELICS.** Fragments of a Life. By FRANCES MACNAB. Crown 8vo, cloth, 6s.

## Popular 6s. Novels.

**THE TOWER OF TADDEO.** By OUIDA, Author of "Two Little Wooden Shoes," &c. New Edition. Crown 8vo, cloth, Illustrated, 6s.

**THE MASTER.** By I. ZANGWILL. With Portrait. Crown 8vo cloth, 6s.

**CHILDREN OF THE GHETTO.** By I. ZANGWILL, Author of "The Old Maids' Club," &c. New Edition, with Glossary. Crown 8vo, cloth, 6s.

**THE PREMIER AND THE PAINTER.** A Fantastic Romance. By I. ZANGWILL and LOUIS COWEN. Third Edition. Crown 8vo, cloth, 6s.

**THE KING OF SCHNORRERS, GROTESQUES AND FANTASIES.** By I. ZANGWILL. With over Ninety Illustrations. Crown 8vo, cloth, 6s.

**THE RECIPE FOR DIAMONDS.** By C. J. CUTCLIFFE HYNE. Crown 8vo, cloth, 6s.

**A VICTIM OF GOOD LUCK.** By W. E. NORRIS, Author of "Matrimony," &c. Crown 8vo, cloth. 6s.

**THE COUNTESS RADNA.** By W. E. NORRIS, Author of "Matrimony," &c. Crown 8vo, cloth, 6s.

**THE NAULAHKA.** A Tale of West and East. By RUDYARD KIPLING and WOLCOTT BALESTIER. Second Edition. Crown 8vo, cloth, 6s.

**AVENGED ON SOCIETY.** By H. F. WOOD, Author of "The Englishman of the Rue Cain," "The Passenger from Scotland Yard." Crown 8vo, cloth, 6s.

**THE O'CONNORS OF BALLINAHINCH.** By Mrs. HUNGERFORD, Author of "Molly Bawn," &c. Crown 8vo, cloth, 6s.

### Five Shilling Volumes.

**THE SECRET OF NARCISSE.** By EDMUND GOSSE. Crown 8vo, buckram, 5s.

**VANITAS.** By VERNON LEE, Author of "Hauntings," &c. Crown 8vo, cloth, 5s.

### Two Shillings and Sixpence.

**THE TIME MACHINE.** By H. G. WELLS. Cloth, 2s. 6d.; paper, 1s. 6d.

**THE DOMINANT SEVENTH: A Musical Story.** By KATE ELIZABETH CLARKE. Crown 8vo, cloth, 2s. 6d.

## The Pioneer Series.

12mo, cloth, 3s. net; or, paper covers, 2s. 6d. net.

*The Athenæum.*—"If this series keeps up to the present high level of interest, novel readers will have fresh cause for gratitude to Mr. Heinemann."
*The Daily Telegraph.*—"Mr. Heinemann's genial nursery of up-to-date romance."
*The Observer.*—"The smart Pioneer Series."
*The Manchester Courier.*—"The Pioneer Series promises to be as original as many other of Mr. Heinemann's ventures."

**JOANNA TRAILL, SPINSTER.** By ANNIE E. HOLDSWORTH.
*The Saturday Review.*—"So grave in subject, so passionate and earnest in treatment, and so absolutely right in morals, that one might suppose it intended to lead into high regions of pure reason."

**GEORGE MANDEVILLE'S HUSBAND.** By C. E. RAIMOND.
*The Athenæum.*—"A most excellent and powerful piece of work."
*The Pall Mall Budget.*—"Clever, biting, and irresistible."

**THE WINGS OF ICARUS.** By LAURENCE ALMA TADEMA.
*The Daily Telegraph.*—". . . Nothing has been more impressively told in the pages of modern fiction than the *dénouement* of this sad but deeply fascinating story."

**THE GREEN CARNATION.** By R. S. HICHENS.
*The Daily Telegraph.*—"One of the most brilliant expositions of latter-day humour that has been brought to the public cognisance for many a day."

**AN ALTAR OF EARTH.** By THYMOL MONK.
*The Saturday Review.*—"Exceedingly well written: there is pathos and genuine power."

**A STREET IN SUBURBIA.** By E. W. PUGH.
*The Sketch.*—"By humour and pathos of a healthy kind, and not a little literary skill, Mr. Pugh has given some very vivid pictures of poor London life."

**THE NEW MOON.** By C. E. RAIMOND.
*The Daily Chronicle*—"A story that moves us, and we must own to having read the last pages with breathless interest and emotion."

**MILLY'S STORY.** By Mrs. MONTAGUE CRACKANTHORPE.
*The Pall Mall Gazette.*—"A very clever account of a nervous, invalided woman. It is very readable."

**MRS. MUSGRAVE — AND HER HUSBAND.** By RICHARD MARSH.
*Vanity Fair.*—"The interest is absorbing from the first chapter, in which the keynote is artfully struck, to the logical climax."

**THE DEMAGOGUE AND LADY PHAYRE.** By WILLIAM J. LOCKE.

**THE RED BADGE OF COURAGE.** By STEPHEN CRANE.

**SOME FRIENDS AND A WOMAN.** By C. G. COMPTON.

**PAPIER MACHÉE.** By CHARLES ALLEN.

**THE NEW VIRTUE.** By Mrs. OSCAR BERINGER.

**ACROSS AN ULSTER BOG.** By M. HAMILTON.

*Other Volumes to follow.*

*UNIFORM EDITION OF*
# THE NOVELS OF BJÖRNSTJERNE BJÖRNSON

Edited by EDMUND GOSSE.

Fcap. 8vo, cloth, 3s. net each Volume.

### Vol. I.—SYNNÖVÉ SOLBAKKEN.

With Introductory Essay by EDMUND GOSSE, and a Portrait of the Author.

### Vol. II.—ARNE.
### Vol. III.—A HAPPY BOY.

*To be followed by*

| THE FISHER MAIDEN. | MAGNHILD. |
| THE BRIDAL MARCH. | CAPTAIN MANSANA. |

AND OTHER STORIES.

*UNIFORM EDITION OF*
# THE NOVELS OF IVAN TURGENEV.

Translated by CONSTANCE GARNETT.

Fcap. 8vo, cloth, price 3s. net each Volume.

### Vol. I.—RUDIN.

With a Portrait of the Author and an Introduction by STEPNIAK.

### Vol. II.—A HOUSE OF GENTLEFOLK.

### Vol. III.—ON THE EVE.

### Vol. IV.—FATHERS AND CHILDREN.

### Vol. VIII., IX.—A SPORTSMAN'S SKETCHES.
(Two Volumes).

*To be followed by*

Vol. V. SMOKE.

„ VI., VII. VIRGIN SOIL. (Two Volumes.)

## Heinemann's International Library.
### Edited by EDMUND GOSSE.

*New Review.*—"If you have any pernicious remnants of literary chauvinism I hope it will not survive the series of foreign classics of which Mr. William Heinemann, aided by Mr. Edmund Gosse, is publishing translations to the great contentment of all lovers of literature."

*Each Volume has an Introduction specially written by the Editor.*
Price, in paper covers, 2s. 6d. each; or cloth, 3s. 6d.

**IN GOD'S WAY.** From the Norwegian of BJÖRNSTJERNE BJÖRNSON.

**PIERRE AND JEAN.** From the French of GUY DE MAUPASSANT.

**THE CHIEF JUSTICE.** From the German of KARL EMIL FRANZOS, Author of "For the Right," &c.

**WORK WHILE YE HAVE THE LIGHT.** From the Russian of Count LEO TOLSTOY.

**FANTASY.** From the Italian of MATILDE SERAO.

**FROTH.** From the Spanish of Don ARMANDO PALACIO-VALDÉS.

**FOOTSTEPS OF FATE.** From the Dutch of LOUIS COUPERUS.

**PEPITA JIMÉNEZ.** From the Spanish of JUAN VALERA.

**THE COMMODORE'S DAUGHTERS.** From the Norwegian of JONAS LIE.

**THE HERITAGE OF THE KURTS.** From the Norwegian of BJÖRNSTJERNE BJÖRNSON.

**LOU.** From the German of BARON ALEXANDER VON ROBERTS.

**DOÑA LUZ.** From the Spanish of JUAN VALERA.

**THE JEW.** From the Polish of JOSEPH IGNATIUS KRASZEWSKI.

**UNDER THE YOKE.** From the Bulgarian of IVAN VAZOFF.

**FAREWELL LOVE!** From the Italian of MATILDE SERAO.

**THE GRANDEE.** From the Spanish of Don ARMANDO PALACIO-VALDÉS.

**A COMMON STORY.** From the Russian of GONTCHAROFF.

**WOMAN'S FOLLY.** From the Italian of GEMMA FERRUGGIA.

*In preparation.*
**NIOBE.** From the Norwegian of JONAS LIE.

**NIELS LYHNË.** From the Danish of J. JACOBSEN.

## Popular 3s. 6d. Novels.

**ELI'S DAUGHTER.** By J H. PEARCE, Author of "Inconsequent Lives."

**INCONSEQUENT LIVES.** A Village Chronicle. By J. H. PEARCE, Author of "Esther Pentreath," &c.

**HER OWN FOLK.** (En Famille.) By HECTOR MALOT, Author of "No Relations." Translated by Lady MARY LOYD.

**CAPT'N DAVY'S HONEYMOON,** The Blind Mother, and The Last Confession. By HALL CAINE, Author of "The Bondman," "The Scapegoat," &c.

**A MARKED MAN:** Some Episodes in his Life. By ADA CAMBRIDGE, Author of "A Little Minx," "The Three Miss Kings," "Not All in Vain," &c.

**THE THREE MISS KINGS.** By ADA CAMBRIDGE.

**A LITTLE MINX.** By ADA CAMBRIDGE.

**NOT ALL IN VAIN.** By ADA CAMBRIDGE.

**A KNIGHT OF THE WHITE FEATHER.** By TASMA, Author of "The Penance of Portia James," "Uncle Piper of Piper's Hill," &c.

**UNCLE PIPER OF PIPER'S HILL.** By TASMA.

**THE PENANCE OF PORTIA JAMES.** By TASMA.

**THE COPPERHEAD;** and other Stories of the North during the American War. By HAROLD FREDERIC, Author of "The Return of the O'Mahony," "In the Valley," &c.

**THE RETURN OF THE O'MAHONY.** By HAROLD FREDERIC, Author of "In the Valley," &c. With Illustrations.

**IN THE VALLEY.** By HAROLD FREDERIC, Author of "The Lawton Girl," "Seth's Brother's Wife," &c. With Illustrations.

**THE SURRENDER OF MARGARET BELLARMINE.** By ADELINE SERGEANT, Author of "The Story of a Penitent Soul."

**THE STORY OF A PENITENT SOUL.** Being the Private Papers of Mr. Stephen Dart, late Minister at Lynnbridge, in the County of Lincoln. By ADELINE SERGEANT, Author of "No Saint," &c.

**NOR WIFE, NOR MAID.** By Mrs. HUNGERFORD, Author of "Molly Bawn," &c.

**THE HOYDEN.** By Mrs. HUNGERFORD.

**MAMMON.** A Novel. By Mrs. ALEXANDER, Author of "The Wooing O't," &c.

**DAUGHTERS OF MEN.** By HANNAH LYNCH, Author of "The Prince of the Glades," &c.

A ROMANCE OF THE CAPE FRONTIER. By BERTRAM MITFORD, Author of "Through the Zulu Country," &c.

'TWEEN SNOW AND FIRE. A Tale of the Kafir War of 1877. By BERTRAM MITFORD.

ORIOLE'S DAUGHTER. By JESSIE FOTHERGILL, Author of "The First Violin," &c.

THE MASTER OF THE MAGICIANS. By ELIZABETH STUART PHELPS and HERBERT D. WARD.

THE HEAD OF THE FIRM. By Mrs. RIDDELL, Author of "George Geith," "Maxwell Drewett," &c.

A CONSPIRACY OF SILENCE. By G. COLMORE, Author of "A Daughter of Music," &c.

A DAUGHTER OF MUSIC. By G. COLMORE, Author of "A Conspiracy of Silence."

ACCORDING TO ST. JOHN. By AMÉLIE RIVES, Author of "The Quick or the Dead."

KITTY'S FATHER. By FRANK BARRETT, Author of "The Admirable Lady Biddy Fane," &c.

A QUESTION OF TASTE. By MAARTEN MAARTENS, Author of "An Old Maid's Love," &c.

COME LIVE WITH ME AND BE MY LOVE. By ROBERT BUCHANAN, Author of "The Moment After," "The Coming Terror," &c.

---

DONALD MARCY. By ELIZABETH STUART PHELPS. Author of "The Gates Ajar," &c.

IN THE DWELLINGS OF SILENCE. A Romance of Russia. By WALKER KENNEDY.

LOS CERRITOS. A Romance of the Modern Time. By GERTRUDE FRANKLIN ATHERTON, Author of "Hermia Suydam," and "What Dreams may Come."

## Short Stories in One Volume.

Three Shillings and Sixpence each.

**EPISODES.** By G. S. STREET, Author of "The Autobiography of a Boy."

**WRECKAGE,** and other Stories. By HUBERT CRACKANTHORPE. Second Edition.

**MADEMOISELLE MISS,** and other Stories. By HENRY HARLAND, Author of "Mea Culpa," &c.

**THE ATTACK ON THE MILL,** and other Sketches of War. By EMILE ZOLA. With an Essay on the short stories of M. Zola by EDMUND GOSSE.

**THE AVERAGE WOMAN.** By WOLCOTT BALESTIER. With an Introduction by HENRY JAMES.

**BLESSED ARE THE POOR.** By FRANÇOIS COPPÉE. With an Introduction by T. P. O'CONNOR.

**PERCHANCE TO DREAM,** and other Stories. By MARGARET S. BRISCOE.

**WRECKERS AND METHODISTS.** Cornish Stories. By H. D. LOWRY.

## Popular Shilling Books.

**PRETTY MISS SMITH.** By FLORENCE WARDEN, Author of "The House on the Marsh," "A Witch of the Hills," &c.

**MADAME VALERIE.** By F. C. PHILIPS, Author of "As in a Looking-Glass," &c.

**THE MOMENT AFTER:** A Tale of the Unseen. By ROBERT BUCHANAN.

**CLUES;** or, Leaves from a Chief Constable's Note-Book. By WILLIAM HENDERSON, Chief Constable of Edinburgh.

---

## THE NORTH AMERICAN REVIEW.
Edited by LLOYD BRYCE.
Published monthly. Price 2s. 6d.

## THE NEW REVIEW.
*NEW SERIES.*
Edited by W. E. HENLEY.
Published Monthly, price 1s.

---

LONDON:
WILLIAM HEINEMANN,
21 BEDFORD STREET, W.C.

Lightning Source UK Ltd.
Milton Keynes UK
UKHW011032271118
333020UK00011B/1528/P